LIBRARY - GREENVILLE TECH

000
210101

D0148673

89 3

Reproduced from the collection of the Library of Congress

THE CHICAGO RENAISSANCE IN AMERICAN LETTERS

A Critical History

BERNARD DUFFEY

GREENWOOD PRESS, PUBLISHERS
WESTPORT, CONNECTICUT

31095

State Board for Technical and Comprehensive Education

The Library of Congress has catalogued this publication as follows:

Library of Congress Cataloging in Publication Data

Duffey, Bernard I   1917–
    The Chicago renaissance in American letters.

    Bibliography: p.
    1. American literature--Chicago--History and criti-
cism. I. Title.
[PS285.C47D8 1972]   810'.9'977311   72-6193
ISBN 0-8371-6461-3

Copyright 1954 The Michigan State College Press

All rights reserved

This edition originally published in 1956 by The Michigan
State University Press

Reprinted with the permission of The Michigan State
University Press

Reprinted by Greenwood Press, Inc.

First Greenwood reprinting 1972
Second Greenwood reprinting 1977

Library of Congress catalog card number 72-6193
ISBN 0-8371-6461-3

Printed in the United States of America

LEARNING RESOURCES CENTER
GREENVILLE TECHNICAL COLLEGE
P.O. BOX 5539
GREENVILLE, S. C. 29606

Acknowledgments

AN extended period of work upon this book has made me much aware of the communal nature of scholarship. I owe a debt not only to those who have extended a personal hand, but also, as my list of sources indicates, to the labors of numerous writers, living and dead. Though my work has thus been a cooperative one in a most pleasant and helpful sense, that fact does not relieve me in any way of responsibility for its errors or omissions. The final judgments have been mine in every case. I am pleased, however, to record here my chief obligations.

The Rockefeller Foundation, through the agencies of the Newberry Library and the Midwestern Studies Committee of Michigan State College, has underwritten a large part of my labors, and the administration of Michigan State has been generous in granting necessary leaves of absence. The directors of the acting Rockefeller agencies, Dr. Stanley Pargellis and Prof. Russel B. Nye, have been far more than mere administrators. Their friendship and humane interest were a constant personal resource. From a number of the persons who were active in the Chicago Renaissance I have received direct and uniquely valuable aid and counsel. In this wise I must especially record the courtesy and warmth of Mr. Ralph Fletcher Seymour, Mr. Vincent Starrett, Mr. Roger Sergel, Prof. Ferdinand Scheville, Mr. Francis Hackett, Mr. Pascal Covici, and Mr. Floyd Dell. Mrs. Sherwood Anderson's friendship and encouragement was of deep importance to my work.

Among my professional resources, staff members of the various libraries in which I worked have been of primary importance. Mrs. Amy Nyholm and Mrs. Gertrude Woodward of the Newberry have in their skillful keeping the greatest single asset to this study, the Newberry Library collection of the papers of midwestern authors. My personal debt to Mr. Ben C. Bowman of the Newberry is a

surpassing one. Miss Anna Lauren, now retired, and Mrs. Judith
Bond of the Harper Library at the University of Chicago were of
the greatest help in the use of its crucial materials. The friendly
cooperation of Mr. John Alden, curator of rare books at the University of Pennsylvania Library, together with the permissions of
Prof. Sculley Bradley, gave me a much needed assistance. And the
staff of the New York Public Library opened and ordered essential
records for my use.

The list of persons, institutions, and publishers who have given
me permission to quote from documents and books within their
control is large.

I am indebted to the Newberry Library for permission to quote
from their collections of the papers of Henry Fuller, Francis Fisher
Browne, Joseph Kirkland, Eunice Tietjens, Floyd Dell, and Sherwood
Anderson; to the New York Public Library for their permission to
quote from letters contained in the Richard Watson Gilder collection; to the University of Chicago Library for permission to quote
from papers contained in the Robert Herrick collection and the Harriet Monroe collection; to the University of Pennsylvania Library
and to Mrs. Edgar Lee Masters for permission to quote from papers
contained in the Theodore Dreiser collection and elsewhere; to the
University of Michigan Library for permission to quote from papers
contained in the Maurice Browne-Ellen Van Volkenburg collection;
and to Mr. Maurice Browne for permission to quote from a letter of
his to the author.

In addition, the following publishers and holders of copyright have
given me permission for substantial quotation from published work
in their hands. Mrs. Edgar Lee Masters has allowed me to quote the
poems "Adam Weirauch," "Lois Spears," and "Conrad Sievers," from
Edgar Lee Masters' *Spoon River Anthology*. The selection from Sara
Teasdale's *Strange Victory*, copyright 1933 by the Macmillan Co., is
used with their permission. Henry Holt and Co. have allowed me to
quote the poem "Who Am I?" from Carl Sandburg's *Chicago Poems*.
And Mr. Nicholas C. Lindsay and Mrs. Susan Russell, together with
Charles Scribners Sons, have allowed me a quotation from Vachel

Lindsay's college notebooks as reproduced in Edgar Lee Masters' *Vachel Lindsay* and from certain of the poet's letters.

More familiarly, my daughter Nora was a constant help in compiling the index—and to Edith Duffey, for her help in a myriad of ways, my life-long gratitude.

Table of Contents

Part One

PROTEST AND SEARCH

The Larger Pattern

CHICAGO itself is the midland metropolis. It sits heavily upon the lowest point in the low divide that separates the Great Lakes valley from that of the Mississippi, and into it flow, almost by gravity it would seem, the products, the people and the interests of all the greater Midwest. But Chicago is more than midwestern. The greatest railway transport point in the nation, it maintains connections with New York, Atlanta, New Orleans, Albuquerque, and San Francisco; there is hardly a city in the land to which it is not bound. It is largely without glamor or charm. Its interest is mercantile and industrial. The higher culture of America, the expression of its mores, imagination, and feelings, is not often thought of in connection with its name.

Yet, had Chicago no claim except that of its continentally strategic location, it must command the attention of the historian. For, as it has become the nation's transfer point, so it has typically concentrated a mixed and often muddled national character more overpoweringly, perhaps, than any other American city. Its creators, as was inevitable in the 1830's, were largely from New England, New York, and Pennsylvania; yet its first civilian inhabitant was a free Negro whose name, Jean Baptiste Point du Sable, suggested Louisiana or Canadian origins. Its site had been visited by French missionaries and traders in the seventeenth century. The British had wished to fortify it, but in 1803 Fort Dearborn was erected by Americans. Though the town's early population was heavily Anglo-Saxon and North-eastern in origin, a portion of settlers came from the South, both tidewater and upland, and its first major captain of industry was a Virginian, whose loyalty to the Old Dominion was overcome only by the great commercial opportunities he saw in the city as a manufacturing and distributing point for his newly con-

3

trived reaping machine. By 1861, Cyrus McCormick's southern loyalties fell apart, in typical Chicago fashion, under the pressure put upon his business by the Civil War. Mr. Secretary Stanton went so far as to say that without McCormick's reaper to take the place of the thousands of northern farm hands who left for the army, the defenders of the union might well have lost a critical advantage.

Perhaps the bond between North and South could be achieved more easily in Chicago than elsewhere because of the presence of the hundreds of thousands of European immigrants who, beginning in the forties, continued to arrive without great abatement until the quota acts of the 1920's. In the face of such an alien and ambitious horde, the gentlemen of North and South could, for a large part, swallow mere sectional differences. But one of Chicago's most popular mayors, the first Carter Harrison, also a Virginian, declared that he was so enamored of the city that he must take it as his bride, all of it for better or for worse. So he did, speaking throughout his tenure of office during the eighties and early nineties for Chicago's whole population, insisting (against a complaint of Marshall Field) that the least of Chicago's citizens had as much right to the mayor's attentions as the city's wealthiest man. The least citizens for whom he spoke were of a polygot sort. They came during the forties and fifties from Ireland, Germany and the Scandinavian countries. They came later from Austria-Hungary, the Balkans, Greece, Italy, Sicily. And in great numbers, after the first World War, they came from the southern United States—Negroes who sought in escaping the South to find some measure of social and economic opportunity. Where the original settlers of Chicago, or at least those who found the city good to them, had made Chicago their home, these later comers tended to make their homes in Chicago. As a result, there grew up Kilgubbin, Conley's Patch, Germantown, Bronzetown, Little Italy, and even, during the twenties, a substantial colony of Persians on the near north side, the complete and homogeneous inwardness of which defied any attempts at nicknaming. But as Chicago grew in size and in diversity of existence, it also became more and more a microcosm of the nation as a whole.

What was dilute in the nation, was concentrated in Chicago, and where in the nation lines were blurred, not easy to define, in Chicago they were as distinct as city blocks could make them.

Ranking all others were Chicago's powerful men, Field, Pullman, Armour, Yerkes, Insull. The goods in which these oligarchs dealt (and it is revealing that most of them dealt in goods rather than the intangibles of banking and stock ownership) were of the stuff of life itself. Field, through his retail and wholesale stores, clothed and furnished a whole area. Armour and Swift, and their less well advertised counterparts on the Board of Trade, sold a nation its meat and its grain. Potter Palmer, though perhaps longest to be remembered for his queen-of-society wife and his ornate Palmer Houses, owned the east side of State street and did much to create the business district in which the others worked. And even Insull, who will always be thought of as the conscienceless juggler of lighter-than-air holding companies, boasted the Commonwealth Edison Corporation as a chief possession and through it supplied Chicago and much of the adjacent region with its vital electric power.

Chicago was, and is, as diverse as the nation's races, religions, occupations, classes, and inherent hostilities could make it. But from these it has produced nothing which was not endemic to its own and the country's nature. It is the chief city of a multifarious region, and it concentrates the forces of that region through its heavy lens. The result is great heat, but the cause of its heat lies in the number of things, and the power of the things, which Chicago concentrates. Its character is generic rather than special.

Throughout its hundred odd years of existence Chicago has been a city in rushing transition—always hurrying on. As its characteristics have been those of the region and the nation of which it is the hub, so the phases of its transition were those of the larger wholes. It was to begin with a fort and a trading post. In 1833 it declared itself a town, and it grew in a decade or two into a city. In 1871 the great fire all but destroyed it. But between 1871 and 1910 it became a metropolis, not just the chief town of a limited region, but the chief town of several such regions and the chief among their notable cities. From then to the present it has been converting itself into megalopolis—huge in size, diverse and anonymous in character, and one of two or three cities in the land which recognize each other's substantial equality and hold their superiority to all others. These stages mark the larger Chicago transition. Though the present concern is with only selected aspects of this process, and with only a portion of it in time, the larger pattern underlies the more special interest. It is the broad frame upon which all our later details must be hung.

By an inevitable if inexact usage, the continuous wave of literary activity in Chicago, beginning in the last decade of the nineteenth century and continuing through the first two decades of the twentieth, has come to be known as the Chicago renaissance. It was, of course, not a re-birth but the working out within the city of creative forces common to the nation at that time. The Chicago writers worked from diverse impulses, and with some mutually felt hostilities, but they also shared a common awareness which bound them up in a common group and gave to their efforts a common stamp. The Chicago renaissance spanned precisely those decades during which serious American literature was shifting from its native romantic moorings to a berth somewhere on the periphery of American culture. The idealists of an earlier day had attacked much in America which offended them, but the tendency of the nation had been to honor them, if only formally, as legitimate albeit starry-eyed prophets. One needn't worry too much in this context whether or not Henry Ford spoke with any truth when he said that Emerson was his favorite author. The significant thing was that he allowed the statement to be reported. One cannot imagine him saying under any circumstances that Sherwood Anderson, for example, was his favorite author.

By the early nineties and the first dawnings of the Chicago renaissance, it became apparent that the American writer, who during the previous decades had functioned under a charter drawn loosely from the principles of a diffused romanticism, was about to have his prerogatives lapsed. In Chicago, certainly, he could have no further existence. With its apparent commitment to the culture of business, to a career of gain and loss, to greatness measured by railroads, stock yards, bank balances, and market raids, to gentility as the sweetening of life, and to a grimy democracy as its political actuality, there was no place or honor for the seer whose individual destiny and vision were so compelling as to require his own full devotion, and a public's respectful attention. Romantic seers had no place on the Board of Trade, they would have outraged a Congregationalist church and bewildered a west side crowd. The romantic image of the author could scarcely be contemplated, much less imitated.

The writer needed a redefined lease on the national life. During the nineties, and continuing indeed up to the present times, his efforts to make new terms were to be various and without a final success. He was to invoke the moral and aesthetic prerogative of an attenuated genteelism. He seized upon the claims of a realism extended far and ambitiously beyond its humble origin in descriptive writing. He was to dabble with the world-rejecting precocity of the aesthetes, he was to attempt a new application of Whitman's unfulfilled claim to a popular poetry, and he was finally to resort to outright hostility, inwardness, or shock in an effort to define his character for himself. The Chicago renaissance included in itself samples of all these efforts, and each of them, in Chicago, was to have a special clarity and, even, a special futility.

Itself a product of the very uncertainty which faced the writer, the Chicago of 1890 to 1910 (those decades during which the first phase of the Chicago renaissance took place), could not help its literature very measurably in achieving character. The city itself, before 1915, offered to the writer only one of three regular roles. There was first that of newspaper columnist, one which gave some notable writers a compromised freedom and support for their work. Eugene Field, George Ade, and Finley Peter Dunne thus gained their eminence as harbingers of Chicago's literary renaissance. Second, the intensification of the city's efforts toward genteel status which had created university, clubs, society, monumental houses, museums, libraries, and philanthropy reached out also for a literary distinction, which it attained in Henry Blake Fuller and, ironically, in Hamlin Garland. Third, the brute nature of Chicago made an obvious foil for the efforts of a group of realists among whom Robert Herrick was the most successful. The presence of a fourth class, that of the purely commercial success like George Barr McCutcheon or Henry Kitchell Webster was too largely accidental and had too little relevance to the spirit of the renaissance to have any real place in it. The first three, however, encompassed a process of search and protest which was to typify Chicago's and America's literary and intellectual emergence into modern times.

The First Estate

EARLY in the October of 1871 Chicago burned. The great conflagration which had been preceded by another major fire only the day before, began on the southwest side of the city in the Irish section. It was driven by a brisk wind and fueled by the drought-dried city, built largely of wood or flimsy stone-faced construction. Without obstacle, it ate its way on through the business district, crossed the river and proceeded through the whole northeast section, destroying slum, business area, and superior residential blocks alike. The tally of its destruction was enormous. Over 17 thousand buildings were destroyed, $200 millions of property in all. Only 250 dead were counted, but the toll had probably been far larger than that, for so intense was the heat that many of the bodies must have been wholly consumed. The numerous eye-witness accounts tell of a constant rain of glowing embers and brands, of panicked multitudes variously fleeing, praying, weeping, and looting, and of a heat so great that workmen trying to save the Tribune building, still some distance from the flames, had to retreat to the lee side of chimneys in order to breathe. When the fire burned out after two nights and two days, the city looked upon its thousands of black acres and wondered if it could ever recover from the harm. Especially did Wilbur Storey, publisher of the Chicago *Times*, despair. The *Times* plant had been destroyed completely, and Storey could see no use in working to re-establish his newspaper in a devastated city. He wept and bewailed his ruin. But one of his employees comforted him with words which carried conviction.

> I think, Mr. Storey . . . that you are mistaken as to Chicago being played out. In fact the real Chicago has not been touched by the fire. We still have our immense system of

9

railways, our sewers, our miles of water mains, our pavements, our lake navigation; in short, all that constitutes the real Chicago has not been disturbed.[1]

Storey's comforter was quite accurate. The "real" Chicago had not been disturbed. In less than a year, the business district and much of the outlying area had been rebuilt. Within three or four years, according to travelers' reports, there was hardly a direct trace of the fire left in the city. The conflagration had become a heroic memory. By 1873 and 1874 tens of thousands of vessels were again clearing the harbor, millions of bushels of grain were stored within the city, millions of hogs, cattle and sheep, were being processed in the packing plants, and the railway mileage of the section had nearly doubled. Chicago's greatest epoch of expansion and wealth had only begun.

The sole stock in trade of Chicago's earlier newspapers had been commercial and political information summarized with a baldness and lack of address which could argue only the journalistic self-sufficiency of these subjects in themselves. John Wentworth's *Democrat*, Joseph Forrest's *Tribune*, or Cyrus McCormick's *Times* were published by and for men of affairs limited largely to business and politics who were concerned only with their affairs. But by the later nineteenth century a change was in process. Its efficient cause was the reaching out of the newspaper publishers for a larger circulation—for a following among those classes to whom the mere news of "affairs" was scarcely a compelling lure. The history of Chicago's innovating newspaper editors and publishers was one principally of the enlargement of the newspaper from a tool of narrow utility to one of the broadest possible appeal. And in this process the special skill and ingenuity of clever writers took on importance. If readers without previously formed interests were to be drawn to the papers, it was necessary to create interests for them. But as imagination and inventiveness thus became commodities, they created a difficulty for the newspaper author. How, in the increasingly tight race for popularity, could he preserve the individual authority essential to his craft?

The process was begun in 1875 by Melville E. Stone who brought to the founding of the *Daily News* a set of ideas then novel to Chicago journalism. "Unlike our competitors," he argued, "we must with single-mindedness accept as our only masters, our readers."[2] This meant, in particular, that the *Daily News* would make no political or advertising affiliations which would diminish its liberty. There were, in Stone's opinion, three ends to be served by his policy of independence and of broad appeal. He would make news as lively and as reliable as possible. He would guide public opinion. And he would entertain his readers. In the latter two of these especially, though they were less crucial to him than the first, Stone created a need for trained writers which jumped them in importance several steps beyond any earlier Chicago practice.

His policy led directly to the acquisition of a locally distinguished staff. John Ballantyne and Slason Thompson, from the defunct Chicago *Herald*, became Stone's managing editor and chief editorial writer. Robert and Elia Peattie joined his paper, and Dr. Frank Reilly, later to be a mentor of Eugene Field, became first a medical correspondent and then a member of the editorial board. Following the practice of the London *Times*, Stone retained editorial specialists to write on their own subjects as the occasion arose. In addition to Reilly there was Prof. W. S. B. Matthews, an expert on music; Col. Gilbert A. Pierce, later a senator from North Dakota, for politics; William Morton Payne, soon to be a regular critic of literature on the *Dial* magazine, for books; Prof. James Lawrence Laughlin, of the University of Chicago, for economics; and Prof. Richard T. Ely, of the University of Wisconsin, for sociology.

From Indiana came John T. McCutcheon, as cartoonist, and George Ade, first as reporter then as columnist. From Denver, Stone brought Eugene Field, for the last ten years of his life a pillar to the popularity of the *News*. From the unlikely neighborhood of Chicago's west side emerged Peter Finley Dunne who served a brief term on the *News* before creating Mr. Dooley, and who was one of the few of his notable writers to escape Stone's grasp. Dunne, while writing on baseball for the *News*—a feature which before his time had been a colorless and largely statistical matter, reportedly created the elaborate kind of lingo which since then has marked the sportswriter's practice. And to George Ade, for his lively and imaginative description of the Corbett-Sullivan fight and the training period preceding it, Victor Lawson, Stone's partner, and later owner of the paper, gave the credit for an increase of five thousand in circulation.

Though entertainment was only one of three items in Stone's theory of editing, its importance was reflected in the rapid promotion of writers who could produce it successfully. As a result of Ade's Corbett-Sullivan success, for example, the reporter earned a column of his own which led directly to his major work, a daily feature called "Stories of the Streets and of the Town," which was to include the fables in slang. And in all cases Stone, or his editorial successor, John Dennis, was willing to put high value upon any man who could increase the power of the News by increasing its appeal. "The reader," explained Stone's memoirs, "was quite likely to find a gem worthy of Douglas Jerrold or Voltaire buried in an out-of-the-way corner, anywhere on the sheet. It paid him well for buying the paper, and the next day he bought it again."[3]

What paid the reader, paid the publisher. In this maxim lay the recipe for Stone's success and the basis for his interest in lively writing. But the result, for American letters, was a compromise, another Grub Street in which popularity and success were identified. What, as the twentieth century wore on, has become the commonplace of Hollywood, the popular magazines, radio, television, and the best-seller market lay, in Chicago of the nineties, in only a hopeful infancy. The child was to be nurtured on ever increasing technological advance into a multi-million dollar maturity, but his original nature was not to change. He was, for the creative writer, a problem then as now. Could an individual talent preserve an identity among the pressures of a business market? Chicago journalism of the end of the century supplied a tentative answer. The writer who had to be popular might also be perceptive, intelligent, and eloquent only as his formulas allowed for the smuggling in of these qualities. He was the jester of the marketplace rather than of the court, but he still had to dress his virtues in a persuasive motley.

I

Though Chicago papers had been served by feature writers before 1883, that year marked the coming to the city of Eugene Field and the beginnings of major literary effort in the Chicago newspaper world. Field was to die in 1895 without opportunity to make anything of the chances that might have come his way in another decade with the advent of newspaper syndicates and the mass circulation magazines, but he had arrived in time to know the strain of a double purpose. His immediate and daily task was the entertainment of *News* readers, but his fundamental drive was one of self-fulfillment—at least at the beginning. Stone had had some difficulty in luring him away from Denver though Field was tired of the city and tired of his job there. But he was equally tired of moving for its own sake. "If he was to make a change," wrote his biographer, "he must be assured that it was to be for his permanent good. He was a newspaper man not from choice, but because in that field he could earn his daily bread. Behind all he was conscious of great capability—not vain or by any means self-sufficient, but certain that by study and endeavor he could take high rank in the literary world and could win a place of lasting distinction."[4]

An idiosyncratic soul from his earliest days, Field nevertheless died like any laborer in the Chicago mill trying to meet the payments on a north side house. And, though he maintained his reputation as a practical joker and eccentric throughout his career, he dutifully filled his long column for twelve years. His politics were regularly Republican. He told Hamlin Garland, "I've consistently jumped on the crowd of faddists but I've never willingly done a real man or woman an injury."[5] And he said to his friend Slason Thompson, "Reform away . . . the world is good enough for me as it is." At the same time, one of the regular duties of John Ballantyne, Field's managing editor, was that of deleting the paragrapher's barbs against the institutions and persons of Chicago's genteel world when they stung too sharply. His position never exceeded that of licensed fun-maker whose liberty went unchecked only so long as it never really threatened the establishment which he amused. And, one might guess, much of his unusual popularity sprang from the ample testimony he provided of his strong basic loyalty. There was the reassuring sentimentality of much of his verse, the dislike of Europe reflected in his communications from London, a concentration of criticism on those who aped

Eastern tastes, and a reliance on home bred sense and common prejudice as the source for his satire.

Field's satirical writing had taken shape in 1881 with his move to the Denver *Tribune* and his composition of the *Tribune Primer*. Made up of paragraphs illustrated by the sardonic cartoons of Frederick Opper, this early and very popular volume suggests clearly the raucous distaste of the wandering newspaperman (Field's occupation for the past eight years) for the shibboleths of domestic sentiment. Its twists were those of a village atheist who had turned his attention from God to the average citizen. His butt was Everyman.

> Mamma is Larruping Poppa with the Mop Handle. The Children are Fighting over a Piece of Pie in the Kitchen. Over the Piano there is a Beautiful Motto in a Gilt Frame. The Beautiful Motto Says There is no Place Like Home.[6]

And the disenchantment so proudly cherished by the newspaper vagabond showed directly in "The Editor's Valise."

> Here we have a Valise. It does not weigh Four Hundred Pounds. It is the Valise of an Editor. In the Valise are Three Socks and a Bottle. Maybe it is Arnica for the Editor's Sore Finger. The Book is Baxter's Saints Rest. The Socks got into the Valise by Mistake. Perhaps the Bottle will get into the Editor by Mistake.[7]

Field's move to Chicago involved two changes in his work. By the first he shifted the aim of his satire from domestic manners generally to those of a prominent and unpopular elite, the very "upward movement" which was to inaugurate the chief work of the renaissance. By the second, he toned down the violence of his writing. In the *Primer* any device had been welcome.

> This is a Gun. Is the Gun loaded? Really, I do not know. Let us Find Out. Put the Gun on the Table, and you, Susie, blow down one Barrel, while you, Charlie, blow down the other. Bang! Yes, it was Loaded. Run, quick, Jenny, and Pick Up Susie's Head and Charlie's lower Jaw before the nasty blood gets over the New Carpet.[8]

Such a paragraph, perhaps, would not have done for a carefully run family newspaper.

A typical achievement of the Chicago period occurred in one of Field's columns for 1890 celebrating the arrival in the city of the stock-broking poet, E. C. Stedman, and the preparations made to greet him by the Chicago literari. There would be, declared Field earnestly, a great parade.

> *Twenty police officers afoot.*
>
> *The grand marshall, horseback, accompanied by ten male members of the Twentieth Century Club, also horseback.*
>
> *Mr. Stedman in a landau drawn by four horses, two black and two white.*
>
> *The Twentieth Century Club in carriages.*
>
> *A brass band, afoot.*
>
> *The Robert Browning Club in Frank Parmelee's busses.*
>
> *The Homer Club afoot, preceded by a fife and drum corps and a real Greek philosopher attired in a tunic.*
>
> *Another brass band.*
>
> *A beautiful young woman playing the guitar, symbolizing Apollo and his lute in a car drawn by nine milk white stallions impersonating the muses.*
>
> *Two hundred Chicago poets afoot.*
>
> *The Chicago Literary Club in carriages.*
>
> *A splendid gilded chariot bearing Gunther's Shakespeare autograph and Mr. Ellsworth's first printed book.*
>
> *Another brass band.*
>
> *Magnificent advertising car of Armour and Co., illustrating the progress of civilization.*
>
> *The Fishbladder Brigade and the Blue Island Avenue Shelley Club.*
>
> *The Fire Department.*
>
> *Another brass band.*
>
> *Citizens in carriages, afoot, and horseback.*
>
> *Advertising cars and wagons.*[9]

Of course, it would be agreed, the Twentieth Century Club should come at the head of the parade, surrounding Stedman. The club consisted of Chicago's notable citizens assembled expressly for the purpose of lionizing visitors. It was a joke throughout Chicago's newspaper world, and half a scandal to itself, though neither fact inhibited its lionizing. Then there was a fitness in having the two hundred Chicago poets go afoot while the exclusive and moneyed Chicago Literary Club, which accepted without complaint the substantially accurate charge that it was the only literary club in existence with no literary men as members, should ride in carriages. The Blue Island Avenue Shelley Club was a comfortable irony since the denizens of that far southerly and westerly thoroughfare had never heard of Shelley and so might safely be laughed at, while Armour's advertising car was just another version of Field's running gag about the incongruity of hogs and cultural pretensions. Chicago was fairly inured to almost any jokes about hogs.

Though Field had begun writing verses as early as his St. Louis days, and had continued in his Denver columns, Chicago gave him increased variety in this regard, but also an increasing conventionality. After a few years in Chicago he achieved what he called "The Golden Week," during which his column for six days was filled with a variety of verses of his own composition—a feat he believed to be unparalleled in newspaper history. These included a comic poem relying on a western miner's attempts to grapple with the French language, some of the early "translations" of Horace, imitations of Beranger, Johann Uhland, and Heine, and a sample of the pastiche Middle English versifying he had picked up from Slason Thompson. Field could read no foreign language, but he delighted in Horace and Heine Englished and in his own talent for a re-versifying of them.

He had been attracted to the book stores of Chicago, McClurg's especially, from the time of his arrival in the city, and it was these, plus his newspaper associates, who created the greatest change in him. Most important by far among the latter was Dr. Frank Reilly. Reilly had followed a busy medical career which had given him experience as a Civil War surgeon, as Secretary of the State Board of Health, and as Deputy Commissioner of Health for Chicago. Throughout his life he had maintained a great interest in literature, its byways more especially, and when an opportunity for association with the *News* came his way, he took it gladly—in time making it a full-fledged professional interest. The precise state of his learning is hard to judge from the scanty reports of him, but, for Field, he compacted a catholic literary culture into his knowledge of two books, Christopher North's *Noctes Ambrosianae* and Francis Mahoney's *Reliques of Father Prout*. The latter, especially, was the doctor's favorite and the key which opened a narrow way for Field into the realms of world literature.

But, according to Slason Thompson, Field's literary development in Chicago took him in circle from a reliance on the society of his own kind, suggested by his satire, to a nearly complete submersion in the narrow and bookish world which came to dominate his later columns. And the change, one from creation to imitation, paralleled his growing success. Dr. Reilly had opened to Field the pleasures of the bookish life and then left him to find his own direction to what his friend Cowan called "the must and rust of bibliomania." Field turned his column more and more toward the "Saints' and Sinners' Corner" of McClurg's bookstore, which he invented and then filled with his friends in imaginary session chatting of their hobby and so escaping the dull world which lay all around them. His introduction to literature had come too late, perhaps, to cut deeply into his consciousness. Certainly it failed to provide him with whatever he needed to deepen his writing or increase its reality. His wit maintained itself to the end, but it had lost its grasp on all but a narrow and artificial experience.

There is no need to argue that Field's career was that of a thwarted genius, but one may suggest that little resistance to the dissipation of his talent was to be found in his Chicago success. So long as he held his readers, his task was done. There was, however, the Field who had come to Chicago to find a fuller exercise for his literary gift and who then lost himself in the curious and trivial. His final relation to literature in the midst of Chicago's business culture was not unlike that of the tycoon, Charles Yerkes, to his collection of paintings. If one's circumstances allowed, one might amass art, or otherwise express his interest in it. But so peripheral was it to the job immediately in hand that no question need arise as to its reality.

II

Of the three most notable newspaper writers of turn-of-century Chicago, it was George Ade whose career was to show most clearly the particular limitations and advantages which the Chicago newspaper might hold for the ambitious man of letters. After graduating from the recently founded and still bucolic Purdue University, he put in a few years of writing for the two Lafayette papers and for an advertising company. When, through the good offices of his friend John McCutcheon he was translated to the metropolis and to the staff of the *News*, he was still young and malleable. He had an indiscriminate taste in reading, a gift of easy and effective writing, and an interest in people and places; but his literary character remained to be formed. Except for his brief career in advertising, where his chef d'oeuvre had been the slogan for Cascarets, "They work while you sleep," his early experience as a writer was confined entirely to newspapers.

Not only did he learn much of his craft after his arrival in Chicago, but the city itself was a revelation. Until he took special assignments in 1892, Ade served the *News* as a general reporter covering labor, thefts, fires, politics, strikes, inquests and all the other doings of a large city, which constitute its news. Unlike Field or Dunne, he worked hard at reporting and from his earliest days showed an unusual talent for the chief need of the newspaper writer—that of dealing freshly with commonplace events. He enjoyed the reportorial side of his career. The newness of his discoveries became the color of his later specialized writing in his column, "Stories of the Streets and of the Town." Where both Field and Dunne, in differing ways and degrees, counted on manner, style, for an important element of their appeal, Ade, like any good realist, worked for transparency and plainness. "My ambition, like McCutcheon's," he was to say later, "was to report people as they really were, as I saw them in their everyday life, and as I knew them to be. Consequently, I avoided exaggeration, burlesque, and crude caricature; and I did not try to fictionize or to embroider fancy situations, as was common in the fiction of that day. In the "Stories" there was not much emphasis upon plot, but instead carefully sketched, detailed incidents in the delineation of real characters in real life, depicting various episodes in their lives as related through the medium of their own *talk*."[10]

As Ade's column progressed through 1894 and 1895 he received letters from Hamlin Garland, by that time a Chicago resident and an aspirant to midwestern literary dictatorship, and from Henry Fuller, whose second excursion into realism, *With The Procession*, had just appeared. Both urged Ade to turn his talents to some form more substantial than that of the newspaper sketch—in particular to do a novel. Fuller was especially effusive, declaring, "When you feel the disposition to write the 'Chicago Novel' that people are beginning to expect of you, I don't know of anybody who wouldn't be glad to pull off to one side and give you all the room you need."[11] Both letters were occasioned by the collection of Ade's "Artie" stories into a book at the urging of Herbert S. Stone, partner in the enterprising firm of Stone and Kimball and son of the *Daily News* founder. This same volume occasioned the high praise of William Dean Howells. "On the level which it consciously seeks, I do not believe there is a better study of American town life in the West."[12]

Though Howells may not, as Ade's biographer asserts, have named Ade as his favorite author, he did certify the Chicagoan's work, his *Artie*, *Pink Marsh*, and *Doc Horne* especially, as acceptable to the realistic canon.

Artie, published in 1896, deserved especially the praise which Howells gave it. The city's new buildings were filled mainly with young men who performed routine office tasks (the ubiquitous female clerk was still largely in the future), and who regarded their white collar jobs both as advancement from usually humble origins and a certification of themselves as men of the great world. Cockily sure of their powers, confident in their associations with the city's business leaders, they developed manners and an argot setting them apart and, in their own opinion, well above the average citizen. Of such was Artie Blanchard. In part he fitted Ade's earlier description of "the Board of Trade young man," " . . . a square shouldered young man, with a small soft hat pulled forward over one eye, a short office coat flapping in the wind, and a general suggestion of good clothes worn in a 'don't care' fashion." But Artie had grown from more humble roots, though he too was at ease in the business Zion and certainly not less knowing, not less a man, than the retainers of the great institution itself.

> You go along Prairie avenue and see all o' them swell joints where the fat boys with side whiskers hang out. Well, them boys all come in from the country, but they had sense enough to saw wood and plant a little coin when it begin to come easy. I'm tellin' you the worst suckers you'll find is some o' these city people that know it all to begin with. They got such a long start on everybody else that they don't need to learn nothin'. If they know the names of the streets, what shows is in town next week, what color of a necktie to flash and what was the score at the ball game they think they come purt' near bein' dead wise..You live here in town awhile and you'll get on to them people. Say! I know a lot o' boys that's got just enough sense to put in workin' hours and then go ridin' a wheel. You couldn't set 'em down and tell 'em a thing. Any of 'em that's got himself staked to a spring suit and knows the chorus o' 'Paradise Alley' thinks he's up to the limit. You can make book that them boys'll be workin' on bum salaries when they're gray headed, and what's more, they'll be workin' for some Reub that come into town wearin' hand-me-downs."[13]

But when Ade moved away from his genre figures, Howells' acquiescence lessened. In particular, the sudden rise to popularity of the fables in slang, first conceived of as filler for Ade's column, constituted a threat to the realistic character of his other work and indeed to Ade's whole concept of himself as a writer. Almost from their start in 1896 the fables created a demand that posed the question of whether Ade could hope ever again to secure a hearing for any of his work except these entertainments. His friends, seeing the success which the fables offered, advised him "to take the gifts that were falling into his lap and not to crave the golden persimmons that grow on the hill tops," and the young newspaperman found such ready reward irresistible.

The result was a conversion from developing realist to master gag-writer, a change which allowed his penetration and his sharp sense of the ridiculous full exercise, but which cut off at the root his concern for the literary substance of real life. The fables were largely held to common prejudices and brash attitudes the better to generate the amused but tolerant sense of incongruity in which their popularity lay. If they aspired to a total disenchantment, their effort was too predictable, too obviously guided toward surface effects, to stir much depth. The result was that of a single joke repeated too often. They represented a startling degree of concentration—the finding of a gag formula so apt that it could serve for decades to entertain its fans and to win new ones. One may dip into the fables at almost any point and find the same elements—an elaborate title; a chief character of whom it is easy to make fun; a set of minor adventures usually consummated in a surprise ending; and a mock moral tag which served as the concluding punch line. There was little variation. Often the fables had shrewdness ("Get acquainted with the Heads of Departments and Permit the Subordinates to become acquainted with You"), but even more often their chief strength was in the simple incongruity of slang itself—the pointlessly flippant expression of situations usually expressed more directly ("Once there was a Financial Heavyweight, the Mile Stones of Whose Busy Life were strung back across the Valley of Tribulation into the Green Fields of Childhood").

Most of all, Ade had abandoned the concern with living speech which had lent the most vitality to his work in favor of a convention. Slang and colloquial language of all sorts had filled his writing, but it had functioned as an aspect of character and situation. Artie's brittle lingo, Pink Marsh's dialect, and Doc Horne's garrulousness had come naturally out of their speakers' mouths. In them, Ade realized to a degree the aim he had originally set for himself—to create the reality of common, contemporary life through the speech of its characters. But the fables divorced speech from living character. Everyone in them either talked slang or had his thoughts paraphrased in slang. The results of concentration, in itself, need not have been bad. But the language in which Ade put his trust lacked resilience or suggestion. It was a shorthand reference to experience for the convenience of those to whom the complexity of experience had small reality. Slang, at its best, might be smart or knowing, and Ade's fables possessed these qualities, but it could seldom be encompassing or wise. In effect George Ade had sacrificed his early interest in life itself, in the human skein from which he might well have woven the qualities characteristic of better realism, for the popularity, the success, attendant upon the gag. He was not unaware of his choice, as a letter to Howells suggested. "It cheers me exceedingly to read your kind words, especially since you choose to remember that picked up and patched together little volume of Doc' Horne. I believe that the sale of "Doc' Horne" has been approximately eight copies— the fables, four million (publisher's statement). Don't cease to hope for me, as I shall get around to the work I like and swear off on Capital Letters sooner or later."

In Chicago's business world, its department of journalism, Ade learned that one might become more a success as he became less an author. Circumstances had at first pushed him toward a degree of personal achievement, but when circumstances were more fully heard from, they required a stricter attention to business—theirs and not the writer's. And, to this call, Ade finally gave his whole heed.

III

Eugene Field and George Ade, comparative strangers to the city in which they brought their careers to fulfillment, found Chicago a new experience. Field's response was to select those few interests which were especially congenial to him and, increasingly, to concentrate on them alone. Ade, to the contrary, took such picturesqueness as was inherent in the life of its metropolitan streets, making of this life the staple of his own work until popular pressure brought him to concentrate on the formula of the fables in slang. Where, to Field and Ade both, the city's newness was its chief stimulus, its familiarity was of greatest importance to Dunne.

But Mr. Dooley was not to achieve his stature from a single cause. He, or rather his predecessor, was first conceived as topical filler for the Sunday edition of the *Evening Post* to which Dunne had moved in 1892. The original version of Dooley was one Colonel McNeery who in turn had been suggested to Dunne by the proprietor of a large Dearborn street saloon much frequented by Chicago newspapermen. McNeery's comments for the *Post* were inaugurated by some remarks the actual saloon keeper, McGarry, had made on the death of Jay Gould. These had pleased Dunne sufficiently so that he worked them, probably with embellishment, into an imaginative conversation between the saloon keeper and John T. McKenna, a ward heeler of Chicago transferred from real life to the *Post's* Sunday issue.

> *Jay Gould is dead, Vanderbilt is dead, Mike Casey is dead. They're all dead and gone, poor men, and none of them took his money with him. Jay Gould had no fun in life. My friend there, little Johnny McKenna, would have more fun at a dance at Brighton Park, ten times over, than Jay Gould had all his lifetime with $100,000,000. Ten times over, for McKenna could get up the next morning and eat a side of bacon, cabbage, and boiled potatoes, put on his cambric shirt and come down town as fresh as e'er a man you know, while Gould, sure, the poor little wisp of a man, if he ate one egg for breakfast, he'd be doubled up with sorrow in his stomach.[14]*

Much, however, of what was to make Mr. Dooley most real was lacking from this earliest version. In particular, Dunne gave only an inkling here of the highly developed and flavored speech which his later character was to use. The free-ranging wit of Martin Dooley was present in spirit, but it lacked the apposite letter. Dunne himself valued Mr. Dooley's dialect for the security and freedom of opinion it made available to him. It seemed possible, he thought, to express all manner of opinion in dialect which, if written straight out, would have enraged not only many readers but often the influential subjects of Dunne's comments. Dooley's brogue was a verbal mask to secure for Dunne some part of the freedom he valued so highly. But more important than this, Dooley's brogue brought an element of poetry into Dunne's apprehension of public matters. It lent both detachment and reality.

Dooley's famous remarks on Rockefeller led not to an arming of the proletariat with pike staffs, but to an ironic comprehension of this hypocrite-seeming man of much wealth.

> He don't care f'r money in th' passionate way that you an' me do, Hinnisy. Th' likes iv us are as crazy about a dollar as a man is about his child whin he has on'y wan. Th' chances are we'll spoil it. But Jawn D., havin' a large an' growin' fam'ly iv dollars, takes on' a kind iv gin'ral inthrest in thim. He's issued a statement sayin' that he's a custojeen iv money appointed be himself. He looks afther his own money an' th' money iv other people. He takes it an' puts it where it won't hurt thim an' they won't spoil it. He's a kind iv society f'r th' previntion of croolty to money. If he finds a man misusin' his money, he takes it away fr'm him an' adopts it.[15]

But the development of both language and character had to wait until the first period of the McNeery sketches had run its course. For the aim of these earliest pieces was linked closely with a simple journalistic desire to crowd as many references to living and notable people into each essay as was possible. They were popular from the start, but their original popularity was like that of the gossip columnists of a later day—the result of a simple pleasure in the doings and sayings of the great. Consequently when the saloon keeper McGarry objected, in 1893, to the use of his establishment as a scene, and of a name similar to his own as a tag for Dunne's chief character, the writer was forced to make some changes which were of major importance in the increased stature of his work.

Martin Dooley, who now appeared for the first time as his chief figure, ran a small establishment which stood in the old Irish section on Archer avenue in the midst of workingmen's houses and cabbage gardens. He retained more of his native Irish qualities than did the thoroughly urbanized McGarry, and it was seldom that one could find in his saloon or among his acquaintance the august personages who formed McGarry's natural orbit. Mr. Dooley, in a word, was thrown very largely on his own, and whatever of interest or value came in his sketches had to rise from himself. Dooley must, it would seem, be eloquent or perish. Happily, the former alternative prevailed, and the history of Dunne's sketches in 1893 and 1894 was one of a rapidly developing central character. After the latter year, Mr. Dooley was fully established.

Above all, a desire for free expression impelled Dunne's progress. In his various moves, from early days down to the latest, his search was for a spot where he might write most nearly from his impulses. Though the Dooley essays never appeared at intervals of less than a week, Dunne's independence made him a flagrant crowder of deadlines, toiling through the last few minutes before press time while an anxious editor stood watch over him. He left the *Post* in 1895 primarily because a change in ownership of that paper had brought Herman Kohlsaat as Dunne's ultimate superior, and Kohlsaat in turn brought a rigidly Republican line to the *Post's* editorial page. Dunne, usually, was Democratic in his views, but he was much more disturbed by Kohlsaat's declaration of a line to be followed than at his publisher's Republicanism. In politics, as in everything else, Dunne was a mugwump. Early in life he had ceased to be a practicing Roman Catholic, but he always maintained a friendly attitude toward that communion. The creator of Mr. Dooley, like his creature, needed space, time, and independence in which to operate. Unlike Field or Ade, he bound himself to no particular paper, refused the financial lure of a daily column, and cut off the Dooley series for good when it no longer had a creative reality for him.

Out of such freedom Dunne made his other self, the saloon keeper in the Archey Road, a spokesman of greater dramatic stature than that of any other character to appear in the pages of a Chicago newspaper. Though, like the Supreme Court in his own characterization of it, his subjects followed the election returns of popular interest, Dunne opined at liberty. Theodore Roosevelt was a great admirer of his, but he was also the victim of Dooley's wit. Strikes, progress, foreign affairs, and high finance, all were brought upon Dooley's stage for their turns. And when in the midst of his remarks he turned his attention to more ambitious subjects and, in these less familiar areas where homely philosophies are most likely to fall under a disproportionate strain, Mr. Dooley maintained his wit and his poise. When Dooley came to speak for himself, he spoke for all.

I'm a house to ye, wan iv a thousand that look like a row iv model wurrukin' men's cottages. I'm a post to hitch ye're silences to. I'm always about the same to ye. But to me I'm a millyon Dooleys and all iv them sthrangers to ME. I niver know which wan iv them is comin' in. I'm like a hotel keeper with on'y wan bed an' a millyon guests, who come wan at a time an' tumble each other out. I set up late at night an' pass th' bottle with a gay an' careless Dooley that hasn't a sorrow in the wurruld, an' suddenly I look up an' see settin' across fr'm me a gloomy wretch that fires th' drink out iv th' window an' chases me to bed. I'm just gettin' used to him whin another Dooley comes in, a cross, cantankerous, crazy fellow that insists on eatin' breakfast with me. An' so it goes. I know more about mesilf than annybody knows an' I know nawthin'. Though I'd make a map fr'm memory, an' gossip iv anny other man, f'r mesilf I'm still uncharted.[16]

IV

Like any journalistic character, Mr. Dooley had his better days and his worse, but if one were to make a selection of the best in Field, in Ade and in Dunne, the last would show a unique distinction in kind—that of creative freedom and dramatic reality. For Ade there was the blind alley of routine entertainment suggested by the fables and by his dramatic pieces. Starting with an ear for the living speech of the city, he moved too willingly away from one kind of literary reality which Chicago offered him. Field, relaxed by popularity and confined by routine, sought a private refuge. But Dunne, clinging to his freedom as best he could, and saturated in the reality of Chicago and American life, made his other self, the saloon keeper in the Archey Road, a spokesman who within his limits rose from the levels of journalism to those of literature. His best discourses accomplished the basic literary act, the transforming of common experience into language so that each of the two elements served in a dramatic context to enrich the other. The key to Dunne's success in transcending the limits of popular entertainment without sacrificing popularity lay in the creation of dramatic character out of the necessities of popular entertainment itself. Only a figure who was as free and as real as he was entertaining could serve the double need.

Henry Fuller

AS CHICAGO moved into the nineties it gave evidence other than journalistic of its sense of self-arrival. For the sixty years preceding, it had billowed out in all directions at a rate of growth unprecedented among American cities to reach a population of well over a million and to assert itself as the commercial and industrial capital of the midwest. All the world, it felt, now knew it to be the busiest, noisiest, dirtiest, and most expansive city of the continent; the seething and polyglot mart of railroads, grain, meat, timber, and machinery; and just possibly the wickedest city of the new world as well. It had little to recommend it except wealth; little beauty, little culture, no tradition, no variety apart from that of its despised but numerous immigrant nationalities. But these things, it felt, came second. Possess the wealth, and you could buy what else you needed. And, by 1890, the money was on hand. The decade began with the incorporation of the University of Chicago, a university at a clap of the hands, paid for by John D. Rockefeller. Plans were afoot for the nationally significant Columbian Exposition. Theodore Thomas' symphony was reconstituted as the Chicago Symphony in 1903 and presented with its hall in 1904. And the city was faced with the possibility of a new character for itself—that of an earnest if uncertain center of culture.

In the pages of Francis Fisher Browne's *Dial*, which for a decade had been attempting to keep the pulse of literary culture beating in Chicago's body politic, and economic, there appeared a wholly natural note of exultation at the sudden flowering. "The Art Institute, The Newberry and Crerer and Public Libraries, the World's Fair Auxiliary, the Historical Society's enlarging quarters, the fact of the new Chicago University and the rejuvenescence of others near by,—all indicate that the city is passing to a higher and maturer stage

27

of civic existence. . . . Centres of social activity are thus forming, in which artists and scholars and educators will gather, at which ideas and ideals will prevail, and which, as an informal 'Academy,' will set standards that shall mitigate and transform the grossness of our hitherto material life."[1]

A moment had been achieved which, in more than one quarter, seemed the beginning of a new epoch. And the *Dial*, in its literary capacity, might have made a little more pointed the importance of Chicago's new upward movement to the city's writers. Where there had been, until this moment, only two very meaningful literary *genres* open to the native Chicago author, those of the popular press and of the new and still suspect realism, there was being created in the prairie a seeming rock on which to stand—that of the eastern genteel tradition. Of the three, the role of genteelist might have seemed most promising. Despite its apparent incongruity in the city of stock yards and the bitch goddess, it held out the best apparent hope of satisfying the writer's own professional needs and the demands of the dominant national literature. It had a pantheon of such deities as Longfellow, Lowell, and Holmes, and a working priesthood made up of Aldrich, Warner, Gilder, Stoddard, and Stedman. It was the obvious heir to the great New England ethical tradition which the Civil War had helped to make the commonly professed creed of the victorious states, and if, in 1890, one chose to be a serious writer, there was scarcely any place except the genteel tradition in which to find regular habitation. Mark Twain felt its pressures and Whitman its censures. The chief literary magazines, the *Atlantic* and the *Century* especially, were in its hands. It formed the taste acted upon by every important publishing house. Any opportunity for individual and romantic quest was largely stifled by the growth of a massive and materialistic age, and there was as yet no coherent bohemian or lyric refuge to which the writer might retreat.

It was this force which literary Chicago responded to. By 1890 tensions in the Chicago world, and particularly that between the older, New-England Chicagoans on the one hand and the newer entrepreneurs such as Charles Yerkes on the other, were beginning to come clearly into the open. Yerkes' sin, interestingly enough, was that of a great desire to make money, a wish which the leading citizens of Chicago had heretofore respected wholly. Yerkes came late, however, and with a bad past. He had been imprisoned briefly in Philadelphia for having in his possession certificates of indebtedness which belonged to the city and, though he disclaimed any guilty intention, there can be little doubt that he had, as traction speculator in Philadelphia, learned rules useful for getting his way with city corporations. Chicago, upon his arrival, presented great opportunities. Its inhabitants were moved from place to place on a few lines of slow moving horse cars, most of them owned by separate companies. All combined failed to provide the transportation which the spreading city required. Yerkes' work consisted, first, of buying control of the scattered lines and then of unifying, multiplying and electrifying them. During the eighties speed was increased chiefly by means of cable trains, and during the nineties Yerkes introduced trolley cars. While thus giving the public better service, the entrepreneur proceeded to assure his own interests by the time-honored method of watering his substantial issues of stock—of capitalizing his holdings for sums far beyond their real worth or future expectation. To preserve his interest it became necessary to assure his ownership of the lines. Since he held these under short-term franchises from the city, there was always the possibility that the city might destroy him by cutting off the tenure of his franchise at its expiration. Yerkes took the simplest and most direct method to prevent such a contingency. He bought the votes of a majority of the city's aldermen sufficiently large to give him what measures he desired and to pass them over the mayor's veto when that was necessary.

In 1893 there was formed the Civic Federation, headed by Lyman J. Gage—a chief banker of Chicago and sponsor of a public discussion group out of which the Federation had grown. The Federation's chief initial objective was the removal of Yerkes from control of the city government and from Chicago itself if possible. For five years it conducted a campaign of exposure and civic virtue during which Yerkes' men, one by one, were removed from City Hall. By 1900 success had been won, and Yerkes fled to London where he set about satisfying that city's need for transportation. He had not given up easily however. Among other things he had bought J. Y. Scammon's conservative paper, the *Inter-Ocean*, to promote his cause, and had come close to bribing the state legislature into giving him a fifty year franchise.

Though the Civic Federation, and its *ad hoc* agency, The Municipal Voters' League, were open to public membership, they were headed and sustained by prominent and successful citizens who were the masculine counterparts of Chicago's "Society" women. It was the women primarily who organized and supported the social events, clubs, and cultural and philanthropic institutions which, beginning in the seventies became increasingly prominent in Chicago's social life. "My culture," commented Philip Armour, "is mostly in my wife's name."[2] The Civic Federation could not be described as a function of Chicago's Society, but its work in ousting Yerkes, in instituting a civil service law, in organizing relief during the black winters of 1893 and 1894, of closing Chicago's open gambling houses, of instituting a municipal court system to replace the older justice courts (which had come so largely into the hands of political bosses and their immigrant constituents that a gentleman could get no justice from them), and of promoting Daniel Burnham's "Chicago Plan," which was to change at least the face of the city in the next two decades—in all of these things the Civic Federation, like Society, was extending the culture of Chicago, heretofore so deeply committed to business for business' sake, in a new direction.

For the upward-movers, the issue largely took the form of an effort to elevate the taste and social tone of the shoddy, brick-built wilderness with which increasingly they felt themselves at odds. As more of them were jostled in the economic pre-eminence which in the early decades of the city's history they had enjoyed, so their efforts to assert their leadership partook increasingly of those qualities in which they claimed a special excellence. In the sacred names of Decorum, Culture, and Good Taste, of Education and Self-Improvement, they found the tokens which might restore a partially compromised status. The genteel tradition, as it was exercised in Chicago, was in part an effort to assert one kind of value over another—to declare that in manners and taste there lay distinctions which were as real as that of dollars and which might be maintained against that of dollars.

The Chicago novelist, Henry Fuller's account of the upward movement, which he wrote for the *Atlantic* in 1897, was an effort to survey all of the forces which, to his mind, were making for the right in the midst of most inhospitable circumstances. Done with a characteristic irony, his essay nevertheless took full cognizance of the reality of the issue. In Chicago, he noted, "we are obliged to fight—determinedly, unremittingly, for those desirable, those indispensable things, that older, more fortunate, more practiced communities possess and enjoy as a matter of course. As a community, we are at school; we are trying to solve for ourselves the problem of living together."[3] Nor did he overstate the case. For if one were to subtract from the life of the present day city all that the upward movement gave to it, one might have some notion of the moral and intellectual wilderness which faced the aspirant to "higher things" of Fuller's time. The Civic Federation did not succeed in transforming Chicago into a paradise, but it heightened its civilization. Such educational institutions as the Art Institute and the University of Chicago brought to the city its first very successful efforts to understand something of the life of mind and imagination. Before Theodore Thomas inaugurated the presence of symphonic music in Chicago, before the Public Library, the Newberry and the Crerar Libraries began to make available at least a selection of the instruments of a culture not purely mercantile, there was no generally available arsenal for those who might wish to oppose the notion that the making of money formed, exclusively, the proper study of mankind. One may well argue that the upward movement, the expression of genteel standards in Chicago, was less than a triumph, but it would be impossible to deny its perceptible effect in mitigating some of the bleakest and most hopeless aspects of Chicago life. For Fuller, its enemies were the forces of "Greed" and "Slouch." Whatever in the city's life, in his opinion, was not to be dominated by these two masters, could come only from a dedication to higher things, to things largely imported from more fortunate regions, particularly the East. Possibly, he felt, the battle was hopeless, but there was no other choice.

In particular, the upward movement first defined the Chicago literary renaissance and made a place for Fuller, Herrick, Garland, Hobart Chatfield-Taylor, Harriet Monroe, Edith Wyatt, Joseph Kirkland, and the other Chicago authors by creating for them, as Browne had suggested in his *Dial* editorial, the role of aesthetic and ethical arbiter, or inspiring them at least with this ideal, in imitation of their eastern peers.

They had a heavy lump to leaven. Marshall Field as sole tenant now occupied Potter Palmer's building at the corner of State and Washington streets and was fully embarked on the merchandising career which was to leave him a fortune of $120 millions, the largest in Chicago. This was four times greater than Philip Armour's estate, but the latter's $30 millions were well into the making upon his arrival in Chicago in 1873 to oppose successfully the established packers, Nelson Morris and Samuel Allerton. Of him, his great rival Gustavus Swift said, "He was a born speculator, and coupled with the power to speculate safely, he had the faculty of being able to keep a great number of irons in the fire all of the time."[4] Swift's own talents were different. He avoided speculation, except when the maintenance of his business itself demanded it, and concentrated upon the conversion of meat packing from butchery and pickling to a fully developed industry. It was he who began utilizing the by-products of the carcasses in which he dealt and who led in developing the trade in fresh dressed meat which today constitutes the bulk of the packer's business. He was quick to see the possibilities of refrigerator cars and bludgeoned their use upon the railroads when the latter rejected the lower income they brought. As Armour was a speculator Swift was an industrialist, but both lived for their work, commonly spending ten to twelve hours a day at it. It was from Armour that the most concise description of business motives came. "I have no other interest in life but my business. I do not want any more money; as you say, I have more than I want. I do not love the money. What I do love is the getting of it. All these years of my life I have put into this work, and now it is my life and I cannot give it up. What other interest can you suggest to me? I do not read. I do not take any part in politics. What can I do?"[5]

The reporter whom he thus questioned had no answer, or at least none is recorded. But as Armour waxed rich he did give some attention to symbols of bourgeois achievement other than dollars. His greatest philanthropy resulted, in 1893, in the founding of the Armour Institute, now the Illinois Institute of Technology, with the popular Chicago preacher, Frank Gunsaulus, as president. He also founded a day nursery and presented several items to the collection of the Art Institute. With this latter benevolence, a visiting English journalist, George Steevens, was much struck. "Mr. Phil D. Armour, the hog king, giving a picture to the gallery, and his slaughter house man painfully spelling out the description of it on Sunday afternoon —there is something rather pathetic in this, and assuredly something very noble."[6]

But where to Steevens the incongruity of hogs and fine art was striking, it was possible to see in Armour's later-day philanthropies a larger problem to which the upward movement addressed itself— that of the business success trying to define and believe in a culture from which his activities had excluded him. For Armour, as later for Marshall Field, the business world had been sufficient unto itself. The idea of breaking its rules, of giving money away for reasons which had no connection with the making of it, was strange enough so that these men and others like them found it hard to understand. The idea might, like Armour's culture, be presented to them in their wives' names, or it might be acceptable within the familiar limits of charitable and church giving, but any other motive required a different rationale. It is not surprising that the Armour Institute should have been devoted to useful arts only, or that the Armour day nursery should have been established for working mothers. Such establishments did relate to the business culture and could be explained in its terms. But when the founders of the University of Chicago approached Marshall Field for a gift of ten acres of land upon which to build the school, they were kept waiting for weeks before any answer was given them. Field, by nature, was a cautious and thoughtful man. Being of a temperament which required good reasons always, he may well have spent the time defining the coordinates by which he might evaluate this unprecedented action. "He never gives a note," said one of his partners, "he never buys a share of stock on margin; he is against speculation; he has made it a point not to encumber his business with mortgages; he does business on a cash basis; he tries to sell on a shorter time than his competitors; he tries to sell the same grade of goods for a smaller price; he holds his customers to a strict meeting of their obligations."[7]

II

In describing the upward movement's attack on the business Philistia, Henry Fuller had been occupied with an entity to which, by birth and upbringing he was committed, one which made demands on his loyalties, and one which by his own standards was doing a needed and genuinely good work. But for all his identification of himself with a "better class," and for all his concern with Chicago's struggles toward a better day, he could not keep his article free from a continual ironical play of tone about the uplifters. He had been born into the third generation of a New-England Chicago family— one which had come West early and prospered. His fate, however, was to find himself unable to give more than a qualified allegiance to his family background, unable to give any allegiance to other parties in Chicago, and possessed of literary talents and tastes which were at least sufficient to keep him throughout his life aware of his unrealized possibilities. He is, without doubt, the chief literary representative of Chicago's genteel culture, and his unsettled mind, his permanent bachelordom, his eccentric habits and solitary life prefigure amply the tentative and unrealized nature of his writing. The wonder is that his work achieved distinction at all. It does not possess major status, but it is acute and imaginative. Its limitations are those created by a compromised temperament, but its qualities, being genuinely literary, survive the circumstantial failure. For Fuller, the problem was that of living in his Chicago a life which a man of his tastes and feelings might tolerably endure.

Not surprisingly, the original and pervasive force in his work was a centripetal one—away from the work-a-day Chicago which was the overwhelmingly triumphant reality, outward toward whatever momentary point of rest suggested itself as a refuge from the chaotic center. In this center his grandfather had established a family fortune, and his father continued to serve a less distinguished but solid career. For Henry B., however, the center was never to be anything but a subject for probing and study; he was the exile at home, a dispossessed one surrounded by massive evidence of the cause which he had deserted—or which had deserted him. Moving alone among the deepening canyons of Chicago's streets, regarding their inhabitants with a gaze compounded of detached perception and obscure loyalties, finding his acquaintances only among the few persons he chose as congenial to his needs, his mannered figure became the archetype for all his writing. Few novelists have vested their creations more sharply with a sense of their author's loss, his need for a point of rest, or, finally, his inability to discover one.

Paradoxically, it was the failure of Fuller's quest, the unresolved difficulty both of his life and his work, that gave the latter its distinction. Many of his contemporaries saw him, either approvingly or disapprovingly, as a snob—whether aesthetic, intellectual, or social was harder to say—but most of them recognized also that his work was more than a mere record of snobbery. It was well wrought and filled with a genuine expression of its author's self, and if that self was after all a minor and contorted one, there were none who gave a sharper sense of its limitations than Henry Fuller. Though his immediate problem was that of making something of a diminished thing, he seldom tried to solve it by pretentiousness.

The title of his first book set the angle at which he was to regard both himself and his world throughout his career. *The Chevalier of Pensieri-Vani,* the knight of idle thoughts, was a phrase which had a greater resonance than that of the immediate *fin de siecle* tenor within which the book grew. It suggested also that earlier knight who, like Fuller, set out to meet the world equipped originally with a high, romantic notion of his own destiny. Unlike Don Quixote, however, Fuller suffered early and thorough disillusion. His original dedication, interestingly titled *Pensieri Privati,* had occurred in an unpublished, juvenile poem which declared, in its final stanza,

> *I'd see and hear the best of all the good;*
> *And if it were forbid me to create,*
> *I still could love, admire, appreciate;*
> *Here such a life is not e'en understood.*[8]

But this private ambition came to an unhandsome end which was recorded, with a good deal less circumstances, in his journal for 1874, "Ovington's Crockery—122 State St." Fuller had left school and gone to work.

He returned to public high school after a brief session at Ovington's crockery establishment and graduated with high marks in 1876, but his life from then until 1886 was only a series of minor jobs, none of which compelled his interest or loyalty. In 1879 and 1880, and again in 1883, he spent several months in Europe, two periods of travel which gave him his only substantial relief from routine occupation during the ten years preceding the composition of his first major work. The detailed journal of his first trip, containing a minute account of his activities from his embarkation on August 20, 1879, through his tours of England, France, and Italy, offered a vivid insight into the sources of the *Chevalier* and its significance. Their minute detail and copperplate hand revealed the highest order of meticulous and indefatigable tourist. All points of interest were scrupulously attended to and recorded. Not only was Fuller the careful observer, but also he gave occasional flashes of a critical intelligence which was engaged in making judgment out of the wealth of tourist's experience to which he exposed himself. He was inclined to dislike Pompeii, for example, because of its nouveau-riche character, but he noted with pleasure, "The House of the Faun is one exception among all the cheap and meretricious glitter of the town. I fancy this as inhabited by some wealthy, old-fashioned family . . . desiring to withdraw themselves as much as possible from the sham and frivolities of the new order of things."[9]

The taste which governed Fuller's observation on the House of the Faun was formed prior to his travels. It was reflected in much of his unpublished juvenalia, as in the *Pensieri Privati*, and stood, from the earliest pages of the *Journals*, as a point of reference for evaluating what he saw abroad. He was by no means the conventional American *arriviste*, rushing out to embrace all things European because of an assumption of their necessarily greater elegance. Rather, he visited Europe as a critic and connoisseur whose taste was competent to sorting out the good from the bad among what it had to offer him. His upbringing and education had taken place among the Chicago gentry, and his New England consciousness of integrity and, perhaps, superiority, was fully up to taking Europe without obeisance or prostration before its wonders. Occasionally he struck the lyric note, "Oh, this question that troubles me so much, what, after all is civilization?"[10] But his lyricism was reserved for something greater than the sights which he was bent upon seeing.

The decade, 1876-1886, was also the period during which Fuller's mature writing began. It included, for certain, the composition of "Pasquale's Picture," a sentimental Italian tale which, his first important publication, appeared in 1884, and may well have included the essay, "Howells or James," which was certainly written before 1888. Fuller chose Howells over James, a choice he reaffirmed later in a series of lecture notes on the novel in which he declared his preference for the social as opposed to the psychological novel. "Instead of a searching and indelicate analysis of the individual," he declared, "I . . . favor the study of a group of individuals in their relation to the community."[11] Herein he formulated concisely the pattern upon which his two realistic novels were based and, indirectly, described also the perennial conflict of all his work.

But Fuller's first major expression of his maturing point of view was not to come until the commencement of the *Chevalier* in 1886 at a point when its author was again trapped among the toils of a Chicago business house and three years removed from his second trip abroad. He was prevented, he noted in his unpublished manuscript, "My Early Books," from taking a desired journey abroad by "family circumstances,"—one of the hints Fuller occasionally gave of the diminution of his family's wealth after the death of his father. But, he concluded, such a journey might be taken "by mind and pen" if not in actuality. As a result he began on what presumably was to be a fondly-made substitute for a further escape from Chicago, a purpose for which his immediate surroundings must have given him a spur.

> The Chevalier of Pensieri-Vani *was written in a business office on Lake Street, Chicago. The office was a small one, where little business was done and where the personnel*

(myself excepted) would often be absent. I had a desk beside the manager's own. Mine was as large as his; my waste basket too. One day when alone, I reached down into the waste basket fished up a discarded envelope, and began; 'It was the Chevalier of Pensieri-Vani who halted his traveling carriage—' if that be the way in which the book, the first page of which I have not seen for years, really starts.[18]

He had undertaken a series of sketches, stories—if that term by virtue of each items' centering around a plotted incident may be applied to the slight pieces which were to fill his volume. Each contained as central figures one or more of a fixed group of characters,—the Chevalier himself; his friend and comic opera prince, the Prorege of Arcopia; the Prorege's antagonist and foil, the Contessa Nullaniuna; and the Chevalier's friend, the affetuoso Seigneur of Hors-Concors. What the characters shared in common was an elevated taste, time, and a set of projects worthy of such leisured and cultivated gentry. They perhaps were no more European than they were Chicagoan, for in the development of his work, Fuller created not a substitute for the Europe of his travel journals but an ideal land. The milieu was of no recognizable sublunary kind; rather it yielded engaging, entertaining, and acute comments on the kind of life that one Henry Fuller of Chicago might conceivably have led if circumstances, the human race, the universe, had been of a different order. The difficulties which the Chevalier encompassed, when they were not the mere properties of an engaging fiction, were of the kind which Fuller could not quite encompass in actuality. His defeats were consoled for with the kind of consolation which would apply to Fuller's loneliness.

At the end of the book, with the characters marrying off, with the tissue which had sustained them fading rapidly away, the Chevalier took comfort. "He could still congratulate himself on his exemption from the burdens of wealth, the chafings of domestic relations, the chains of affairs, the martyrdom of a great ambition, the dwarfing provincialism that comes from one settled home. Others might falter, but he was still sufficient unto himself, still master of his own time and his own actions, and enamored only of that delightful land whose beauty age cannot wither and whose infinite variety custom can never stale."[13]

Thus Fuller cheered himself up. The net achievement of his book, for himself, had been to create an imaginative atmosphere in which such a conversion of isolation and alienation into not only bearable but desirable qualities might take place.

One need not labor the worthiness of Fuller's conclusions, nor even apologize too much for the Shakespearean cliché in which he formulated his ideal, to make the point that the *Chevalier* was a serious attempt to create some acceptable version of the good in the midst of many alien circumstances. Its surface sentimentality could be penetrated without difficulty. Its foundations rested upon an effort little short of heroic to find a way in which the good life might be put in terms which, to Fuller in the Chicago of 1886, might have validity. During one of the adventures detailed in the book, the Prorege of Arcopia debates with his American friend, George W. Occident, the relative virtues of the Italian and the English civilizations. His problem is to make a proper apology for what seems to Occident the decadence of "southern" culture. What he has to say, however, is of more than peninsular importance; it may safely be taken as Fuller's developed comment on the culture with which he felt himself so outvantaged a fighter.

> The civilization of the South was a superstructure on a wavering and insecure foundation; the civilization of the North was a mere foundation with scarcely any superstructure at all. Now every structure, no matter how strongly founded, was destined to ruin in the end: such being the case, which sort would his young friend choose,—the graceful and pleasing fabric of the Italian civilization, erected on such unstable masses of debris as a ruin-strewn past might offer and honeycombed by a certain political and financial incapacity, or the abortive and truncated effort of the Anglic civilization,—a foundation whose stability, indeed, had as little to fear from the disintegration of deficit as from the shock of invasion, but whose jagged top-courses called, and seemed to call in vain, for the superstructure that in right should crown it.[14]

Again there was the fin-de-siecle sense of evil times come upon us, but one which, in the sequel, does not seem wholly ill-founded. At any rate, the Prorege had an advantage over his author; for him there was the fictitious Italy in which he lived—a super structure which, when its decay was matched against that of the abortive "Anglic" foundations, came off superior in its congruity to his needs. For Fuller, however, the real choice was that indicated by his conclusion. It was his imaginative self, the Prorege, and not he that could choose Italy, for the choice became available only by the fictitious terms of the argument. The real choice—to join the dominant Chicago or to preserve what was possible of a personal identity against it,—remained. And though the bleakness of his selection was here cushioned by a thin rag of sentimentality, Fuller himself did not blink its uncompromising terms. One must choose to be largely alone.

But the more durable version of Fuller's self-imposed alienation is to be found in his "realistic" novels, The Cliff Dwellers and With The Procession, where he was enabled to examine in immediate and relevant terms the nature of the dilemma which faced him. The Chevalier had been published in 1890, and was followed in 1892 by The Chatelaine of La Trinite, a less personally grounded continuation of the genre represented by the first volume. But, recognizing perhaps the Chatelaine's lesser stature, Fuller turned to the realistic mode for his next two books. These appeared in 1893 and 1895 respectively, dates which placed them squarely upon the upsurge of realistic writing which followed Howells' advocacy of the new method through the eighties. Though the motives impelling Fuller toward realism remain incompletely known, it seems likely that, sensing its relevance to his basic theme, he allowed himself for the time to be carried forward by its growing general impetus. In any case, Howells recognized his work handsomely. In a letter of congratulation following the appearance of With The Procession, the critic declared that Fuller's writing had so satisfactorily caught the essentials of Howells' own practice that its author should be recognized as heir to his mantle. Such congratulations, however, may have been more a tribute to Howells' desire for the increase of realism than to the literal similarity between Fuller's work and his own. For, while Fuller's realism was filled with sharp observation and effective writing, it was less valuable as a transcript of the life with which it was concerned, or as a general moral inquiry, than as a personal testimony of Fuller's situation. Hobart Chatfield-Taylor could feel that Fuller had caught the essence of Chicago life in *With The Procession*, but it would, perhaps, take a fellow New England-Chicagoan to make just that judgment.

Of course Fuller had complied with the basic tenets of Howells' theories in his two realistic novels—he had, that is, set his story among familiar and contemporary scenes and had allowed his characterization and motivation to grow out of such familiarity. He had avoided the melodrama of romanticism, though he was not to be entirely free from a sort of realistic melodrama. But within these limits, he so selected and arranged his characters and events that they emerged, finally, as elements in a kind of morality play whose aim was to work, as best possible in a moral vacuum, toward the right. Like the other Chicago writers, he was primarily concerned with the impact of the dominant business culture upon older, antipathetical values, and the interplay between these forces was a lyrical occasion rather than a realistic one, strictly speaking. *The Cliff Dwellers* took its title from one of its main symbols, that of the Clifton—an eighteen story skyscraper of the sort which, in the nineties, was impressing itself on the city as perhaps the most overwhelming symbol of its new status and age. But Fuller did not rely very heavily on the Clifton itself or on its multitude of tenants to carry forward his tale. His central problem was that of the genteel sensibility faced suddenly with the black city. His hero, George Ogden, goes to work in the Clifton for The Underground National Bank which is housed on the building's lowest floor and presided over by Erasmus Brainerd, who helps forward the imagery of the title not alone by dwelling in the sort of man-made cliff which the building represents, but also by displaying the primitive code of behavior presumably commensurate with cliff-dwellers. Two other persons in the Clifton tie closely to Ogden's fortunes, his brother-in-law, George McDowell, a real estate agent, and one G. Walworth

Floyd, a fellow New England emigré who gives an indifferent attention to the western office of The Massachusetts Brass Co. and allows
himself to be won over by the slovenly forces native to Chicago
business.

Fuller's chief concern with characterization seems to have been
that of achieving a spectrum of business men to suggest the dominant
tones of Chicago life. There was Brainerd, proprietor of the Underground National, with whom the most somber hue is achieved.

> He had never lived for anything but business. He had never
> eaten and drunk for anything but business; his family shared
> his farm-like fare and his primitive hours. He had never built
> for anything but business; though constantly investing in
> grounds and buildings, he had occupied his own home for
> fifteen years, as a tenant merely, before he could bring him-
> self to a grudging purchase. He never dressed for anything
> but business—he had never worn a dress coat in his life. He
> wrote about nothing but business—his nearest relative was
> never more than "dear sir,"—he himself was never otherwise
> than "yours truly," and he wrote on business letter-heads even
> to his family.[15]

George McDowell, the real estate dealer, was of a newer and
somewhat lighter headed school, a go-getter to whom Chicago's
business culture was a lively and fascinating game of chance with
large possibilities of reward.

> You've got to have snap, go. You've got to have a big new
> country behind you. How much do you suppose people in
> Iowa and Kansas and Minnesota think about Down East?
> Not a great deal. It's Chicago they're looking to. This town
> looms up before them and shuts out Boston and New York
> and the whole seaboard from the sight and the thoughts of
> the West and The Northwest and the New Northwest, and
> the Far West, and all the other Wests yet to be invented.
> They read our papers, they come here to buy and to enjoy
> themselves.[16]

At the far end of the scale was another banker, the conservative
Fairchild, enlightened beyond the capacities of McDowell, and far

beyond those of Brainerd, but still accepting Chicago and its ways as an apotheosis of American life.

> *Fairchild leaned back his fine old head on the padded top of his chair and looked at his questioner with the kind of pity that has a faint tinge of weariness. His wife sat beside him silent, but with her hand on his, and when he answered, she pressed it meaningfully; for to the Chicagoan—even the middle-aged, female Chicagoan—the name of the town in its formal, ceremonial use, has a power that no other word in the language quite possesses. It is a shibboleth, as regards its pronunciation, it is a trumpet call as regards its effect. It has all the electrifying and unifying power of a college yell. "Chicago is Chicago," he said. "It is the belief of all of us. It is inevitable; nothing can stop us now."[17]*

Underlying the world of these business men lay another world which remained largely remote and unreal to Ogden as it did to Fuller himself, but which, occasionally, was brought to his attention as on the occasion when he went into the rooms of the public library, along with many others from the streets, to escape a heavy rain.

> *The downpour without seemed but a trifle compared with the confused cataract of conflicting nationalities within, and the fumes of incense that the united throng caused to rise upon the altar of learning stunned him with a sudden and sickening surprise.[18]*

As far above the realm of the business man as the laborers were below it dwelt the last of the major elements in Fuller's pattern of Chicago—the business man's wife. Here, as in his article "The Upward Movement," Fuller saw in her the prime mover to her husband's world as the flame is prime mover to the moth. It was she, idle and destructive, for whom her husband drove himself and his fellows. For her beauty and ease the ugliness and toil of Chicago existed. In the person of Ogden's first wife, Jessie Bradley, she pushes a sensitive and confused husband to despair, and in the person of Cecilia Ingles, wife of the Clifton's owner, she condemns a multitude, "It is for such a woman that one man builds a Clifton and that a hundred others are martyred in it."

Despite such occasional oversimplification, Fuller did not retreat from the complexity of his problem by making any too simple opposition between a hypothetical set of genteel values and the values of Chicago. Walworth Floyd, a New Englander, was ineffective both as business man and person. And the hero of the book labored more in suffering incompetency than heroic conflict. He settles into Brainerd's bank and turns to choosing a wife from one of two possibilities. On the one hand is Abbie Brainerd, daughter of his employer, though quite unlike him in her abundant possession of simple virtues. On the other is Jessie Bradley who comes to Ogden under the New England auspices of Floyd and from a family blessed with a much greater civility than that of the ineffable Brainerd. Ogden, out of snobbishness, chooses Jessie, but his unworthy motives are rewarded justly when Jessie turns out to be a climber and as much a devotee of the "high" business culture as Brainerd himself is of the low. In the end, Jessie dies and Ogden turns to Abbie, chastened with the knowledge that virtue cannot be identified by the society it keeps.

If, in *The Cliff Dwellers*, Fuller's initial quest be taken as that of a life acceptable in moral and aesthetic terms, then his resolution must be understood as one achieved apart from Chicago's own power to resolve. The fact that Abbie Brainerd should turn out to be the virtuous vessel of Ogden's search was a sportive occurrence, one which the logic of her situation in no way made probable. Further, Ogden's New England sense of decorum led him to make the nearly fatal choice of Jessie Bradley. The whole of *The Cliff Dwellers'* action, in these terms, was one of rejecting what the life of Chicago, high or low, had to offer. Ogden wins an embodiment of humble virtue as foreign to Chicago's gentry as to its entrepreneurs. For all, as in the person of Floyd, the initially amiable New Englander, Brainerd, the solid farmer gone wrong, or even Cecilia Ingles, the beautiful and gifted, if wholly selfish, symbol of Chicago's luxury, are corrupted by the city and the culture to which they are bound, and the ultimate villain of the book is no person, but rather that city and that culture. The fault is with Chicago itself. Its gentry, its tycoons, and even its odorous immigrants suffer the same taint.

The nature and scope of this taint were made plainer in *With The Procession* which hinges entirely around the central irony of the efforts of Jane Marshall, daughter of an old Chicago family, to bring her people abreast of the stream in which all of Chicago's inhabitants swim. Though her origins were similar to Fuller's own, and her motives of the best, the only outcome of her struggles to woo her family out of their old fashioned and modest ways into the brilliant life which their wealth and social position promise them is tragedy. Her father, bewildered and defeated by the events which she has set in motion, takes to his bed and a bitter death. Her brother, Truesdale, just home from Europe where he has devoted himself to becoming a dilettante of the arts and a master of the leisured life, succeeds only in making an ugly kind of fool of himself in Chicago and in driving his younger sister into a pretentious and hollow marriage. Though Jane marries happily, the only reparation she can make for the ruin she has brought upon her family is to endow a building at the new university. Once again, neither her motives nor her understanding of them is at fault; it is Chicago, a city which requires keeping up with the procession but yields only empty prizes. What can one expect from an effort to heighten the tone of life in a city which, as one character puts it, labors under a peculiar disadvantage? "It is the only great city in the world to which all its citizens have come for the one common, avowed object of making money. There you have its genesis, its growth, its end, and object; and there are but few of us who are not attending to that object very strictly. In this Garden City of ours every man cultivates his own little bed and his neighbor his; but who looks after the paths between?"[19]

Fuller's realism veered strongly toward outright plaint. In the novels his characters, and not he in his own person, suffer the indignities of Chicago life, but, like Fuller, their only refuge from suffering is lament; they are helpless to do anything. George Ogden, only by luck, finds Abbie Brainerd and through her realizes some of the moral order which he sought. Jane Marshall marries solidly, but she suffers a continuing guilt for the misery which she has brought upon her family and can expiate it only through the secular ritualism of contributing to the University. Direct action, even that of secession, seems beyond possibility. Fuller's realism took on its lyrical tone precisely through this inability of its characters to move toward their own restoration. His stories were *exempla*, but the good works which they might otherwise have invoked were lost among the sands of regret for his own lack of opportunity.

It may have been in justification of his own developing practice that Fuller wrote a "Plea for Shorter Novels," in the *Dial* for August, 1917. This essay urged not only brevity as a virtue of the novel form, but also suggested that much of the extensive textural development of the novel bound up with realism could well be dispensed with. Novelists, he argued in effect, should give up elaborating the obvious. Let the reader's imagination play a more active part in furnishing detail. Scenes, actions, sensory perceptions—these things could all be supplied. The author's function was primarily to show the consequences of actions and the subtleties which the reader might not furnish for himself. Certainly Fuller's own work hewed increasingly to this sort of practice. *With the Procession* was by far the most fully written of all his novels. After it, he grew increasingly fond of an anecdotal technique, content to find his particular exercise in the construction of dry and ironic commentaries upon the slight action of his plots.

In 1900 he had returned to the romance genre of the *Chevalier* and the *Chatelaine*, but brought to it a sharper, bitterer and even more artificial approach. *The Last Refuge* was again a European tale filled with fanciful characters whose adventures formed an analysis of Fuller's own preoccupations. The setting again was Italy, the hero another minor nobleman with elevated tastes, a restless temperament, and abundant leisure. But the Freiherr von Kaltenau, unlike the earlier Chevalier, set himself from the first upon a quest which, though essentially hopeless, was of the highest moral importance; his story was little graced with the playfulness and charm which had so marked that of the Chevalier.

Feeling his advancing years, the Freiherr sets out to find an ideal young friend, one who can help restore his own youthful joy in life. His search however, is long conducted without any fruitful outcome.

Each of the young men thrown in his way has some important failing. They are indolent, irreverent, self-indulgent, stolid, or over susceptible to young women, and for these failings the Freiherr has no tolerance. At length, however, he encounters the young Bruno who promises to satisfy his high requirements. "He likes ruins . . . idyllic landscapes . . . Guido's Aurora . . . medieval frescoes . . . catacombs . . . gardens." Further, he is Roman Catholic, and the imaginative warmth of that religion appeals strongly to the Freiherr though he retains his own "pale Lutheranism."[20]

Bruno is agreeable to the Freiherr's overtures, so the two strike a pact and set out to travel Italy together with the hope that Bruno's youth may refresh the Freiherr's love of the land. No sooner is the travel undertaken, however, than the paragon Bruno falls in love with a beautiful lady, Violante, whose travels parallel theirs, and the Freiherr's hopes crumble. But, after holding debate with himself, he decides that if he is to have youth, he must allow its nature some expression, and agrees to help Bruno in his pursuit of Violante. At this point, the story suddenly takes a different direction. As Bruno and the Freiherr travel along, they meet diverse people, all of whom are traveling to Sicily, wherein each seeks to find his own "last refuge." The disillusioned and wearied philosopher, Balanzoni, seeks hope; an unsuccessful painter desires beauty; a man of feeling, without the gift of language, desires fluency that he may become a poet; the Lady of Quality, a wealthy American, seeks Glory; a vengeful and mysterious Italian woman, Monna Clothilde, wants vengeance.

After a series of adventures in which each character has a chance to demonstrate his particular need, the whole party arrives at the edge of the Sicilian city which promises itself to each as the last refuge. Before entering LaFelice however, they stop at an inn, the Villa dei Dubii, where each find a quality sufficiently restful so that he is deterred from entering the city, unfavorable reports of which are beginning to reach the searchers. In the end, only Bruno and his beloved Violante, escape from the inn to the town. The others continue their travels in different directions or remain at the villa. The earlier words of the Freiherr are fulfilled. "Let the rest go. Light your fires before youth, pour out your richest libations, pipe out the fullest sweetness stored within your double pipes; make any sacrifice to keep it, for no sacrifice can ever bring it back. . . . Youth includes all: Beauty, Love, The Hope and Glory of the World . . . we weary, world-worn mortals should humbly prostrate ourselves in the outer court."[21] Thus, the last refuge itself, which each had sought so eagerly, turns out to have no existence. It is illusory, and the only reality, once youth is gone, is mundane existence.

It is curious to witness Fuller in the contorted and confusedly allegorical tale regretting the passing of a youth which, to judge by his own record of it, was far from robustly satisfactory. But the important thing, perhaps, was that his own youthful *Chevalier* had accomplished an end which, fifteen years later the Freiherr found unattainable. The *Chevalier*, that is, had created an anti-Chicago; its possibly naive aestheticism, its acceptance of loneliness as a desirable status, were acts of hope which the man of forty-three could no longer complete. The plaintive tones of Fuller's realistic novels were sounded again here, but more loudly and assertively. The Freiherr is the Chevalier grown older and sadder. His situation differs little from that of the younger adventurer, but the personal resources which he brings to its allegation are diminished. As the realistic novels had scrutinized the insuperable odds which Chicago and its life put before Fuller, and lamented their insuperability, so *The Last Refuge* looked at the other side of the picture, the possibility of a personal escape which the first novel had offered, and found that now to be wanting also. The trap was closed.

Fuller continued to endure a life which he found full of difficulty and unhappiness. Why was he not numbered among the exiles who found more congenial situations in Europe than in America? He always made much of the claims which bound him to Chicago. After his father's death in 1885, he became the head of his family of mother and sisters, and, though his inheritance was not large, it required management. After his mother's death in 1907 he moved from the family home, lived in furnished rooms, and ate in restaurants. But even so he continued to look after the family investments, mainly in rental properties. While it was conceivable that some arrangements might have been made to give him more freedom than he allowed himself, Fuller took few if any steps to attain it. Except for his five European trips, which were never of more than a few months duration, he continued to live in Chicago and continued, so doing, to hug its incompatibility close to him.

His intense egoism, his endless preoccupation with his own plight, prevented his taking any real steps to end that plight. By destroying his unhappiness he would have destroyed his profession. From the start, Fuller possessed a critical sense of sufficient magnitude to poison for him the character of almost any conceivable situation. Though he found happiness at school, he seems to have been unable there, or in later settings, to make close friends, and at least one entry in his early journals laments the unsuitability of such candidates for friendship as did present themselves—a parallel to the Freiherr's difficulties. An acquaintance could scarcely remember his making a complimentary observation. His travel journals, as has been noted, gave indications of an early developed sharpness as little ready to spare Europe as America. Certainly the genteel literary circles in which Fuller moved, with their easily violated sensoria, would have done little to build up an attitude of acceptance within him. And his own intelligence and experience may well have informed him that Chicago, though extreme in degree, was scarcely unique. Like his Freiherr, Fuller had elected to take up permanent residence in the Villa dei Dubii, but his choice had occurred long before youth and hope were gone.

He published much after 1900. *Under the Skylights* (1901), *Waldo Trench* (1908), *On the Stairs* (1918), *Bertram Cope's Year* (1919), *Gardens of This World* (1929) and *Not On the Screen* (1930). These were his principal titles, and there were others, mainly essays and short stories. But the cycle of hope, disillusion, and despair which had been established by the early works was not repeated. Rather, through all his later work, Fuller alternated the most apparent sort of trivia with expressions of the defeat which first appeared fully in *The Last Refuge*. Maintaining the themes and methods used in the earlier books, sometimes portraying modern life and sometimes reverting to the world of fancy, he came to regard the more passionate images of his earlier period, both the evil and the good, as material for a dry and rather terrible comedy in which success and failure lost all potency and were seen simply as cluttering up their own pointless existence. His restrained and limited technique developed both flexibility and sureness beyond its early uses, but increasingly it limited and restrained his expression. While suitable for the slight and simplified material of these later works, it never proved capable of major utterance.

But in the end, a personal rather than a stylistic difficulty must bear the principal burden of blame for Fuller's failure to create major literature, for with him the style was truly the man. His most obvious inadequacies were those of a too narrow and too shallow set of sympathies and understandings. What he might have made of his native talents under different circumstances, can only be guessed. But that he was secretive, lonely, an avoider of new ways and new persons, and apt to take refuge in a forbidding precision of manner are all facts. One can, in the end, come only to the testimony of his writing. He was puzzled, irritated, and finally conquered. His defeat was made inevitable by an alienating process begun in early youth which failed, however, to supply him with any real alternative to the thing he shunned. In the eyes of history he may be seen pathetically, as the victim of a massive cultural change, but as a writer the quality he did gain inheres in such reality as he made of an ineluctable and unhappy fate.

The Genteel Protest

A MONG the various havens opened by the upward movement to writers, the most notable and longest lived was undoubtedly that characteristic institution known as "The Little Room." The phrase was the name given to regular meetings, held each Friday afternoon following the matinee concert of the symphony, at which a more or less constant group of persons interested in literature and the arts met for tea and conversation. The group had taken its unusual title from a short story written by Madeleine Yale Wynne, one of its number, about a New England homestead in which there is a mysterious little room which at intervals appears and vanishes. Because of the intermittency of meetings, and as a suggestion of ephemeral status, the phrase was considered appropriate to these assemblies of Chicago's artistic elite. It stuck firmly to them during the thirty odd years of their existence.

The group's origins were intimately associated with the general upward movement. In the middle eighties, the firm of Adler and Sullivan was called upon by a group of Chicago promoters headed by Ferdinand W. Peck to design a large structure containing a hotel, an auditorium, and an office building which could be given over to housing artists, writers, impresarios, and other persons associated with Chicago's artistic activities. The result was the ensemble which still today stands on Congress street filling the block between Wabash and Michigan avenues. The auditorium is no longer in use, but the hotel on Michigan at present houses Roosevelt College, and the office building on Wabash, though filled with run-of-mill enterprises, stands as a grimy memorial to one of Chicago's better impulses. Upon its completion in 1889 the Auditorium, as the ensemble came to be called, provided the finest kind of testimony to Chicago's new intentions. The hotel itself was widely recognized as one of the most luxurious and complete in the nation. The auditorium proper was immediately invoked for the use of Theodore Thomas' symphony orchestra and for traveling attractions, like opera, which needed a large hall to pay their way. The office building, unfortunately, never succeeded in its announced aim because of the high rents which its owners were forced to put upon its rooms.

Sullivan's project was architecturally a triumph. Though to the modern beholder, the heavy masonry walls, the torturous system of partitioning, and the general mien of the building so clearly inspired by Richardson Romanesque seems clumsy, the acoustics of the auditorium and the beauty of the hotel were then the city's admiration. Adler and Sullivan had successfully completed the largest and most complex building which the Chicago of that day had seen, and had done so with taste and originality. No sooner was the building completed than Sullivan became one of its most constant patrons, making the enormous and palatial bar of the hotel on Congress street his nightly headquarters.

The commencement of The Little Room dated from after the orchestra's use of Sullivan's building. With Thomas installed in the new auditorium, it became the duty of all right minded Chicagoans to attend his concerts, and the Friday matinee was a favored hour. After the matinee came leisure for tea which could be pleasantly filled with a congenial group, and from such Friday afternoons The Little Room was born. Just when the birth took place or who assisted at it remained obscure even to members of The Little Room itself. In the fall of 1917 the group held a twenty-fifth birthday party for itself, which would suggest a founding date of 1892. But in one of its last meetings, in 1929, the same group recorded its own founding date as 1896. Hamlin Garland put himself down as a founder along with Henry Fuller, with Garland's brother-in-law, Lorado Taft, and the painter, Charles Francis Browne, dating the first meetings sometime in 1893 or 1894. But, though Garland was an inveterate founder and joiner, the insatiate *amour propre* displayed in his autobiographical writing, coupled with the testimonies of The Little

Room itself, makes this claim less than compelling. The earliest direct record is contained in an autograph book presumably signed by persons present at a meeting which must have taken place between 1894 and 1898, the years during which Harrison Rhodes, one of the signers, was present in Chicago. Such a meeting might have been the first of the regular series, but it may equally well have been the first after the group settled upon Ralph Clarkson's studio in the Fine Arts building as its regular meeting place in 1898. The best conclusion possible is that sometime between 1892 and 1896 The Little Room came into casual existence to fill the hours after the orchestra matinee; that at first it met sometimes at Taft's, sometimes at Bessie Potter's studio, and perhaps elsewhere as well; and that Fuller, Garland, Harriet Monroe, William Morton Payne, and Anna Morgan were among its early members. By 1898 Charles C. Curtiss finished the present Fine Arts building at the corner of Van Buren and Michigan; a number of The Little Room members took studios in it; and the group chose Ralph Clarkson's studio on the tenth floor as its Friday afternoon location.

To conclude a musical afternoon by calling in at Clarkson's studio was a pleasant way of meeting with other persons of artistic tastes. These were numerous and varied. The tenants of the Fine Arts building made up a part of The Little Room. Lorado Taft, sculptor to the rich whose work still dots' Chicago, was a pillar of the group. It also included Charles Francis Browne; Frank and Joe Lyendecker, whose painting adorns panels on the tenth floor of the Fine Arts building; Ralph Clarkson, painter and regular host; Mrs. H. C. Chatfield-Taylor who had opened an arts and crafts bindery in the building; Anna Morgan, dramatic coach and elocutionist; and Ralph Fletcher Seymour, artist, illustrator, and publisher.

Among those members of a literary persuasion, Henry Fuller was chief. And Hamlin Garland, after his arrival from Boston in 1893, threw himself as avidly upon The Little Room as he was to throw himself on any institution or person who promised him a congenial or profitable association. Many other names were to be found among its regular and occasional members. There was Lucy Monroe, Harriet's sister, who was to become chief editor for the Chicago publishing firm of Stone and Kimball, later H. S. Stone and Co. Both Stone and Kimball themselves attended. The architectural brothers, A. B. and I. K. Pond were constant, while Sullivan himself sometimes appeared. Emerson Hough, I. K. Friedman, Elia Peattie, Keith Preston, H. K. Webster, Wallace Rice, Alice Gerstenberg, and Clara Laughlin were regular members as were such later intellectuals as Francis Hackett and Llewellyn Jones. The number of transients too was large. There were those in Chicago who maintained a distant relationship, like Robert Herrick, and any visitor with artistic pretensions and a Chicago acquaintance was sure to be introduced to the group.

Though The Little Room was mainly social in its activities, its meetings sometimes centered in special events such as a literary lecture by Fuller or the production by Anna Morgan's school of an interesting and little-seen play by Shaw, Ibsen, or Maeterlinck. These latter, indeed, provided one of the group's clearest distinctions. It was in 1900, for example, that Miss Morgan, whose activities were among the earliest in America to suggest the nature of the later little theater movement, produced Shaw's *Candida* for the first time in America. The production was witnessed by William Archer who advised Shaw that his play had fallen into competent hands. As a result, the Irish dramatist established cordial relations with the Chicago drama coach which lasted for several years and led to another first American production by Miss Morgan, this time *Caesar and Cleopatra*. Fuller wrote most of the Maeterlinckian fantasies contained in his *Puppet Booth* for production by Miss Morgan. But as a rule, The Little Room confined itself to tea and sociability. The tea was made in a prized samovar and served with ceremony among the lighted candles and ornate Spanish furnishings of Clarkson's studio. Plates of peppermints stood on the tables and the other refreshments were usually sandwiches or cakes. As for the sociability, it was as discreet as the refreshments. Though the tea might be laced a little with brandy, and the emotional tone heightened with whispers of illicit love affairs, hoped for or real, the importance of a mannerly atmosphere was as important to the group as its devotion to the artistic life. When Fuller came to write *The Downfall of Abner Joyce*, detailing the fall of Hamlin Garland from a state of austere idealism to a condition of acquiescence with the "necessary" and pleasant compromises of life, he placed his hero squarely in the midst of The Little Room, transformed to paper. Abner's great difficulty, he discovered, was a lack of sophistication, a failure to understand that only through the niceties of behavior is such good as exists in an imperfect world to be had. Filled with a conscientiously rough and ruthless devotion to his western loyalties, Abner had done more harm with his boorishness than he could make up with his impeccable intentions.

The Little Room was neither exclusively intellectual nor exclusively artistic; its importance lay not in its production of art, but in the degree to which it both comprised and symbolized the largest official acceptance of the arts as a living cultural force which Chicago had been able to achieve. It provided an identity for the writer not by serving as a meeting ground for artists and intellectuals alone as did the bohemias of both Chicago and New York, but functioned as a bridge between the Chicago artist and his local society. Mrs. Arthur Aldis, wife of one of the city's important real-estate developers, was a Little Room member and exercised in the group the kind of twofold activity with which it was concerned. As a playwright, she came to The Little Room with the same sort of status as Fuller or Garland, that is as a writer drawing together with other writers and artists. But as a wealthy patroness of the arts, the wife of one of Chicago's chief citizens, the owner of a large Lake Forest estate, she approached The Little Room as a member of society interested in its concerns, anxious to forward them and to give them a better recognized status. Toward this end she established a little theater on the grounds of her Lake Forest home. Chatfield-Taylor, a member of The Little Room, was similarly a novelist, but by his assistance to Harriet Monroe in the establishment of *Poetry*, he functioned as a wealthy and solid member of society lending his patronage to the arts. The genteel character of the group needs no laboring. It was Chicago's best available substitute for a fully developed, leisured, and cultivated class. For about a decade and a half the club flourished. Between 1902 and 1909 its affairs were pressing enough for it to elect an executive committee to sift applications for membership, collect dues, pay bills, and plan programs. But after 1910, though its meetings persisted, its original impetus wore off. By the mid-twenties members had to be circularized in an effort to bring them to the meetings and arouse their active support. The last meeting recorded in the Newberry papers took place on January 3, 1931.

The Little Room remains an ephemeral phenomenon whose importance and nature are to be gleaned almost entirely from the memories, and memoirs, of persons associated with it. The place in which it met, and some of the atmosphere which the Fine Arts building provided for it, may still be seen by the visitor, but the institution itself is gone. Of its run-of-mine literary production, the bulk exists only in the *Contributors' Magazine*, published in 1893 and 1894 by the Contributors' Club. Many of the literary members of The Little Room figured in this corollary gathering with, once again, a generous cross-section of society folk patronizing the arts. Again occurred the names of Henry Fuller, the Chatfield-Taylors, and Harriet Monroe. But also to be found here were Mrs. William Armour, Mr. and Mrs. Eugene Field, Major and Mrs. Joseph Kirkland, General and Mrs. A. C. McClurg, and Mr. and Mrs. Potter Palmer. Like The Little Room, the Contributors' Club was a device for bridging the gap between the writer and society, but the club favored the writer's terms more notably than did The Little Room. Its activities centered not around tea parties, but rather around the publication of its magazine, composed exclusively of members' contributions. These lacked, however, any real distinction. They included a short story on the Pagliacci theme by Chatfield-Taylor; a defense by Lucy Monroe of *vers de societé*; a lament for the lost art of conversation by Walter Larned of the Art Institute; some short selections from Kirkland's *Zury* not used in the novel; "Holy Week in Seville," the reworking of a passage from one of Fuller's travel journals; and, filling one whole issue, pieces from foreign contributors on a variety of themes. When the Contributors' Club came to an end, it was because not enough contributions were forthcoming from its members either to be read at its quarterly meetings or published in its magazine.

II

But The Little Room was only the center, the meeting place of the larger number of individuals and institutions comprising Chicago's genteel protest. Mrs. Elia Peattie, who from 1901 to 1919 was literary editor for the *Tribune*, turned the genteel influence into the long stream of criticism, novels, historical romances, children's books, and patriotic writings which tumbled from her pen. And, before the genteelists produced a literary organ in the short-lived *Contributors' Magazine*, Chatfield-Taylor and Slason Thompson had given them a more generally representative voice in their magazine, *America*. From 1884 to 1887 the genteel protest against Philistia had been voiced in the ephemeral *Literary Life* which for a time was edited by Grover Cleveland's sister from her home in New York —a relationship which was felt to bring great credit to the magazine. And from 1880 until 1915 its standards found at least an indirect expression in Francis Fisher Browne's *Dial*. During the nineties it had a partial voice in determining the course of Chicago's publishers. A. C. McClurg and Co., headed by the socially prominent and carefully conservative General McClurg, published some of its work. Herbert Stone and Ingalls Kimble, though possessed of a broader and much more advanced taste than the General, looked on a part of the genteelists' writing with favor and, in the firm's later years, employed Harriet Monroe's sister, Lucy, as their editor-in-chief. Likewise both the colorful Way and Williams and the ambitious Francis J. Schulte gave a precedence to them, though the latter was also anxious to forward a more strictly regional kind of writing. Thus, from 1885 until about 1905, there was a stream of periodicals and publishers through which the genteel tradition maintained itself in print and attempted to establish itself in fact as the dominant cultural element in Chicago.

The magazine *America*, published from 1888 to 1891, was a notable case in point. Its co-originator, Hobart Chatfield-Taylor, had been born in Chicago in 1865, brought up in the heart of its old, New England west side, and educated at Cornell. From there he returned to Chicago in 1886 possessed of some means, though as yet unembarrassed by the hyphenated name which he assumed in later years to secure his full inheritance. He had done some writing in college and was determined to give himself over to the literary life. His original hope was that of founding a literary and cultural magazine in Chicago to compare favorably with anything else the nation had to offer, and particularly with those of the East. Like most of the genteelists, Taylor was genuinely devoted to raising Chicago's taste and tone. His first impulse was a missionary one, and if he found much in the city which disturbed him, he felt always that there remained the possibility of converting it to better ways. In his writing for *America*, as in many of his books, he expressed a kind of absolute faith in the gentlemanly ideal and in the possibility of its establishment in mid-western life which, in the sequel, seems fantastic. The same faith, however, dominated the whole of Chicago's upward movement. It assumed that if the upper classes conducted themselves properly, if through organizations and persuasive writing they gradually disseminated good taste and high standards of behavior, if their wealthy members founded a sufficient number of universities, libraries, museums, and symphony orchestras, and if, without forgetting that there was a difference between the gentle and the vulgar, they faithfully practiced *noblesse oblige*, Chicago might yet be changed into the garden city which its old motto, so battered by unfriendly circumstance, declared it to be.

In this faith *America* began. Taylor was joined by Reginald De Koven, later to be known for his light operatic compositions, who was to write a column on music; and by Harry B. Smith and Charles P. Bryan, businessmen of the city who assisted in financing the venture. For editorial management they selected an unusual Chicago newspaperman, a colleague and biographer of Eugene Field, Slason Thompson. Thompson had been born of Canadian parents, some of whose forbears in turn had emigrated from the United States at the time of the Revolution. He had been trained as a lawyer, but upon coming to the United States, had gravitated into newspaper

work on the west coast. After a series of moves, he arrived in Chicago
as local manager of the Associated Press. He was one of the five
young newspapermen who had combined to form the Chicago *Herald*
in 1881, and one of those who had transferred to the *Daily News*
when the *Herald* came upon hard times in 1883. The group interested
in *America* brought him as managing editor and publisher from
the *News*.

Undoubtedly the policy of *America* was agreeable to all of its five
founders, but it was Thompson who gave it special force. He was the
most active of the group in the management of the magazine, and
the only one who exercised much general interest in the venture.
Taylor was largely occupied with literary and editorial contributions,
De Koven with music, and neither Smith nor Bryan figured largely.
But in any case, *America*, from first to last, displayed a degree of
narrow prejudice and chauvinism which today would make it out-
rageous. In writing a farewell message for the magazine, Thompson
adequately summarized its position, though the restraint of his
language gave no suggestion of the vehemence with which *America*
had pursued its policies.

> The preservation of American manhood by the restriction of
> foreign immigration, the purification of our voting system,
> the enactment of uniform laws regarding citizenship in the
> different states, the adoption of an educational qualification
> for voters, the compulsory diffusion of primary education
> on the American plan in American schools, a firm but
> moderate opposition to the political and educational policy
> of the Roman Catholic Church in the United States, an
> abiding faith in the potency, as well as the necessity, of the
> American common school as the alembic in which all races,
> classes and creeds can alone be fused into the best material
> for American citizenship; these and cognate themes which
> will occur to the reader were the especial campaign of edu-
> cation in which *America* was engaged.[1]

Its "educational campaign" was conducted with no holds barred.
Thompson hired Thomas Nast as cartoonist and paralleled his

dramatic presentations of its point of view with the boldest kind of writing. The magazine featured in every issue a statistical and alarmist summary of the number of immigrants which had arrived at Castle Garden during the preceding week, and combined the most vociferous denunciation of the Roman Church with equally strong attacks upon the political power held by foreign groups in Chicago, particularly the Irish and Germans. One of its essays criticized Jesuitism as despotic and intolerant. Another described France as a modern Sodom. A cartoon showed a conventionalized ape-like Irishman, animated by the Pope, his hands in a money chest labeled "United States." Frequently, however, the magazine protested that it did not ally itself with the Know-Nothing point of view. Its aim was declared to be the establishment of immigration restrictions and quotas so that only the healthy and fit would be allowed into the country. It attacked Roman Catholicism allegedly as a secular force and protested against the concerted political activity of immigrant groups because they could not understand the basic principles upon which the country was founded and so might easily vote away the privileges which were to be theirs under careful management. It aimed, in sum, at the establishment of an enlightened, native aristocracy as the central force of American culture and wished to curb the power of the populace until they could attain enlightenment.

As a literary organ, *America* was likewise anxious to forward what it felt to be native and gentlemanly qualities. It strove especially for contributions from such writers as James Russell Lowell, Charles Dudley Warner, and Julian Hawthorne. So ambitious was it for the right sort of contents that Taylor spent over $50,000 for them before the magazine began publication. Indeed, this expense, and the level of writing it secured, could be maintained only for the first few weeks after which the magazine contented itself with less well-known writers and filled large parts of many issues with items written by Taylor himself, often under assumed names, and by Thompson. *America* was never a commercial success. The largest circulation it ever achieved was 10,000, and this only for a brief period. The bulk of its readers were of Chicago itself, although it had some followers in other parts of the country.

The magazine's rampant aristocracy found expression in ways other than mere abuse of non-Anglo Saxon Americans and their institutions. One unsigned contribution, which may well have been from Taylor judging by its congruence with his later writing, attacked the "sophistry of equality." Let us, said the author in short, admit that inequality in all things is an "invariable law of nature." If this is agreed to, one should then consider whether American civilization has been well served by substituting an inequality of wealth for an inequality of birth. Plutocracy, when balanced against true aristocracy, must come off second best. "A plutocracy must give way to a true aristocracy of virtue, intelligence, and devotion to the state."[2] Another article, perhaps by Thompson, defended the punishment of the Chicago anarchists holding, with Judge Gary, that anarchistic incitement to violence was equivalent to an act of violence. In a third, and revealing case, Andrew Carnegie's gospel of wealth was severely attacked. Carnegie, argued the anonymous writer, was a hypocrite and a fraud. He had made his money principally by cheating his customers and underpaying his workers. Abusing thus the privileges which pertain to aristocratic power, he now sought to make amends by indiscriminate charity. Much better, the article concluded, that a man of wealth leave his money within his own family where it properly belongs while he sees to it that his paternalistic responsibilities are exercised so there can be no complaint about the way he disposes of his fortune.

By striking out at both democrat and plutocrat, America provided a forceful example of the degree to which the genteel tradition sought to be a power unto itself. It could affiliate more easily with rich men, whatever their aristocratic failings might be, than with poor. But it maintained at least a precarious independence of the nearly universal division of the American social world in terms of money.

Its chief writers on literature, Julian Hawthorne and Maurice Thompson, best known perhaps as the author of *Alice of Old Vincennes*, frequently resorted to aristocratic standards, equating them largely with the defense of "romanticism" against the attacks of the realists. One characteristic essay, entitled "Un-American Fiction," held that while America had not an "arch-genius" like George Eliot or Thackeray, it had at least been decently represented in literature by its New England authors. Their force, unfortunately, had been replaced by "an unnecessary and frivolous debasing of personal honor." Among the chief offenders were "Edgar Saltus, Mrs. Atherton, and Miss Daintrey."[3] Thompson took the common stand against realism as an immoral and foreign thing, one which could not produce lasting literature because it was concerned only with ephemeral and specialized problems and scenes. In "The Alien Taint in Criticism" he summarized fully his objections to un-aristocratic, realistic writing. "I can confidently assert the influence of alien literature in debauching a large class of American voters so that they went to the polls intoxicated with the dreams of European socialists and political antinomians. . . . The revolution threatening our country is in its early stage. The progression will be: realism, sensualism, materialism, socialism, communism, nihilism, absolute anarchy. . . . Show me a race of men wholly insensible and invulnerable to romance and I will be sure that it is a race of brutal anarchists."[4]

In similar terms, Chatfield-Taylor, under his own name, conducted an attack upon French realism. "M. Zola . . . admits a void in nineteenth century existence, but he does not admit that this void is in great measure created by his own countrymen. . . . Had there been no *parc aux cerfs*, no philosophers of the Rousseau school, no Voltaire, no revolution, no goddess of reason, and no modern Paris with its dens of socialism and vice, there would in all probability have been no 'continued craving and undefined longing.'

"We need writers who will direct material drawn from actual life to some good end. We need more writers like Charles Dickens and Charles Kingsley, and no more Tolstois, Zolas, Ouidas, Jameses, and Saltuses."[5]

III

No one can determine with any accuracy the degree to which *America* was given the whole hearted support of the Chicago aristocracy except to infer from its circulation of several thousand, largely in Chicago, that it was found at least tolerable. But there was some indication, of a sort occurring in the writing of Edith Wyatt and the earlier poetry of Harriet Monroe, that the ideas upon which it rested were not peculiar to itself alone. Certainly its rabid allegiance to Anglo-Saxondom was not shared by these ladies directly, but its genteelism was clearly the basis of their work as well as America's.

Edith Wyatt was much concerned with American life, and with the ways in which it might best be understood and improved, but her acceptance of it necessitated some careful tidying. Though she was midwestern by birth, having come to Illinois from Wisconsin, her writing sought the same conversion of native ways to a genteel pattern which had been the concern of Taylor and Thompson. Instead of reviling the objectionable, however, she sought to refocus American life to a point where it was acceptable in romantic and genteel terms. Her novel, *True Love*, published in 1903, told a story involving members of the midwestern "aristocracy." Its scene shifted alternately from Chicago to "Centreville," Illinois in the manner of Jane Austen and as though there were no essential difference between the temper of Illinois life in 1900 and that of Jane Austen's England. Her characters moved from the "capital," Chicago, down to the provincial Centreville (even the spelling of which was thus made to conform with good taste). Their activities include a "county ball," in which the provincial ladies are outshone by those from the city, and center around a conflict of sense versus sensibility where sense is shown to reside in the wholesome, native virtues of the story's hero who, bewilderingly, combines all the talents of an ambitious and ethical young American business success with those of a well-behaved member of the English gentry. The country people around Centreville are wholesome and stalwart. They live in the midst of pleasant fields and rolling hills. They are not wholly deracinated, for Miss Wyatt's purpose was to show an American aristocracy in action rather than a British one, but the reader cannot escape an impression of double vision as occasional glimpses of the native scene impinge upon the artificial use of Jane Austen's manner and theme.

This same attempt to transmute the rawness and even the grandeur of America into an aristocratic and aesthetic suitability also characterized many of Miss Wyatt's early poems, collected and published in 1917 under the title, *The Wind In the Corn*, but the complex realities of her subject sank under a broad and sentimental imagery. America was big. It was full of high energy and color with great beauty in its western regions and a fine spirit at its center. The nativism in her point of view shunned the foreign, even as Taylor and Thompson had in *America*, in favor of chauvinistic rhapsody, but what it really praised were only those aspects of American life which could be comprehended within a genteel devotion to "inspiration," "goodness," and "beauty" of the sort which Henry Van Dyke was popularizing. One of her poems celebrated the run of the overland express train.

> Overland, overland, sings the rail
>   Riding from sea to sea.
> The stars sink down past the dwindled town
>   And pale through the flying tree.
> The daystars sink; and the morning's brink
>   Brims through the cinders' flail.
> Overland, overland swings the sun;
>   Overland swings the rail.
> Cut away, cut away, curve through the ridge
>   Sapphire before, next the sky.
> The cool-buoyed river-chords call through the bridge
>   Where the river's arms wave goodbye.
> Through the shantied day on the right of way,
>   By the roundhouse roof, pebbly and tarred,
> Ring your bell, swing your bell, pace and tell
>   Your tale through the switch-veined yard.[6]

Here as elsewhere the terms of her acceptance were those of an uncritical ideal.

Though Harriet Monroe belongs principally to a later stage of this history, one must note that her introduction to literature, and for some two decades her whole commitment to it, was made under the genteel aegis. In 1892 she heard recited at the dedication ceremonies of the Columbian Exposition her "Columbian Ode"

which the governors of the fair had accepted as its official poem.
She, also, sought a conversion of middle-western ways and standards
into aristocratic and even heroic terms as in her "Cantata," sung
at the dedication of Sullivan's auditorium in 1889.

> Hail to thee, fair Chicago! On thy brow
> America, thy mother, lays a crown.
> Bravest among her daughters brave art thou,
> Most strong of all her heirs of high renown.[7]

The poem went on with a series of allusions to Chicago's history.
First, the unpeopled wilderness was described. Then Indians came
to a conclave on the shores of Lake Michigan. Finally, arrived the
settlers, that same greedy and graceless horde who had participated
in the land boom of the thirties. Chicago thus established,

> [The] weary nations heard
>   As they dreamed on the breast of time,
> Till the yearning world was stirred
>   With the thrill of a birth sublime.[8]

In sequence, Chicago's enemies—war, fire, anarchy, and greed—
attacked the city, but these were vanquished in an inspiring victory.

> New thoughts are thine: new visions rise
>   Before thy clear prophetic eyes.
> On to the future, where the light
>   Streams over fields of glory,
> Thy soul doth take its morning flight
>   From slumberous ages hoary.
> Out of the dark an eagle to the sun
>   Speeds on. Awake! 'Tis day! The night is done.[9]

Unlike Edith Wyatt, Harriet Monroe introduced into her verse
a suggestion that the late nineteenth century America might not
be all that the Chicago aristocrats desired. She knew ugliness and
confusion and could feel despair. In her later work indeed, that
collected in 1924 in *The Difference and Other Poems*, Miss Monroe

abandoned wholly the heroic vein of her genteel efforts; no doubt *Poetry* magazine educated her as much as it did any of its readers. But her nineteenth century manner showed its genteel origin. Her sonnet, "On Reading a Modern Romance," looked backward with melancholy to heroic ages and lamented the enfeebled romanticism of her modern times.

> Across a shadow of these morbid years,
> Whose growth luxuriant, tangled, loads the air
> With perfume and decay; whose soil doth bear
> Rich rottenness, while rooted beauty rears
> Heaven-seeking boughs through a hot mist of tears—
> Oh, through this breathless region let the blast
> From happier centuries sweep pure and fast
> And strong upon our fevers and our fears!
> Hark! The clear voice of man's imperial youth
> Cries warning to his weary middle age—
> Sings of the days when newly found was truth
> Nor blasted yet by doubting Time's bleak rage;
> When men bowed low to nature, holiest shrine
> Of God, and, rising, knew they were divine.[10]

IV

But the genteel vine had other fruit yet to bear in Chicago. There was the *Dial* magazine, founded by Francis Fisher Browne and published successfully from 1880 until 1919 when, under new ownership, it moved to New York and became one of the notable organs of post-war writing. Unlike the other genteel figures, Browne was a native New Englander. He had been born in Vermont and raised in Massachusetts where he learned the printer's trade in his father's newspaper office. During the Civil War he fought in a Massachusetts regiment, and after the war he settled in New York state, at Rochester, where he studied law. He spent a short period of study also at the University of Michigan. He seems not, however, to have considered the practice of law as a very deep commitment, for when he came to Chicago he gravitated naturally to literature and publishing. In 1867 he formed an association with the struggling *Western*

Monthly and within a short time became in fact, though not in name, its editor.

Browne's literary taste and standards were formed early and pegged high. He objected constantly to the pressure which the owners of the *Western Monthly* brought on him to accept unworthy contributions or otherwise conduct the magazine with an eye primarily for good business relationships. His desire was to edit a literary review which could devote itself with complete integrity to the best available material. Within a short time he realized at least part of his aim when the *Western Monthly* was reorganized as the *Lakeside Monthly* and Browne was made its editor both in name and fact. Hardly had the *Lakeside* begun however when Browne was stricken with cholera during one of the epidemics that periodically swept the city, and the enterprise was abandoned. From 1874 until 1880 he was occupied with miscellaneous literary work and during the latter years of the period became an editor in General McClurg's publishing house. Hence, when A. C. McClurg and Co. decided to issue a monthly review in order to stimulate the large book-jobbing business which, among other things, engaged them, they turned naturally to Browne as its editor. What struggles may have existed between the publisher, anxious to issue a useful house organ, and the editor, anxious to issue a literary review noted for its integrity, remain unknown; but if there was a struggle Browne triumphed in it. From its earliest days, the *Dial* maintained a high order of intelligence and independence. Under Browne, the magazine devoted itself almost entirely to long and thorough reviews of new books. It emphasized non-fiction, though it had regular columns devoted to current poetry and novels. The latter was for years conducted by William Morton Payne, a Chicagoan who assisted in the editing of the magazine and who maintained regularly the best kind of conservative taste in his reviews.

Except for a regular lead-essay by Browne, the *Dial* was written by its contributors, and these represented something broader than the Chicago culture within which the magazine existed. For the most part they were college professors, scattered throughout the country, who were called on for essays reflecting their special interests and training, although Browne also boasted the services of the Chief

Justice of the United States, university presidents, and distinguished private scholars. Throughout its life, the magazine maintained a circulation of several thousand, much of which was centered in the midwestern area.

Despite its more than local importance, the *Dial* occasionally served to bring into sharp focus issues which had special importance to the Chicago literary world. William Morton Payne in his fiction chronicle reflected genteel Chicago's taste, and from time to time, as in an exchange of letters with Hamlin Garland in 1893, Browne engaged himself in local matters. The exchange between Browne and Garland took place very shortly after Garland's arrival in Chicago during a phase in which he bristled most fiercely with professions of western loyalties. The *Dial*, in the normal course, had sent him a circular couched in the usual flattering terms of such missives inviting him to subscribe to the magazine. Unfortunately, it failed to make any special acknowledgment that this Hamlin Garland was a shaper of western letters. Garland, piqued, returned the circular to Browne with a sharp note scrawled on it. "I'm very glad to know you've heard of me in such a pleasant way. I had my doubts. When the *Dial* gets through with the middle ages I'll see about subscribing."[11]

There followed a conciliatory letter from Browne which, however, failed to impress Garland, who replied, "A journal that will call Riley's work 'doggerel' is not a critical journal, it is a conservative rear guard." Browne's patience was not exhausted however. In a long letter to Garland he attempted to make clear the *Dial's* position with regard to midwestern writing.

> Shall a literary fact or a critical opinion not be given because it would be 'disloyal'? Shall criticism be geographical? . . . For twenty-five years . . . I have been devoted to [western literature's] development and advancement. This devotion is not now to be impugned by eleventh hour converts who think that because I, through The Dial, will not make it my mission to exploit them and their narrow cult, am unable to see anything 'this side of England'. . . . We must show

> *that we are willing to have it tried by the standards of world literature, rather than by the standards of the back settle-ment.*[12]

The issue could not have been made more explicit. For Browne, like the genteelists in general, literary quality had a being which was without regard to time or place but dwelt in that much cherished nineteenth century temple of "greatness."

Browne's horizons were by no means those of the sentimental and narrow gentility of a Chatfield-Taylor, but inevitably his loyalties linked themselves more easily with the upward movement than with Hamlin Garland's populism. Like the other members of the upward movement, Browne looked with great favor and hope on Chicago's intellectual and moral growth. In 1892, that *annus mirabilis* of the midwestern metropolis, the *Dial* in a single issue published one essay hailing Chicago's "higher evolution," another in which the magazine welcomed the advent of the University of Chicago, and a third, a letter from Stanley Waterloo, exulting in Chicago's new literary possibilities.

A selection of its critical opinions from the eighties and nineties would reveal its essential good sense. In 1881, for example, one anony-mous writer refused the current American (and British) dismissal of Oscar Wilde as a mere poseur and charlatan: "Most readers of poetic taste will agree that there is something in this young man from Dublin not discovered by the caricaturist of 'Punch!'" In 1882 the *Dial* found itself unable to accept Whitman's poetic radicalism ("his virility as applied to the purposes of poetry, seems to us not unlike what the virility of a buffalo bull might be as applied to carriage purposes"), but by 1889 William Morton Payne could com-pliment *November Boughs* for its "absolute honesty," and "genius for style," and in 1892 John J. Halsey found it possible to make an Arnoldian acceptance of Whitman in terms of his "profound and serious conception of what makes men great." In 1891 Payne found himself enthusiastic over Emily Dickinson: "the form [of her poems] is rugged, but when a thought takes one's breath away, as Colonel Higginson observes, merely formal defects do not shock us." At the same time, of course, the magazine was printing lengthy and fulsome tributes to Longfellow's genius, it was regretting the decline of the great New England tradition, and looking always among writers of the present for "worthy inheritors of the past."

v

If *America* had represented most immediately the genteel group in Chicago, the *Dial* spoke to a broader, conservative, but more enlightened taste in Chicago and the Midwest generally. In a similar fashion, with at least one anchor fixed firmly in Chicago's genteel world, the publishing firm of Stone and Kimball was to swing from its original moorings into the mainstream of American and European literary thought. Its interest in authors of two continents, its fondness for fine bindings and elaborate design, its advanced and cosmopolitan taste, and its magazine, the *Chap-Book*, all had support in Chicago's genteel culture but included much that was foreign to that limited milieu. After publishing a guidebook to the world's fair of 1893, the firm began with a bibliography of American first editions largely compiled by Herbert Stone himself. Garland's volumes were among its early efforts as were books by Joaquin Miller, Eugene Field, Maurice Thompson, George Santayana (his first volume of poems), Robert Louis Stevenson, W. B. Yeats, Maurice Maeterlinck, Henrik Ibsen, and the complete works of Poe edited by Stedman and Brander Matthews. The list continued with Paul Verlaine, Chatfield-Taylor, Harold Frederic, Gabriele D'Annunzio, George Ade, Henry James, George Bernard Shaw (his first American publication), Will Payne, Robert Herrick, George Moore, and George Barr McCutcheon. In addition it published the *Chap-Book* from 1894 to 1898 and *House Beautiful* from 1897 until 1905, after which the latter was continued as an independent venture by Stone until 1912.

Clearly Herbert Stone, who was the originator of the firm and the more important of the partners, had created an institution which brought a real distinction to Chicago's cultural life. He was the son of Melville Stone, founder of the *Daily News*. As such, he was fortunate in being born into a family wealthy enough to support his original efforts (though they became self-supporting at an early date) and to give him an impetus toward whatever high culture, Chicago's upper classes, and Harvard College could yield. Both he and Kimball were members of the class of 1894 at Harvard, and much of the specific stimulus to their work came from their university experience. At college, Stone was a member of a group of literary aspirants which called itself "The Visionists." It included Bliss Carman, Charles G. D. Roberts, Harrison Rhodes (who was to be associated later with Stone and Kimball and to write *Ruggles of Red Gap*), Bertram Goodhue, and Richard Hovey. The Visionists, and others like them wrote poems and stories which they published in such bibelots as *The Knight Errant* and *The Mahogany Tree*. They drank ale and smoked meerscham pipes in the taverns where they were fond of meeting, and enjoyed hugely an exuberant and innocent bohemianism in which Cambridge of the nineties acceded. They read and admired the *Yellow Book* and later the *Savoy*; much of their writing, publication, and book design was directly modeled on that of the English aesthetes. After Wilde's conviction in 1895, the *Chap-Book* protested against the pleasure which many commentators seemed to take in "kicking a man when he is down," though little trace of the immortality or the *langeur*, of the English aesthetes was to be seen in the work of the Harvard bohemians. Stone, indeed, noticed the perversity of Beardsley's work (which he had been using both in the *Chap-Book* and other publications) only when it was called specifically to his attention. Harvard aestheticism was a youthful and naive affair.

It was directly under the aegis of such well behaved and moneyed adventuring that the firm was founded in Cambridge in 1893 while both the partners were still undergraduates. During 1893 and much of 1894 their books carried the imprint, "Cambridge and Chicago," and most of their early work, which luxuriantly embodied their taste for fine bookmaking, was printed at the Harvard University press. By 1894, however, they were settled in Chicago ready to assume a full-time interest in their business. Stone had enlisted the aid of Eugene Field and George Millard, the manager of McClurg's rare book department, in preparing his bibliography of American first editions and was to make use of other Chicagoans in launching his new business. W. Irving Way, who, with the help of Chauncey

William's money was to inaugurate the publishing activities of Way and Williams in 1895, suggested at this period that Stone might be interested in him as a partner. Stone, however, preferred Kimball's proved business head. Way maintained his interest in the firm in spite of Stone's refusal and featured their work in certain articles he wrote on bookmaking for the *Inland Printer*. During 1893, just before Stone and Kimball left Cambridge for Chicago, they enlisted the aid of Francis J. Schulte, whose own firm was temporarily suspended, in looking after the Chicago end of their enterprise.

One of their first acts upon the full establishment of their firm was to inaugurate, in 1894, the *Chap-Book*. Like General McClurg in the case of the *Dial*, they undertook the magazine primarily as a means of publicizing their books and promoting sales, but it was not long before the *Chap-Book* transcended its original purpose. Small, well designed, handsomely illustrated and adorned, and displaying the work of such a variety of contributors as Paul Verlaine, Thomas Bailey Aldrich, Madison Cawein, Stephane Mallarmé, and Hamlin Garland, the *Chap-Book* was much more than a mere advertising dodger. It was *avant garde* in format and content as was no other American magazine and, even more, was alone in supplying the want of a lively, current literary periodical. It was both amusing and useful. Each month its appearance was heralded at news stands across the country with the flaunting of a *Chap-Book* poster, most of them the work of contemporary American artists, but one from the hand of Toulouse-Lautrec himself. Both the *Chap-Book* and its publishers flourished, for a few years at any rate. But by 1898 a combination of circumstances caused Stone to abandon the magazine. Harrison Rhodes, who had come to Chicago from Harvard with Stone and Kimball to give much of his time to the periodical, left the firm to take a new job. The Spanish American War drew interest away from artistic and literary enterprises. And, perhaps the most important, Harry Thurston Peck's *Bookman*, founded with the support of Dodd, Mead and Co. in New York, gave the *Chap-Book's* skillful but amateur quality the competition of a large publisher's knowing hand and deep purse. In 1896 the two partners had separated, and Herbert Stone was left to carry on the firm by himself, which he did until 1905.

VI

The upward movement, however, was only in part concerned with literature, and its interest lacked too much the element of positive and creative imagination. Its chief weapon, like the genteel tradition as a whole, was that of taste, and its characteristic act was that of rejecting whatever—like Yerkes, the immigrant, Whitman's poetry, realistic fiction—did not suit its taste. Its chief monument, perhaps all the more so because of its very temporality, was the Columbian exposition; and on all sides the exposition was admired as a triumph of taste secured against enormous odds. The wonder and admiration which this world's fair of 1893 called forth from most beholders, and especially from those who had had much experience of Chicago, is almost beyond belief to later generations raised in their turn, on Louis Sullivan's doctrine that the world's fair was probably the single most disastrous event in the history of American architecture. But, precisely because it was such a triumph of what "ought" to be over what was, did it appeal to its creators and contemporaries. They were schooled in the negative faculty. The leaders of Chicago's upward movement, though they were pleased to make a place for the writer, could provide him only with a narrow critical attitude. The "artistic gang," as Hamlin Garland was to call it, of *fin de siecle* Chicago was too much the product of its cultural context to do otherwise.

Even such enterprise as that marking the career of Stone and Kimball was marked for ultimate failure. By 1905 or thereabouts the upward movement in Chicago, especially its literary contingent including magazines, publishers, perhaps two-score writers, and its always nebulous public had spent most of its original force. Both Fuller and Garland were to continue writing into the twenties, as were many of its less notable representatives, but only with a growing sense of malease and purposelessness. The publishers were out of business and the magazines, except for the *Dial*, suspended. The Little Room continued, but its importance diminished each year. Not all was quite lost, for it was the Chicago gentry, notably those who were associated with Harriet Monroe in the founding and financing of *Poetry*, who were to provide at least one important impetus for the second generation of Chicago writers. But genteelism as a method of writing, as an attitude, and as a solution to the midwestern author's problem of identity had, by 1905, largely proved its inadequacy. Its nearly twenty years of supremacy had failed to establish the kind of social or intellectual structure which could support a major literature.

Of its writing, Henry Fuller's novels are doubtless the most impressive achievement to which must be added whatever of interest remains in the earlier Harriet Monroe, the later Hamlin Garland, in Edith Wyatt, Hobart Chatfield-Taylor, and, collaterally, Robert Herrick. Other names might be added, but they would only serve to stress the fact that the efforts of Chicago society to patronize, even to create the writer trailed all too rapidly into a form of proprietorship, so that society and not the literary effort dominated in the end. Under its influence only the occasional devoted individual, like Fuller, could hope to preserve his integrity as a creative worker. An offshoot of The Little Room, and perhaps its legitimate heir, was the Cliff Dwellers' Club organized by Garland from among the male members of The Little Room in 1907. Fuller refused to come in (though the club took its name from the title of his first realistic novel) and it would appear that his choice was a sound one. For the Cliff Dwellers, launched by Garland to heighten the status of artists and writers, grew into a comfortable urban club, but one without great creative importance to the practicing artist—if, indeed, he could hope to afford its fees.

Finally, and ironically, the upward movement in Chicago which had bidden so well in the beginning to give the writer a sense of identity, failed in the end to preserve its own being. Between the business enterprisers and the polyglot multitude it led too narrow and precarious an existence. Though traces of the genteel spirit remain, its substance has largely vanished with changing times and conditions. The society from which it sprang altered, its standards lost relevance, and its hopes became a travesty. The civilizing of the world by leisured and cultivated mentors had fallen under too dim a prospect.

Hamlin Garland

FULLER had tried the spinning of a highly personalized cocoon which, in the end, failed its intended purposes of incubation. For another, Hamlin Garland, the problem of identity was best attacked in terms of violent attachments to a series of literary institutions and groups which, variously, seemed to offer an answer to his overpowering need for place and definition. Garland's famous switch of allegiance from realism to something much more like popular romanticism was only one of the many signs of tension in his career. His problem, in its multiplicity of factors, was perhaps more complex than Fuller's, if less profoundly rooted in his very nature, but it grew out of a similar bed of discontent and confusion. Fuller spent the bulk of his career fitting and re-fitting the few pieces of a personal puzzle. Garland, to the contrary, brought resource after resource to bear on his situation so that he presented a less static picture than Fuller—one in which the representative moment was one of shift from the old to the new. He conducted a never-ending and never very successful search for a solid element which might bear the weight of his needs.

From the first, his life had in it the elements of conflict and contradiction which were to determine its course throughout. His father, Richard Garland, was one of the multitude of western settlers whose sole philosophy of adaptation was that of "moving on." If the fields of his Wisconsin farm seemed limited and small, unrewarding of his efforts to make them yield large crops, he moved to Iowa. When in Iowa he heard of new land and more room, he moved to Minnesota. When favorable news of the opportunities for farmers in Dakota came to his ears, he moved to Dakota. When the Dakota farm failed to come up to expectations, he moved to the village of Ordway and became, temporarily, a town dweller. Throughout his long life, he regarded his present situation only as a preparation for the next one. His family necessarily suffered the continual uprooting and continually renewed hardships of a frontier farmer's life. His wife acquiesced, with increasing reluctance, in his peripatetic plans, but to her children she made clear her longing for her original home in Wisconsin with its greater comfort, its relatively fixed circle of family and friends, and its sense of settlement. When, however, after his first successes, Garland was able to buy a home in West Salem, Wisconsin, for his mother and so fulfill a dream which had long dominated him, she delayed making the move back until her husband could be persuaded of its advantages. It was not until his very advanced age that he greatly valued the domestic comforts which his son offered.

In a sense, Garland's mature destiny was prefigured by the restless current which had swept along his childhood and youth. Not only a continual movement from place to place, but also a growing series of internal tensions led, in spite of conscious direction, to his choice of a literary career as the best way to prestige and wealth. Richard Garland's family enjoyed few of the advantages which might predispose its eldest son to a literary career. Books played almost no part in his childhood, and all those concerned understood that he was being raised to serve his father's devotion to farming. For Richard Garland, a life which had no direct reference to farming was one with small reality, and he brought his son along the path which he himself necessarily followed. As it happened, Garland was later to make use of a selection of experiences from his early life, and of memories of farm existence largely related to him by his mother, for his most significant works, *Main Traveled Roads* and *Prairie Folks*. But no such concept could enter his youthful head. His paternal grandmother, bringing with her from Maine a devotion to New England's standards and ideals acted as a carrier for that seemingly remote culture by giving her grandchildren an early fondness for the poetry of Whittier and Lowell, and Garland's family itself, especially in its maternal branch, was versed in the tunes and ballads of the West, "Money Musk," "Over the Hills in Legions Boys," and the like. But always these were relegated to the evenings and to holidays when, for the moment, the demand of the farm had momentarily lessened.

Garland's first introduction to "literature" came, as it did for so many midwestern farm children, through his schooling and particularly through the selections from Shakespeare and Milton with which McGuffey had supplied his reader. Dime novels were available, and made an especially intoxicating delight, but they had to be stolen away from time which should have been given to farm duties and so bred a sense of guilt in reading and perhaps a persuasion that literature necessarily conflicted with the "real" business of life. When the Garland family settled in town in Hamlin's sixteenth year, his father was with some difficulty persuaded to let him attend the Cedar Valley Seminary, located in Osage, where his education in the anomalous discipline of "oratory" commenced. His reading at this time went far enough to include Eggleston's *Hoosier Schoolmaster*, then in serial publication, but there was little at the seminary, and nothing in the milieu which supported it, to establish anything like a real literary predilection.

Cedar Valley nevertheless gave Garland his first intellectual ambition, that of being an "orator," though the form his oratory was to take seemed nebulous. He apparently had no thoughts of the ministry, his political ambitions and knowledge were scarcely formed, and though he later showed a half hearted interest in law, the actual practice of that profession was remote to him. His choice was determined by a triumph in the oratorical exercises which were a regular and featured part of the seminary's discipline. Though, at the outset, these had formed a fearful obstacle for him to overcome, his sense of fulfillment at his final success was all the greater for his initial fears. He enjoyed the speaker's spotlight, the rapt attention of large groups, and the sense of power and self-command which the orator's role afforded him. But the demand for orators who had little more than their elocutionary gifts to offer was limited in middle border life. As a result, Garland graduated from the Seminary in 1881 with a training which could be of little practical use to him and one with small relation to the world in which he had been reared. Following upon a tacit agreement with his father, moreover,

Garland had now to regard himself as independent of his home ties for support. He was, in his twenty-first year, thrown upon a world which he was notably unequipped either to understand or to take a part in.

His immediate response to it was, understandably, that of vagabondage, of a kind of post-graduate effort to look around him and see something more of the circumstances with which he must cope. After a pointless period of months spent in wandering through the Midwest he conceived the notion of visiting New England whence his family had two generations before him emigrated. With his younger brother, he sallied forth on a hard-times tour of the area, one which was to make a major experience. The two boys were deeply affected by such aspects of it as they could understand. Its picturesqueness was one of its chief qualities. After the vastness and the monotony of Iowa and Minnesota, after their slatternly buildings, their lack of amenities, the compact and trimmed New England towns came as a revelation of what civilization might mean. Here were families who had lived for generations in one place, a region whose sense of the past extended beyond the memory of living men. Its spiritual homogeneity attracted them, and when they came to visit Boston briefly they saw it through the eyes of their regionally pious maternal grandmother. The Common, for them, was not only a splendid park, it was the ground which the great had trod—and were still treading. Their visit to Concord was a pilgrimage filled with wonder that they should be allowed to visit such hallowed purlieus. The reasons for their awe were no doubt amorphous, but that did not dim its reality.

After a time they returned to the West and Garland himself now plunged from his eastern revelation into the desolate reality of life in Ordway County, South Dakota, where his father had taken up a speculative claim on some farm land and was keeping a store while waiting his chance for profit-taking. Here Garland himself was pressed into service as a clerk and took up a claim, following his father's advice, though he did no actual farming. The dull hours in the store he filled with systematic reading, the first to which he had brought himself, but he still felt the pointlessness and rootlessness of his existence. The West rankled his soul. He knew as fully as he knew anything that the life of the farmer could not satisfy him, but even with such knowledge he saw no place else to turn. He labored his way through Taine, Greene's history, and Henry George's *Progress and Poverty*. In the latter he found an explanation for the bleakness of western conditions which he was to use for years, but still he had little better notion of his own destiny. By the veriest chance he struck up an acquaintance with a traveling minister, one Bashford, to whom he talked about his confused feelings. Like Garland's grandmother, Bashford had come to the West from Maine, and when he learned that Garland's tastes were literary and oratorical, he insisted that only New England could give him the milieu for which he was looking. Upon Bashford's advice he finally took what seemed a hopeless chance, mortgaged his claim, and prepared to live in Boston as best he could with his small capital. From Bashford he had letters of introduction to one or two local figures, and with these as an almost exclusive apparatus for placing himself in the East, he left South Dakota in 1884.

His first months in Boston were precarious. Living as he was upon a fixed sum, he was caught in the double vise of continually diminishing resources and a frantic desire to make the best of his stay, a desire which threatened to wipe out his money altogether. His letters of introduction proved fruitless, he could not afford to enroll in any regular school, and he had no chance of obtaining any kind of work which would prove congenial to his needs. As a result, he holed up in the cheapest room he could find, ate in greasy restaurants, and spent his days ransacking the holdings of the public library, trying to find among its wildly confusing detail some course of reading which might somehow open to him the status he desired. His first good fortune came by chance when, applying to Edward Everett Hale, a trustee of the library, for permission to take books home with him, he won Hale's interest. Some time later he heard Professor Moses True Brown of the Boston School of Oratory lecture to a young men's group he had joined and, taking his courage in his hands, approached Brown with his problems. Brown proved most friendly. Before long, Garland had a teaching post at the school, was booked for a series of invitational lectures on Edwin Booth whose art he greatly admired, and was installed in decent lodgings in the home of a Dr. Cross in Jamaica Plain.

To him the transformation was magical and astonishing. Somehow the table of Boston had been opened to him, and, though he had no illusions about his position far below the salt, he was so overcome with wonder that his insignificant western self had been noticed at all that he accepted the minor patronage he had been given with immense gratitude. One bit of good fortune led to another. Through his Booth lectures, he came to know Charles Hurd, literary editor of the *Transcript* and obtained not only his friendship but also some minor writing to do—Garland's first published efforts. Through his attachment to the *Transcript* office he achieved an apprentice place in Boston's literary world and was even told that, when the time was ripe, he might plan on meeting William Dean Howells. This initial newspaper experience seems first to have put into Garland's head the notion that he might become a writer. Though he had taught literature at Brown's school, he continued to think of himself in his undefined role as orator. His Booth lectures, for example, grew much more out of his interest in Booth's technique than the literary associations of the actor's roles.

"Each month," he declared of this period, "saw me more and more the Bostonian by adoption." "New York became a mere emporium . . . Chicago was a huge, dirty town . . . Washington a vulgar political camp."[1] The stray had found a home and was grateful for its warmth and stability. But hardly had Garland's informal naturalization finished than he became aware that his new role was to introduce strains of its own. Though he found an iota of security in the East his literary capital lay in the West. His first magazine publication, a descriptive sketch of an Iowa farm husking, appeared in the *New American* magazine, and the editor, William Wyckoff, invited him to submit more of the same thing. A short time later, *Harper's Weekly* accepted one of his poems of the prairies and confirmed Wyckoff's judgment that Garland was principally to be valued as a chronicler of western life. This in itself brought no immediate shock, but its anomaly was apparent. His emotional loyalties had attached themselves to Boston, but the only subjects which could maintain his pen were Western. Nor was there in the Boston culture which he so much admired a really high regard for the sort of reporting on outlying scenes to which Garland seemed largely limited. He found some hospitality for his efforts, but they did not command high pay or prestige, nor did their current form, that of the sketch, offer much in the way of further development.

At about this juncture, 1887, Garland made his first extended return visit to the West where he was shocked by the barrenness of his parents' life, by the hardness of their toil-devoted days. A strong feeling of guilt at leaving them in such circumstances, began to grow while at the same time he felt that only in the East could he hope to find sufficient reward as a writer to better their situation. He looked upon his home area without love, but the very snugness of the East had piled up in him to a kind of surfeit. He could appreciate the space and looseness of his own land if not its harshness and hostility. Though he was disappointed that his father did not take more note of what he felt to be his own considerable achievements, he was pleased when an invitation to speak at a fair betokened some native recognition. On this visit his mother told him the anecdote which he wrote up and entitled, "Mrs. Ripley's Trip," the earliest of the *Main Traveled Roads* stories, and the West gave him another impulse toward realism when he visited briefly with Joseph Kirkland who urged him to write of the western farmer with unsparing candor. Kirkland, said Garland, realized he had been unable to achieve such fulness in his own novels and felt that Garland should be just the man to carry forward the project.

Howells, whom he first met in 1885, had encouraged him to use the realistic method, and realism had for him the inestimable advantage of being the only literary technique by which he could hope to use his knowledge of western life. Taking a gamble, he elected to place his destiny in its power upon his return to Boston when, in 1889, B. O. Flower, editor of the newly organized crusading magazine, *The Arena*, made it plain he would accept any and all material with a reformist aim which Garland sent him. Then, in 1891, Flower collected a number of his tales and published them under the title of *Main-Traveled Roads*.

By this zig-zag route Garland came to his best known work. Like most of the choices which dotted his literary career, this one was made primarily out of his need for immediate place and function as a writer. He was in great luck actually, for he had turned to realism at precisely the moment when he might hope to benefit substantially from it. Howells and Flower between them took him up and, respectively, pled his cause and published him. As his literary interests had developed, so had his public advocacy of radical economic theories, particularly those of Henry George, and these he now used to define his career.

A crucial duality remained however. In his association with Flower, the reformer, Garland was primarily the socially conscious realist, anxious to bend his art any way to achieve the ends which his editor approved. For Flower, he wrote the dull and crude play, *Under The Wheel*, in which he was wholly the social critic content to write little more than a tract. It was also Flower who inspired *A Member of the Third House*, an anti-lobbyist argument little superior to his play, and the somewhat more successful *Spoil of Office*. In 1891 and 1892 Garland accepted Flower's offer to make an extensive tour of the West gathering material on the reform movement which was to come to a head in the Populist campaign of the latter year. On the other hand, for Howells, Garland took his stand as a regionalist and local colorist rather than reformer. It was from Howells that he received a commission to become the chronicler of the West, and he later made a comparison of his own work of this period with the local color of James Whitcomb Riley, George W. Cable, and John Fox Jr. As New England, the Southeast, and the old Northwest were receiving attention, so in Garland's mind the middle border became a property chartered to him especially. In his own comments, he always emphasized this regional aspect of his work rather than the reform writing done for Flower, though he actually came riding into the nineties behind a confused double hitch of realism and local color. His *Main Traveled Roads* was followed by *Prairie Folks* in 1893, and in 1894 appeared *Crumbling Idols*, his realistic manifesto.

This work, confusingly, post-dated *A Little Norsk* of 1892, written to order for Richard Watson Gilder and committed wholly to a saccharine local-color, while it preceded by a year *Rose of Dutcher's Cooly*, the last of Garland's realistic works. Scarcely had he found a position sufficiently important to make a manifesto of than he moved away from it.

The force exerted by Richard Watson Gilder, editor of the *Century*, had moved Garland from the start. Gilder, above all others, embodied genteelism in American magazine editing, and, since the magazines represented a source of income and prestige superior to those which book publishers could offer, Gilder's position as literary dictator was created almost automatically as a function of his editorship. Garland, from the time of his return to Boston in 1887, wooed Gilder's favor. "My plan of battle," he said of this period, "was to 'aim high and keep shooting,' and to Gilder of the *Century* and Henry M. Alden of *Harpers'* (high judges and advocates of local color in fiction) I sent the first of my almost illegible manuscripts."[2] He had put himself on a reasonably friendly level of correspondence with the editor before 1890 when he described himself as "praying like a Dervish that *Jason Edwards* may have won your sympathies to the point at least of giving me a chance to make his story suitable for your use,"[3] an indication of the earliness and eagerness with which Garland had opened himself to other mentors than the reforming Flower and the realistic Howells. As realism had been a first opportunity for Garland to crack open the inhospitable purlieus of American publishing, so genteelism was a greater opportunity, one which he felt small qualms about seizing so long as it gave him the opportunity which was most important to him. Garland's declaration that he wished a chance to make *Jason Edwards* suitable to Gilder's use did not involve its author in an act of bad faith since he was free to choose whatever manner of writing he wished. But it suggested that Garland's devotion to realism was, from the start, that of opportunist rather than convert. Opportunism was a necessary tactic for him if he were to locate himself as a writer at all. He had come to Boston without consuming convictions, though he counted himself a follower of Henry George. As his Boston years passed he found that thanks to the conjunction of Flower, Howells, the single-tax doctrine, a realistic method, and a western background, he was suddenly possessed of a fulfillment for his unlikely hopes. Having achieved so much, he was more than willing to press his luck further, to see if there were not greater and more rewarding eminences which he could scale. Though Garland's early letters to Gilder were often devoted to a defense of his realistic practices, he almost always finished them by accepting Gilder's suggestions. On one occasion he declared that the language of the common people was "beautiful, pictorial, and splendidly dramatic," but that "I want to bring beauty and comfort and intelligence into the common American home," and that, therefore, "I shall soften down the lingual sins of Albert."[4] In another undated letter from this early period, he gratefully acknowledged Gilder's acceptance of a story and went on to explain, lest he be suspected of ultra-radicalism, "the single tax with me means International copyright, the Sermon on the Mount, and . . . vacations for everybody."[5]

The central theme of Garland's manifesto, *Crumbling Idols*, was the regional one he had learned from Howells and expressed particularly in "The Local Novel." This, characteristically, took the form of urging the inevitable success of localism rather than its inherent moral or literary superiority, though the latter were not without a pious reference. "The local novel seems to be the heir apparent to the kingdom of poesie. It is already the most promising of all literary attempts today; certainly it is the most sincere."[6] And as a representative of both localism and political idealism Garland pressed himself upon Chicago in 1893. He came expecting to be lionized. Not only, he felt, was he the most fully developed author which the windy city had yet seen, if some of the newspaper men whom he despised were excepted, but he was the friend and by this time the associate of such acknowledged lions as Howells and Gilder. His purposes in moving seem to have been confused between a desire to establish a midwestern school of writing in the capital of the West and at the same time to take advantage of the upsurge of western publishing and interest in things literary already under way. Important also was the private motive associated with establishing his mother at New Salem, Wisconsin, in a house which, with her, he referred to as "the old homestead," but which in his correspondence he was fond of calling "my summer place." According to his own account, he maintained carefully his connections with *Harper's* and the *Century* as a present safeguard, though like any Chicagoan he was willing to trade in futures. But, equally by his own account, he was at work during his early Chicago years on a manuscript to be called *The National Spirit in American Art*. It was symptomatic of his thorough confusion, of his complete inability to find an identity for himself, that he should have met Lorado Taft while lecturing upon French impressionism garbed on principle in his Western frock coat.

Garland found in Chicago not a group of Yahoos whom he might lead and educate, but the upward movement which had created the local advantages he sought, and to this he gradually yielded. He was at first unwilling to allow Stone and Kimball to take any of his material. But after some consideration, he did give them *Main Traveled Roads* to re-issue and brought together the essays contained in *Crumbling Idols* for their purposes. Both these books were put out in tasteful though strongly marked fin-de-siecle formats which caused the *Atlantic* reviewer of the second volume to comment ironically on what appeared to be a division of purpose in Chicago culture. His remarks seemed justified by the larger occasion also. Garland lost no time, however, in taking advantage of all possible opportunities. He assisted in the early stages of The Little Room and struck up a friendship with Fuller which endured, as deeply as Fuller would allow any of his friendships to endure, for all of the time that Garland was in Chicago, and later as well. Their relations seem to have been unaffected by the lampoon of Garland in "Abner Joyce." Spending his time alternately in Chicago and in West Salem, he soon became enough of a notable in the metropolis to cause Eugene Field to make some *Sharps and Flats* pleasantry over Garland as realist and to declare his own preference for Mrs. Catherwood's romances.

About the only work of significance performed by Garland during his Chicago years was *Rose of Dutcher's Cooly* (for Gilder he spelled the word Coolé) which was written largely in Chicago and West Salem and published in 1895. In it he reffected the nature of his new environment as surely as his earlier work had been formed by his western origins and his association with Howells, Flower, and Gilder. For one thing, *Rose* was a Chicago novel—one set in that city and given to a study of the problem which that city raised, adaptation. Like the protagonist of many another Chicago novel, Rose came to the metropolis from a small town, was at first appalled by it, and then became gradually naturalized to it—this time by an acceptance of its upper-class standards. The story reflected Garland's own life, though transmuted in its incidents. As in reality he was always the country boy coping with the big city (Boston, Chicago, New York), so his heroine brought a country freshness and wholesomeness, Garland's youth idealized, to her problem. Industrial Chicago was the anti-self; Rose needed re-making.

Garland solved the difficulty in terms which mirrored his experience of city ways. Rose's problem, as it developed in the novel, was that of adjusting an ideal vision to the demands of reality. When younger she had been taken to a circus and there had experienced an epiphany upon beholding a handsome and graceful trapeze artist. His image persisted in her imagination as a symbol of all that was good and beautiful, and her Chicago career, after beginning in a romantically ideal atmosphere, turned rapidly to realizing her ideal among her upper-class acquaintance, particularly in her love affairs. After several hard knocks, she marries a pipe-smoking and urbane journalist, who, if less ideal than the trapeze artist, brings her a more solid and socially acceptable role. In *Rose*, as in his life, Garland acted out a compromise and made it one which was not too hard on either his heroine or himself. Mason, Rose's husband, is shown to have hold of things by the right handle; both Rose and her author approve his mildly cynical acceptance of imperfection.

It was not long after he moved to Chicago that Garland began to look around for a more secure situation. *Rose* was coolly received, "and this criticism," Garland noted, "saddened and depressed me. With a foolish notion that the Middle West should take a moderate degree of pride in me, I resented this condemnation. 'Am I not making in my small way the same sort of historical record of the west that Whittier and Holmes secured for New England?' I asked my friends. 'Am I not worthy of an occasional friendly word, a message of encouragement?' "[7] His notebook for 1895 carried an entry on the vanity of "this bitter war of Realists and Romanticists" declaring that it meant nothing really (this was one year after *Crumbling Idols*), and in 1894 he made the first of the trips which was to give him the locale for his later romances. Each year from 1894 to 1897 saw him in the far West for several months. In 1898 he ventured to Alaska. And in 1899 he married Zulime Taft, took her on a Western honeymoon, and also took his first European trip: to England. It was in preparation for this journey that his epochal struggle over adopting dress clothes occurred, and in this case even Garland was aware, though with inflated seriousness, of the symbolic importance of his decision. He was told again and again that if he was to go to England and consort with the leading literary men he must possess and appear in regulation dress clothes, and for months he worried his conscience about what to do. "To continue on my present line of march," he declared (that of wearing a frock coat and broad-brimmed hat on all occasions), "would be to have as exemplars Walt Whitman, Joaquin Miller, John Burroughs and other illustrious non-conformists. . . . To take the other road was to follow Lowell and Stedman and Howells."[8] He left America without the troublesome garments to put his problem in the hands of his host, Israel Zangwill, when he arrived in London. Zangwill advised conformity, and Garland agreed. The rightness of his choice was made apparent to him at a formal dinner which followed soon after. "Sitting there in the faces of hundreds of English authors, I achieved a peaceful satisfaction with my outfit. A sense of being entirely inconspicuous, a realization that I was committed to convention, produced in me an air of perfect ease. By conforming I had become as much a part of the scene as Sir Walter or the waiter who shifted my plates and filled my glass. 'Zangwill is right,' I said, 'the clawhammer coat is the most democratic of garments.' "[9] No critic of Garland could be more revealing. His place and identity were at last assured—by his clothes. He was as much a part of the elite world as Sir Walter Raleigh—or the waiter. He had proved himself a thorough democrat by adopting the dress of aristocracy. He could return home to write his western romances with a good conscience.

Garland grew less and less attached to Chicago. It had too fla-
grantly failed to give him what he most needed. His literary technique
came from the publishing houses of the East and his subjects from
the mountains of the far West. His clothes were now from London,
and his identity, he felt, from a choice of the best the world had to
give. Chicago was ungrateful. "Delegations of school children did not
call upon me, and very few of my fellow citizens pointed out my
house to travelers at that time. In truth, little of New England's
regard for authorship existed in the valley and my head possessed no
literary aureole."[10] Though Garland was a regular in The Little
Room, the founder of the Cliff Dwellers, a founder of the Society of
Midland Authors, and a member of the American Academy, Chicago
refused to submit to his scoldings or to do him honor. He complained
that he was not a beloved institution. When he moved to New York
in 1915 and found himself suddenly unable to attend the testimonial
dinner which the Cliff Dwellers, over whom he had presided since
their beginning, had planned for him, the Dwellers were seized with
a fullness of spirit which his straightlaced omnipresence had heretofore restrained. Roswell Field, who was at the dinner, hurriedly
sent out for some bottles and set himself up as bartender, and Will
Payne scrawled out a large sign for the wall, "This Place has Changed
Hands."

But whatever of Garland's difficulties sprang out of the simplicities
of his nature, more were owing to his genuinely anomalous situation
—that of the nineteenth century westerner with a literary bent. He
found himself in a real difficulty, however absurd some of his reactions to it may have been. And it was to be deepened. For when
Garland finally made the break from Chicago (he waited until after
the death of both his parents), the eastern literary world to which
he committed himself was also in a tottery condition. On a return
visit to Boston, the appeal that city had had for him in his youth
was gone; it was growing more like Chicago every day. He noted that
there was no younger generation to carry on its great tradition, and
that such young writers as did appear made their way speedily to
New York. In the latter city Gilder greeted him with congratulations
on *Her Mountain Lover*. "I predict a great success for it," he said,

"It has beauty . . . I am always preaching beauty to you, but you need it! You should remember that the writing which is beautiful is the writing which lasts." But Gilder was growing old, Garland noted, and a few days later he was saddened by the death of Charles Dudley Warner. He returned home, urged by thoughts of mortality, to work on an autobiographical manuscript which he had begun in Chicago, that of *A Son Of The Middle Border*, and to complete the final chapter of his more than curious career with his remaining six volumes of mixed memoirs and self-glorification.

Though Garland is a minor writer, he remains a major symbol among the mid-western authors of his time. Raised in a cultural tradition given over to the utilitarianism of city or farm and without a literary sense, committed to middle-class practicality, touched freakishly with a desire to write and a vestigially romantic trust in the writer's identity, he struggled throughout his life to make these netherest of ends meet. He could not abandon one or the other. He had tried that briefly in Boston when he turned his back on the West and had found his pen run dry as a result. His separation from letters during his youth, his opportunistic choice of realism, its failure to give him the place he had conceived for himself, and his eventual espousal of the popular romance, all these condemned him to the largely empty and circumstantial career which was his. Genteelism, though it promised prestige and wealth, was imaginatively sterile. It was Garland's additional misfortune that, forced finally onto himself, he should find so little there.

The Real World

JUST as the genteel tradition was imported to Chicago from the East, so the second major force in the city's literary renaissance, realism, came also from that benign direction. It was more adaptable to the West than the genteel impulse. There is, indeed, a half-truth in describing realism as an eastern influence since it had found western practitioners in the seventies and early eighties in such figures as Eggleston, Howe, Kirkland, and Mrs. Catherwood. But so much of its reputation and its establishment in the West, and in Chicago especially, came through the labors of Howells, that one has difficulty in divorcing the movement from him. Further, the eastern influence incorporated an impact from continental writers, French and Russian particularly. Garland found the primary impetus to realism, to the literary method, through Howells and Flower, though he provided a store of western matter for that method to deal with. Fuller, likewise, was encouraged in his realistic efforts by Howells and looked to Howells' novel of society as the modern fictional form most worthy of imitation. Robert Herrick, who had the advantage of Harvard, found that de Maupassant, and later Tolstoy, were useful mentors. Theodore Dreiser had provincial and romantic scales torn from his eyes by Balzac, and Sherwood Anderson, despite his contradictory statements about the matter, was at times willing to attribute something of his developed method to George Borrow, Chekov, and Turgenev. It thus would seem a mistake to insist upon realism as primarily an awakening and outpouring of the native Midwestern spirit. The method was one which many Americans found difficult to master, and which was slow in winning over native taste. It took something like three decades to naturalize it fully to the American scene, and during most of that time it was opposed by both high-brow and popular critics. Its defenders were often described as a special and limited group, a coterie devoted to unwholesome ways, whose foreign allegiances threatened the main lines of British and American fiction.

The commonest defense, that upon which Howells based his arguments, was of the opposite tenor—that realism was especially suited to picturing the American habitat, character, and mores. By its means literature once again might be brought into close touch with life. As Howells was primarily a writer of fiction, and as his criticism was mainly an elucidation and defense of his own practice, so he had a chief concern for the ways in which fiction had renewed itself, and fiction had depended upon life, upon reality. As the main line of British fiction in the eighteenth and nineteenth centuries had in part perpetuated itself by discovering new kinds of life to treat—rogues, country gentry, urban characters, high aristocracy, the clergy—so Howells proposed to advance American fiction by bringing into it kinds of American life not hitherto pictured. His disciples' achievements, he noted again and again, were those of opening new territories or new social strata for fictional purposes. Garland's use of the middle border was only one case in point.

Realism, thus, offered itself to its earlier American adherents not so much as a literary technique proper but as a substitute for technique. It succeeded in making the writer's primary burden one of presenting a subject faithfully and then asking that he be judged in terms of his fidelity to subject. It had little concern for his skill beyond that of presentation. It talked little of imagination and not at all of stylistic achievement. There should be no surprise that realism spread so rapidly among untutored writers like Eggleston, Garland, or Dreiser—those raised without a devotion to or much knowledge of letters as a discipline. For above all it offered a method for becoming a writer upon the capital furnished by one's non-literary experience, the only capital that many midwesterners had. Not all American realists originated in sub-literary ranks, but few of them achieved the high and mordant skill of a Flaubert. The Frenchman's devotion to style, his fondness for irony over mere presentation, were largely beyond their grasp. There were exceptions to this rule, like

Henry James, but for most of the turn-of-century realists, the method was characteristically an abjuring of the literary discipline rather than an advancement of it.

At one jump, realism offered a unique opportunity for the farmer's son to become an author—he had only to write about the farm. And in various circumstances, changing as the individual changed, realism offered a similar opportunity to almost anyone. It is not surprising that, from the first, a strong lyrical element should have been combined with the realistic method as it was in both Fuller and Garland. For, whether one came from the farm or not, a chief if unprofessed incentive to realism was the opportunity for singing oneself along with things familiar to oneself. This could not be done with the unabashed lyricism of a Whitman,—the self had to be hidden in some way beneath an objective looking disguise, but once the disguise was complete, the demands of objectivity were satisfied. The chief personal or ethical preoccupation of Fuller, Herrick, Dreiser, and Anderson, that of the individual pitted against the world, could be exercised easily within realistic limits, and so formed the staple conflict of their work. Not only were they thus enabled to express deeply private interests, but they could do so without violating the prejudice of the age against outright lyricism. Dreiser's Sister Carrie or Solon Barnes took on a compelling objectivity and could be contemplated without direct reference to their author. But the fact remained that scarcely one of Dreiser's protagonists failed to express something of Dreiser's own burdens and needs.

Realism gave not only a literary opportunity to the aspiring writer, but a generally intellectual one as well. It was, in its early days, of the vanguard; and to profess realism was to profess one's advanced thinking. For Garland, realism was bound up with social reform, for Herrick with a superior morality, and for Dreiser with Spencerian mechanism and a variously harbored mystical thought. Howells himself had advanced to Socialism, if not through realism, at least in congruence with it, and the realists of the thirties, like Farrell and Halper, who accepted the original mantle with least alteration, possessed strong political convictions. The intellectuality which accompanied realism was typically concerned with reformist causes, though this was not to identify realism wholly with the reform impulse. But, as the literary method focused its attention upon the real world, so the writer naturally turned to ideas which could be manifested in the real world; these, mainly political and ethical, were by definition the most real to him.

His subject was the dramatic and often overpowering effect of his immediate world upon the turn-of-century writer. Frequently that world had only to be reported to be made into moving and genuine literature. Its exciting, if often appalling nature, and its blatant contradiction of its own professed ethics were immediately at his hand and heart for what use he cared to make of them. If an author could not create epic, irony, tragedy, or comedy, he could see these spread in abundance around him invested with the appeal of newness and immediacy and could hope to report them in his work. His success, of course, was not assured, but its possibility seemed more immediate this way than any other.

Early realism existed, however, in a twilight zone where the writer's way was obscured by the shadow of the earlier local-color writers whose success dated back into the early century. Local color had much in common with realism; it too was concerned with presenting the characteristic life of a region or a time. But, unlike developed realism, the local colorist gave an allegiance to the traditional values of popular literature also. It was his duty to entertain, usually with humor or pathos, using as his subject selected elements of characteristic, common life. He was expected to be faithful to this life within limits, but where it might offend by its coarseness or dullness he was to revert to the entertainer's role and to expunge or heighten as the case might require. Life, for the local colorist, was not the equivalent of literature; it needed sweetening or spicing. For the realist, at least in theory, it was all.

I

It was out of a twilight zone between local color and realism that Joseph Kirkland emerged. Judging by his advice to Garland, he was more aware of the only partial success of his realistic efforts than many later historians, content to emphasize the realistic elements in his work, have been. Kirkland's three novels made continually increasing concessions to the demands of popular taste. Unlike Garland, who had made a similar compromise, Kirkland showed little bad conscience about his writing and never displayed the gnawing uneasiness and sense of frustration which marked the careers of so many of the Chicago group. As a writer and as a man he was bouyant and assured. It was he who had phrased the *Dial's* limitation of realism, "Let the truth be told, and not all the truth," and his career showed at every point the same willingness to conform to the demands of time and place.

But then Kirkland was not a literary man primarily. He did not depend upon literature for either an inner integrity or an outer security. He turned to serious writing late in life, and though his last years were those of a professional man of letters—a condition which would apparently have continued except for his sudden death —it was as mine operator, lawyer and journalist that he found his place in Chicago life. In a word, he did not depend on literature for personal necessities as did both Garland and Fuller. To him it was an absorbing avocation, but by no means one to which he was wholly committed. The difference was crucial.

He was further aided by his family circumstances. Though he had been born in New York state, his boyhood was spent partly in backwoods regions of Illinois and Michigan, and he was thus brought early to an awareness of western life. Moreover, his awareness was sharpened into something like a literary perception of that life through the influence of his mother, Caroline Kirkland, who wrote penetrating sketches of the rural doings of central Michigan. Young Joseph received little formal education; his learning came almost entirely from his mother and father. And both of them displayed to an unusual degree an acceptance of frontier life made possible, perhaps, by a literary detachment from and pleasure in it. From the first, Kirkland was taught to regard the wilderness as something intriguing. He was by no means of it, though he happened to be living in it some of the time. The one or two of his boyhood letters which survive are remarkable for accurate reporting, complete with dialect, which reflects an acquiescent superiority to his subject.

Kirkland's was a pleasure in rural events and persons displayed by one who belonged to another order of things.

He first came to Illinois in 1856 to work for the Illinois Central Railroad and soon extended his interests to some of the early coal-mining operations in the neighborhood of Danville. From these early years in south-central Illinois he drew much of the experience which was to show itself in his only notable work, *Zury, The Meanest Man in Spring County.* From 1875 to 1880 he was an employee of the U. S. revenue service, spending much of his time in Washington. In the latter year he returned to Chicago to practice law until 1890. His last four years were spent largely on his novels, together with contributions to the Chicago *Tribune* and the *Dial.* That the attitude displayed in Kirkland's boyish letters was not a merely passing one is made certain by the closeness with which he modeled *Zury* upon actual characters of the Danville period, probably of 1868 and 1869. Zury himself was drawn from one Usual H. Meeker. Though the name became Usury Prouder for Kirkland's purposes, much of the original's character remained in the fictional hero.

Kirkland's story was compounded of two elemental purposes which suggest clearly the compromised realism in which he worked. On one level, Zury, a study in character and setting, devoted itself to the accurate rendering of life in Illinois during the early 1800's. On another, it was a concocted romance in the course of which Anne Sparrow succeeds in reforming Zury's meanness to a state of happy benevolence. Like Garland, Kirkland confined his realism largely to setting and character, spinning his plot out of sentiment and melodrama. Unlike Garland, however, he took pains to make his characterization complex and genuine. Zury's mixed motives grew naturally out of his life. His "meanness" did not stem from active cruelty but was rather a devotion to hard work, and money, for which he was more admired than not by his neighbors. Full of humor, completely down to earth in all his feelings, but at the same time capable of suffering and confusion, he was believable in every particular except the plot which Kirkland visited upon him.

Further, Kirkland strengthened his portrait by a skillful and unashamed exercise of middle-western rural dialect the importance of which he acknowledged in a glossary of terms appended to the end of the novel where such expressions as "clamp down," "close call," "a go," "O.K.," "peter out," "swap," "talk turkey," were given origins in rural middle-western speech. Though he occasionally made his dialect a subject for amusement, Kirkland generally hewed to a realistic treatment of it. He accepted it, that is, as the natural speech of his characters and was concerned more with its authenticity than its peculiarity. For any whose ears have been exposed to such gen-uinely rural and native midwestern speech as still remains, a conver-sation between Zury and his father, over the construction of a wooden shovel, must carry a familiar ring.

> "Shell split, Zury, sur's ye're born!"
> "Mebbe so, dad, mebbe not."
> "Ye'll see,—right where ye got t'set yer foot, she'll split square off."
> "Yew jes' hold yer hosses."
> "Ye can't dig nothin' with that thar slopin' tool,—no place t'set yer foot on, 'n so all-fired long in the bit."
> "Din't I tell ye t'hold yer hosses."
> "Lop-sidedest tool ever I see. One shoulder 'baout six inches higher 'n t'other."
> Zury did not deign to reply to this taunt.
> "Bain't ye a-goin' t'hew that shoulder daown level with t'other."
> "Guess that shoulder's 'baout right," answered the youth, who delighted in mystifying his father.
> "Wal, ferever!" said the mother.[1]

Kirkland's realistic characterization went beyond Zury himself. The protagonist's father and mother are genuinely earthy pioneer-farmers. The Peddicombe sisters, whom Zury marries, *seriatim*, before coming to Anne, combine the ignorance and the drabness of the farm wife's existence. The land which each brings her husband, and which passes immediately into his control, is the only motive for his perfunctory wooing. Though neither is abused by Zury, each must find such love and joy as is possible in rare intervals of their work-filled days and without reference to him. Mr. and Mrs. Anstey, Zury's poor neighbors, demonstrate a genial sloppiness and durability native to their kind. Anne Sparrow, coming from New York state to teach school (as Kirkland's father had in Michigan), is a less impressive achievement, but even here, a recent study suggests, Kirkland may have begun with a fully developed figure which he felt constrained to reduce for prudential purposes. Anne, in the revised novel, is lively, but priggish and manipulated by obscure motives. Kirkland's original plan may have been to make her more resolute and clear-cut. In the revision of the novel for its second printing, Kirkland deleted several passages which suggest that Anne was a Fourierest, a free-thinker, and a pioneer feminist, and that the author intended a contrast between such enlightenment as Anne's and the prejudice and ignorance of the frontier.

In the novel as it stands, Anne does enlighten Zury, but not in dangerous or debatable ways. She makes him realize that his "meanness" is excessive and inhumane, that people should be handled with kindness and understanding rather than as assets or liabilities. As a climax, she rebuilds the ugly, stark house in which Zury has lived most of his life. Under her hands it emerges complete with a new kitchen, a laundry, a windmill, and a summer house. In short, she makes a pioneer farmer into an ideal modern farmer. How much Kirkland may have suffered under the necessity of making Anne a popularly acceptable heroine cannot be ascertained. Certainly the comments in his private papers indicated a great fondness for the character without any reservations, and, through them all, there was evidence of his willingness to bow his desires as a writer to the demands of the society in which he had won a fair place. In 1894 he approved the utilitarian dictum. "'Genius is an infinite capacity for taking pains.' The antipodes of Browning—not to say Walt Whitman who is unspeakable."[2] Garland, of course, had made much at one time of his own similarity to Walt Whitman. But Kirkland had, in private, a patronizing tone for Garland. "Hamlin Garland spent Saturday night and Sunday forenoon with me. Enthusiast—country boy— farmer's son—largely self-educated—wants to reform the literature of our country! Reconstruct it on a realistic basis. Hates Lowell, Holmes and the other fossil representatives of classicism. Loves Walt Whitman and Howells and Howe . . . and *me*. Has a great work on hand, 'Literary Democracy,' apotheosis of common things and common people. Wants me to devote myself to literature even at the sacrifice of business."[3] For Kirkland, literature was literature and business was business. There was no doubt about which came first.

Both because such doubts were non-existent for him, and because his works were well-liked, Kirkland was an anomaly among the early realists. But his aims were different from theirs. Without a true villain, *Zury's* story was told essentially as an act of acceptance and written with considerable zest, with an essential joy in its subject—though its bleakness was not scamped. For Kirkland, Zury and his neighbors lived a real and tolerable existence. He had known them, and he was able to communicate their vitality and their resilience to his reader. He wrote not out of personal frustration, nor did he commemorate a stored-up unhappiness. His was genuine fiction—not a metamorphosed lyricism.

II

Kirkland's personal success, coming at the beginning of Chicago realism, served ironically to introduce the personal failure of his immediate followers. Will Payne, William Vaughn Moody, Robert Morss Lovett, and Isaac Kahn Friedman managed to go beyond Kirkland in that there was nothing of the local colorist in their work; they were among the creators and practitioners of the Chicago novel. But for each the city, either in itself or as an epitome of modern civilization, was a recurrent theme, and for each the theme was an unhappy one. These writers fall within Parrington's class of "critical realists" in the sense that they used their novels or poems primarily as weapons against the culture which surrounded and threatened to destroy them. But "critical realism," as Parrington used the phrase, suggests a programmatic and essentially political approach to the writer's concern, and Chicago realism was primarily that of a personal ethic.

Just as the upper levels of the heretofore homogeneous business culture were branching out into new directions, splitting off from the parent in directions different from its own bent, so in the roots of business, in its utter dependence upon large numbers of workmen, basic changes were taking place as the workers discovered that they need not be content to devote their lives wholly to the success of someone else's concern—that they too might hope and work for an independent place, a culture or sub-culture of their own. The riots of 1877 had taught them that they were necessary and powerful enough to warrant the intervention of federal troops against their insubordination. The riots of 1885 had grown at least partly out of the anti-business rationales conceived for them in socialism and anarchism. And a third major wave of labor troubles, those of 1894, were to give them a degree of power, in the emerging fact of union organization, sufficiently strong to rock the whole nation's economy. It was the Pullman strike which set off this latest occasion. The Pullman shops, slowed down by the depression of 1893 and 1894, had reduced wages thirty to forty percent and laid off a third of the working force. The workers struck against these actions in May of 1894, and for about a month were without support. During June, however, the American Railway Union, presided over by Eugene Debs, met in convention and voted to boycott the handling of Pullman cars on all American railroads. Quickly Chicago became the center of violence as the originally peaceful intention of the union changed to open warfare against the General Managers' Association. Again the strife was settled by the intervention of Federal troops, sent this time over the violent protests of Governor John Altgeld, and at its conclusion Debs and a number of the other leaders were jailed for six months after a conviction of conspiracy was returned against them.

As Chicago had grown bigger and more stratified, its original homogeneity of business aims and business rewards had begun to break down. There were too many people whose interests were too discrete for it to do otherwise. Business remained at the core. But, as the genteelist had criticized the business culture for its vulgarity, the Chicago realist attacked its immorality. The law of the business world was too much the law of the jungle in a new setting. Its fierce competitiveness, devotion to the main chance, and acceptance of triumph-or-die as the rule of life offended radically the ethic which a liberalized Christianity and an idealistic view of human nature had bequeathed to the nation. If the genteelist demurred in the name of a romantically conceived culture, the realist criticized in the name of a romantically begotten moral law.

The Chicago realists concerned themselves with their city in deeply personal ways. It seemed, first and most important, an inescapable fact sprung into their lives like some massive geologic extrusion. Whatever else, and almost all else about it was doubtful, it was pre-eminently there. All cogitation, all marshalling of response, had to start with its overpowering presence. So insistent was its reality that all must deal with it. The upward movement had sought its translation in terms of aristocratic hopes; the naturalists were to account for it by re-defining and analogizing the laws of nature. But, after these had finished their exorcistic work, the city triumphed. Whatever ideas and attitudes were brought in to play, it remained.

No wonder, then, that the Chicago realists, faced with living in their great urban anarchy, should have been predominantly ethical in their concern. Their literary code bound them to deal with the city, as did its own power of fascination; and their values were deeply affronted by what they beheld. Henry Fuller, in his *With The Procession*, had the Marshall family destroyed precisely through the impact of the city upon their conventional and unready morality. For Garland, the "portentous presence" of the city was "like an eagle, whose hovering wings extended from south to east, trailing mysterious shadows upon the earth."[4] For Robert Herrick there was to be the question, "But what use in all this multiplication if it meant no gain in quality, no finer fibre, no higher life of the mind or of the soul!"[5] And his question was echoed poignantly in dozens of novels of Chicago life. For all, there was a flat contradiction of accepted ways by a force which could not be ignored. Such a contrast formed the commonest source of imaginative concern with Chicago. The techniques which the realistic imagination might summon to its aid were only necessary properties.

Caught, as most of the realists were, in a local situation which ramified out at a dizzying rate, few had the resource to do anything but protest in the name of the double ethic most readily at hand, that created by the New England mind in a fusion of Christianity and idealism, and spread across the land by lecturers, schoolteachers, and the printed page. Now this force was challenged by what seemed moral chaos come again. For the Chicago realist, the great anarch was the new-risen business man—the giant tycoon who had somehow placed himself to command the full force of the new wave, and, by its force, lift himself to a bad eminence of power. Business was immense and startling; by its nature it transgressed the old law. In this combination lay the indictment of the realists against its domination of Chicago.

One may not dismiss the justice of the realists' charge by arguing that it had elements of melodrama and over-simplification. The authors were right in what they examined even though their examination lacked depth. For them the pertinent reality lay in such a figure as Yerkes (who reappeared under various names throughout their novels), because it was Yerkes, of all the local tycoons, who most patently and carelessly flouted the conventional moral professions. He had never defended himself except to say that everyone was doing it so why not he, but such a defense was the opposite of reassuring. It acknowledged, in effect, that the moral law had ceased to prevail except as a nominal entity. In the new world (the point upon which the naturalists seized) only power counted. Might did not make right, but that was only because right seemed to have no possibility of existence. Might was all.

Thus did the novels of Will Payne, in their totality, form a symbolic record of his own brush with the city—encounter, bewilderment, moral defeat. This last, to be sure, earned him a solace—he became in time a regular and well-paid contributor to Lorimer's weekly journal of reassurance to the middle class, *The Saturday Evening Post*. But his winning through to this attainment had its cost. In 1896 his first novel, *Jerry The Dreamer*, could concern itself with that constantly recurring prototype, the young man just come to Chicago, as the crucial object of study. Jerry's struggles to find a place, his partial success, his involvement with a struggling Socialist paper, his growing attachment to its ideals, his marriage to a thoroughly native middle-class girl, and a breach between them which

Payne could heal only by conjuring with the thin ritual of sentimental romance—all these symbolized as clearly as possible the kind of alienation which Chicago was to force on many of its young men. They must cut themselves off either from their origins or from Chicago itself. The problem of making a harmony of the two was over-difficult. Payne, in his novel, solved the problem by a liberal administration of narrative convention—love, in a word, found a way, though the reader was less than fully enlightened as to what the way might have been.

Jerry's problem with Chicago existed on two levels. There was the city itself—a generalized and impersonal opponent, and there was his wife, Georgia, a product of the city, accepting it thoroughly, bringing its reality as close to Jerry as marriage itself could, making it as poignant to him as a deeply personal relation must inevitably make it. His wife's idea of the future, Jerry learns after he has accepted the ethical idealism of his Socialist weekly, *The Call*, is "that he should make more money. . . . She could not conceive of any reasonable or even sane scheme for the future of two young people living on $1800 a year which did not include more money."[6] Georgia is without meanness or special avarice. She genuinely loves her husband. But she can see nothing more in their relationship than the comfort and security which success can achieve for it. Other questions of better or worse have no reality.

Jerry's reaction to his plight gives an inevitable consent to the pressures of Chicago. He admits the defeat of the idealism which, through his Socialist connections, he has come to cherish. As he watched a group of street urchins cheating and battling each other over a pitch-penny game in an alley, "He no longer wondered that men strove for money. It seemed wonderful to him, rather, that they preserved any semblance of honor, of generosity, of kindliness in their strife for it; that they did not rush out like wolves, pillaging and killing to get the counters that would insure their own against the misery and shame of poverty."[7] The old morality did not fit the new city.

In this first novel Payne preserved some shreds of regard for the old law. It was a code which, though inapplicable, still had a residual force—enough in Jerry's case to set him searching for a statement of it which seemed better to suit the facts, a search which led him into Socialism. But Payne's partial disillusionment here contrasted startlingly with the deep cynicism, the complete abandonment of any law, to which his experience of Chicago and the modern world later led him. In 1916, twenty years after *Jerry*, he wrote to Robert Herrick about the war. "I . . . predict that the war probably will change nothing whatever; that Europe a year after peace will probably be just what Europe a year before the war was except much poorer, less populous, more copiously sprinkled with cripples, and tolerably sodden with hate."[8] Only reality existed. Payne's moral idealism which, in 1896, had been permitted a vestigial existence, was here wholly borne down. Herrick, in 1916, was refueling vigorously, though for the last time, the furnace of his own idealism, seeing momentarily in the war a true conflict between good and evil in which the good was on the side of the allies. Payne, however, refused such a gambit with foreknowledge of certain loss—the good was a function of a way of life now dead. The forces which had killed it were symbolized by Chicago. They were those of the moral anarchy which big business had spawned and by which it was now nourished in a Thyestian feast.

In his novels Payne symbolically recorded the learning of this lesson. He himself had come to Chicago from Whiteside county, Illinois, in 1890, the same year in which George Ade made his arrival, and was a co-worker of Ade's on the *News* until 1896, a period during which he became city editor under Charles Dennis. He spent a year as financial editor of the *Chronicle* and then moved to the *Economist* in 1897 where he eventually became editor in chief. As his novels achieved some success, and as he found that magazine fiction provided a necessary living, he broke his ties with journalistic work to become a free-lance writer. By 1907 he had given up Chicago as a permanent residence. His career as novelist spanned only a decade and a half, fifteen years which were largely given over to completing the conversion which *Jerry The Dreamer* had begun. Of the stages in this process, that marked by his *Money Captain* of 1898 was especially revealing.

His hero, Nidstrom, was the type of passive sufferer which the Chicago novel had made peculiarly its own. Inevitably, the story of

Chicago was a story of what happened to people in the city rather than of what they did; it was a tale of things endured. Sometimes, of course, the hero could be made an opponent of the city, but even in this case defeat faced him so squarely (Chicago, after all, was still there and unchanged), that an author was put to great lengths of narrative ingenuity to end his story short of absolute ruin. There was little or nothing in the logic of the realists' case to allow them active heroes—protagonists. Payne's Nidstrom, private secretary to Dexter, the "Duke of Gas" and overlord of Chicago utilities, suffers long and deeply. At the end of his story he is given a course rather than allowed to choose one, for by the end it has become apparent that only one choice is possible. Despite a few remaining scruples, he joins the forces which Dexter represents, those of selfishness, civic corruption, and devotion to wealth because only by attaching himself to Dexter's career can he hope to secure a place in the real world. At one point he allows himself to think of an alternative. "The only thing . . . is to get away; get into a different atmosphere. Think of that country place! How insane and squalid all this seems beside it!"⁹ But Nidstrom knows well enough that the country place cannot exist for him. He is a city man. He joins the city thus, but without joy or any real hope.

The money captain himself is as much a victim of the business world as is Nidstrom. "Last year," he says, "these companies took in seven and a half million dollars. I'd be well satisfied so far as mere money goes to be guaranteed for myself and my heirs one percent of that amount clear and free. . . . But you want your ideas to win. You want your plans carried out. You think you see opportunities that other people overlook and you want to seize them and show that you were right."¹⁰ The city compelled material expansiveness and acquisitiveness, expression of personality by accretion of the very material goods which, in Emerson's eyes, had been its chief enemy. Things, indeed, were in the saddle, and they rode the self into dreadful and narrow places. Rather than Brahma, the archetype now was the Duke of Gas.

Payne's acceptance of the business world has occasioned his comparison with Norris and Dreiser, but an important difference remains.

Norris and Dreiser, in so far as they accepted the world of big business, did so not in its own terms but in terms of a more or less coherent naturalism. To them the big business world of Chicago was an instance of overpowering forces. Payne's basic ethicalism, as opposed to naturalism, showed itself in his lack of interest in positing for the Chicago world any explanation broader than its own manifest wickedness. If there was no Virgin in his scheme, there was no dynamo either. There were no cosmic processes of the sort predicated by Norris and Dreiser. There was only Chicago, a lumpish symbol of modern life. This he knew intimately as a business writer and lay economist, but he also knew that however far Chicago might be removed from human control, it was not immune to human judgment.

The work of two other writers, faculty members at the University of Chicago, took a further step in the solidifying of ethical realism by bringing explicitly to bear on the symbol, Chicago, a defined and explicitly moral critique. William Vaughn Moody and Robert Morss Lovett both wrote in the name of an advanced idealism which bespoke the New England training both had received. For both, the new age ground moral and rational beings underfoot. It was evil in its nature and must be understood and opposed in the name of morality and reason.

For Moody, poetry had an importance in its own right which far exceeded the esteem of most of the writers of realistic prose for their genre. His commitment to it, like the attitudes he included within it, was exultantly romantic. His belief in his own poetic destiny made him fret with impatience at the necessity of teaching in the "themery," as he called it, which under Herrick had copied Barrett Wendell's theme-a-day plan from Harvard; and his sensitivity revolted at Chicago. He wrote to friends of being "dissatisfied to the point of desperation with the kind of life that is possible out here," and remembered achingly "days in the east when a hedge of lilac over a Brattle Street fence, or a strenuous young head caught against a windy sweep of sunset on Harvard bridge, filled me with poignant perceptions of a freer life of sense and spirit."[11]

For the better part of a year, Moody simmered unhappily in

Chicago. Then there occurred a period of not uncongenial fallow-
ness after which he began again to write. His pre-Chicago work,
though showing some variety, had been largely of a pre-Raphaelite
pastiche kind dedicated to easy ecstasy and embroidered out with
stock feelings and images. According to his own account, however,
the West gave him a new vein and an unsuspected strength. In May
of 1896 he sent to his friend, Daniel Mason, a copy of a new poem
(probably the original version of his "Heart's Wild Flower") with
the hope that Mason would like it "because it is almost the first
thing I have done which has been a direct impulse from 'real' life,
and you know I have theories about that."[12] Whatever the theories
may have been, there can be little doubt that Moody had found in
Chicago the ethical concern with reality which was to mark both his
mature poetry and plays. His writing from this time on was seized
by issues growing out of the real world. Its substance was taken
from the round of ordinary experience (though he maintained his
fondness for the picturesque) while its tension lay in its contrasts
of a deep moral urging with the blatantly amoral culture which faced
its author. In effect, Moody had been converted to a kind of poetic
realism, or at least a poetic attitude congruent with the realistic
concern.

The new interest was epitomized in his poem, "The Brute."[13]
Here a figure Moody had used earlier in reference to Chicago was
broadened and made to apply to the whole of modern culture in
terms of its machinery and factories especially. The brute, symbol of
the nineteenth century's mechanical and business genius, had at first
been meant to serve mankind.

> *They who caught and bound him tight*
> *Laughed exultant at his might*
> *Saying, "Now behold, the good time*
>   *comes for the weariest and the least.*
> *We will use this lusty knave:*
> *No more need for men to slave;*
> *We may rise and look about us*
>   *and have knowledge ere the grave.*

But the brute would not be bound. He rebelled at his servitude and plotted the revenge which Moody could see around him in world-wide abundance.

> *On the strong and cunning few*
> *Cynic favors I will strew;*
> *I will stuff their maw with overplus*
> *   until their spirit dies;*
> *From the patient and the low*
> *I will take the joys they know;*
> *They shall hunger after vanities and*
> *   still an-Hungered go.*
> *Madness shall be on the people,*
> *   ghastly jealousies arise;*
> *Brother's blood shall cry on brother*
> *   up the dead and empty skies.*

For Moody, however, the brute was in rebellion against a human nature innately good; evil was inherent in the modern scheme of things rather than in human hearts. Consequently, a happy ending was possible. The poet could find it in his soul to let the good triumph rather easily because it was good and hence was bound to triumph; the ideal must prevail. As the brute spun his plot, a "still small voice" was heard. Though unidentified, it was that of a conscience still tied to an idealistic hope.

> *Lo, bade them a still and pleasant voice*
> *   none the less rejoice*
> *For the brute must bring the good time on;*
> *   he has no other choice.*
> *He may struggle, sweat and yell,*
> *   but he knows exceeding well*
> *He must work them out salvation*
> *   ere they send him back to hell.*

The poem concluded with a vision of the brute, suddenly redeemed from Hell, standing "Twixt the Lion and the Eagle, by the armpost of the Throne."

Moody's optimism, no doubt, was facile. But it grew naturally in the kind of intellectual climate which he, half unwittingly, shared. To put one's trust in hope and the fundamental goodness of man was an act which the less romantic Will Payne could never have accepted. All around lay evidence of what drastic errors the human will, as implemented by the forces of Chicago, could achieve. For Moody, however, there was the middle-class doctrine of looking to the bright side, and of an instinctive, guilt-erasing allegiance to the belief that, through all errors and viciousness, the right must prevail because it was naturally stronger. Payne, of course, was closer to the durable tragic view. Moody's buoyancy was not the stuff on which a major literary imagination could well work. It dispensed with too massive a complexity too easily.

Such a weakness was generalized and pervasive rather than special, and might, indeed, be discussed under a history-of-ideas rubric as one example of the inadequacy of the liberal ethic to cope with or even understand the late nineteenth-century world. But Moody, like the majority of the Chicago realists, was not deeply affected by idealogical currents. His response to Chicago, as his correspondence suggested, was instinctive and emotional rather than intellectual. He wrote to Mason in 1895, "If you knew the beast Chicago, the pawing and glaring of it, you would not find me hard to forgive. I have been in the condition of the Kluger Schneiderlein in the bear pit: it has taken all my frightened dexterity to keep out of the jaws of the creature."[14] What he felt to be challenged by the city was a whole self. Like Herrick and Lovett, he was a contemporary at the University of Thorstein Veblen, John Dewey and Jacques Loeb. But his writing betrayed no awareness of them or of the extent to which they were busy translating both the Chicago world and his own Cambridgian vision into abstractions variously intended to create a harmony of experience with scientific formula. Science, indeed, along with history, formal ethics, metaphysics, politics, and orthodox religion was notable for its absence from his work. To Moody and his generation, the later concept of the writer as a creative intellectual was unknown. He allowed thought, to be sure, and feeling. But thought had no development for its own sake. Poetry was primarily self-expression and not the imaginative expression of intellect. He took his self as he found it, without further concern, as the proper sieve through which the world was to be strained into his poetry.

The realistic novelists, of course, had a less fervent vision of their literary function, but it was one not greatly different in kind from Moody's. To Herrick, the writer was a person who evaluated life, and Payne had much the same view. Payne's letters to Herrick, whom he admired greatly, were full of references to the writer as an instinctive being—one whose business was twofold: to respond critically to experience and to dramatize his response. What determined his success was primarily the quality of his response; and, plainly, the writer's problem of response in the Chicago world was a huge and unprecedented one. About Robert Herrick's *The Web of Life*, Payne wrote the author, he felt ". . . a sense of proportion and a fine clean stength, but I keep forgetting these things in the power of its truth."[15] Again, ". . . no one could read the last two books without feeling that *The Real World* comes from a richer man, one fuller of experience and sympathy."[16]

Ideas, of course, might be used. Payne had made his Jerry The Dreamer ponder Socialism, and I. K. Friedman was to write novels which recommended a re-making of the world according to Laurence Gronlund's *Cooperative Commonwealth*. But even Socialism, and this was most commonly the idea dealt with by the Chicago realists, was a secondary quantity—an item by which the sort of response characteristic of Moody's poetry could be implemented. The primary subject was always that of the traditionally moral man, adrift in an amoral universe, shocked and distraught that such incongruity could exist.

In his two early novels, Robert Morss Lovett recorded precisely this discovery but could urge only that an ethical structure must, somehow, be found. The pattern of the two books was the same. *Richard Gresham* (1904) was an account of how the hero, having been raised by a strictly moralistic uncle, discovers that the world of business into which he had been introduced is shot through with fraud. His response is to remove himself from its sordid atmosphere and assert thus his uncle's code despite earlier doubts about it. In

A Winged Victory (1907) the story tells of love and tangled personal relationships from which there emerges the conclusion that only the moral man is the good man—that true morality, though unpopular, should prevail despite the general disregard of it. Morality, Lovett would hold, abides. It is the world which changes. In commenting on the modern novel in 1931, he still saw the essense of modern fiction in the ethical search. "The typical modern novel is not the story of how a man struggles to win his own true love; it is the account of how he struggles to win his own true self."[17]

The young man, or young woman, at odds with a world he never made—one which threatened to undo him by forcing him into the power of foreign and hostile circumstances: this was the great preoccupation of Chicago realism. Small wonder the novels it produced were, above all, testimonies of outraged sensibility. They were, as analyses, over-hasty; and as programs for action or definition, they scarcely existed. But they did record the depths of confusion into which Chicago—the immediate and inescapable symbol of a horribly triumphant world—could throw one who had been formed by a friendly, humane, hopeful, and orderly culture. Such a one must, it was clear, look elsewhere than Chicago for a system like that he had known.

Like the early Will Payne, I. K. Friedman seized on Utopian Socialism as the only force in modern culture which gave any promise of maintaining the older, liberal ethic. He was born in Chicago in 1870 and raised in the city. He attended the University of Michigan and did graduate work at the University of Chicago in philosophy and English. Despite these attainments, and despite his reputation among The Little Room habitues for overweening intellectualism, he brought to his novels not only the same outraged sensibility as the other realists, but also an imaginative naiveté far greater than any demonstrated by his colleagues. No depth of bathos was too great for him, no plot-device too mildewed, no character too stereotyped. In his anxiety to proclaim his ethical truth, he rushed impatiently through his stories or bent them at every joint to make them demonstrate his thesis. In *Poor People* of 1900 he was at pains to show how, among slum dwellers, there was an abundance of the very conservative virtues so dear to the utopian socialist. Kindness, sympathy and liberality were all bedecked with a dusty rhetoric which made his characters of the slums (except the comic ones who spoke in stage dialect) talk in copy-book English. The young hero, who suffered the disadvantage of his origin, emerges automatically at the tale's end as a popular and profound playwright.

But Friedman did more significant work in *The Radical* of 1907. Here he had the mechanics of novel writing under better control, and, perhaps, he worked more closely from life. His hero, exemplifying Friedman's sympathies, was a politician who with high motives forged his way ahead from the Chicago city council to the United States Senate to advocate the Cooperative Commonwealth. His hope was to hold the remaining public land for the people in perpetuity so that they might have a safeguard against the growth of business power and as an economic base on which to build the society of the future. Though Friedman's lesson was necessarily more technical than that of the other realists, there can be little doubt that, to him, economics was the only key by which one might unlock the moral resources of the humble folk he had so extravagantly admired in *Poor People*. His aim was not the materialistic paradise of Marx, but the humane and ethical community of the idealistic ethic.

Friedman and the other ethical realists have been left in a curious limbo by the march of history. At the outset, their method promised itself not only as one in which a criticism of their world might be put, but also as a way in which they, as writers, might find a place in modern life. They were, after all, dealing with the real world directly, and the real world was the concern of all. But their efforts failed. The realists could not be laureates. They were men of sensibility and conscience who were forced into an act of judgment by the very nature of the subject with which they dealt. As they became judges, so they were set apart from the thing which they judged and were alienated from it. They could and did plead a common humanity, an all-embracing moral universe, and the best of intentions, but these could scarcely prevail in a world which increasingly knew wealth and display alone. They were not radicals but unpopular conservatives. Theirs was an unsuccessful effort to call an erring world back to a faith which it pretended to accept but which it could not accept and continue to exist. Acceptance, necessarily, was a mockery, and the realists' efforts were fruitless. It remained for the writers of a later generation, a group willing to make the act of estrangement total, to speak commandingly to the American literary community of a need for separation from the claims of the real world.

Robert Herrick

WHEN Robert Herrick, in 1893, arrived at the University of Chicago from Cambridge, he came not only to establish a rhetoric curriculum at the fledgling school. His novels were to be listed in the courts of critical debate over realism. He was to be encouraged by Henry Fuller, patronized by Hamlin Garland, and praised by William Dean Howells. He aroused abusive attack on the grounds of ugliness and obscenity, and he himself was eventually to plead for a recognition of his explicitly non-realistic stories which he came to favor over the realistic. Despite such pleading, his reputation became that of a realist with a developed sense of social justice though one who, somehow, did not manage to achieve a clearly first-rate status.

Herrick's place at the university had been obtained through his friendship with Robert Morss Lovett whom he had known well at Cambridge and with whom he had served on the editorial staff of the *Harvard Monthly* where the two of them, along with William Vaughn Moody, Norman and Hutchins Hapgood, George Pierce Baker, M. A. DeWolfe Howe, and Bernard Berenson had helped create the liveliest undergraduate literary magazine of their day. As an instructor at the Massachusetts Institute of Technology in 1891 and 1892, Herrick had written his first novel, untitled and never published, which somewhat in the manner of Henry James sought to probe the delicacies of choice presented to a young girl and her suitor faced with the knowledge of her father's moral laxness—the whole being situated in the upper class, genteel atmosphere of Cambridge and reflecting the attenuated sense of values characteristic of a fin-de-siecle Harvard graduate of intelligence and taste. In the *Monthly* Herrick had joined the prevailing mode of his group to laud the French realists, de Maupassant especially, but his own early writing, though perhaps owing something to this clipped and spare example, reflected much more directly the chief characteristics of the New England tradition. There was a pleasure in penetrating intelligence, though intelligence always within the bounds of good taste. The problems set and explored were those accruing in a refined society. The complexity and difficulty, or even impossibility, of their solution were given elaborate acknowledgment. And always, the author gave the sense of hovering, albeit anxiously, over his creatures and their difficulties, concerned deeply with them, but loath to mix in the broil for fear of losing his analytic advantage.

Precise information about the development of Herrick's attitude is difficult to find, but, if one may judge by the pattern of misery which occurred in his professedly autobiographical fiction, his upbringing was dominated by a socially ambitious and intensely selfish mother, a father whose essential kindliness was buried under a heavy burden of failure, a nagging if genteel poverty of a sort which frustrated his mother's narrow but intense hopes, his own friendlessness, and a deeply pervasive quality which the novelist characterized as "squalor" —a word covering all the manifold unhappinesses, the essential low-ness, of his earliest associations. From the time Herrick entered Harvard, he was a man in flight, but the very panic which caused him to flee often tripped him into new morasses of misunderstanding and unhappiness. In the novels Herrick's mother was shown sending her son to the Cambridge Latin School because of its supposed social advantages, though that course meant an expensive and unnecessary move for the family. It was she who objected to her son's entrance into Harvard after his father's death as too expensive and fruitless a course, despite his great desire, because she wanted him immediately to make money and achieve a place in the world. Herrick's small pay as instructor at the Massachusetts Institute of Technology was, in fact, taxed by her demands for money, and her later years were punctuated by quarrels with her son. The squalor against which Herrick rebelled was not so much that of physical circumstances as it was a meanness of mind and spirit which his mother somehow centered in herself.

But the evidence of Herrick's later life would seem to raise some of the onus from his mother and place it on his own temperament, one focused in a jealously held self-superiority. His marriage, after a sensationalistic start because he married a first cousin in contravention of Illinois law, led to a bickering and protracted divorce. Though committed to the University of Chicago for his professional life, he could see little there except stupidity, ineptitude, and false assumption. His late novel, *Chimes*, portrayed his early years in the University directly from life, and for all but a handful of his characters, and these largely his fellow Harvardians, he had only withering contempt. A campus legend of his day held that Herrick could not bear to look his classes straight in the face so full were they of underdone westerners. His profile was for them while his eyes sought a refuge in some distant point outside the window. And this attitude persisted despite the generosity of the University to him. He received rapid promotion, a liberal allowance of time free from teaching, and good pay. Despite all these advantages, his correspondence abounded with a sharper than usual joy at his free terms and with constant reference to his distaste for President Harper's creation. Additionally, Hamlin Garland, who during the nineties was playing his self-adopted role as literary dictator to the rising midwestern school, affronted Herrick by his condescension. And, lying behind, pervading all, the ruthless and stark business culture of the midwestern metropolis made a poisoned atmosphere for Herrick in which to teach and live.

Nor, seemingly, did he find much support in his writing. His career was a turbulent one marked by controversy, enmities, and an increasing sense of failure. Twice his books aroused a public discussion which came near gagging him with distaste. Once the matter had a largely local bearing when, in *The Web of Life*, he made a sharp attack upon the raging ugliness of Chicago's south side, and Hearst's *Examiner* leapt to the city's defense. Later, his novel, *Together*, aroused national discussion, and a solemn letter of criticism from Howells, when it seemed to attack the inviolability of marriage in favor of free love. Ironically, *Together* was a best seller, but for the most part Herrick's books received more citicism than praise from the regular reviewers. His realism came in for the usual censure. It ranged in quality, according to its unfriendly reviewers, from "dull" to "morbid." And, though the idealistic branch of his writing, to which Herrick himself became increasingly devoted, was better received, it failed to achieve a major reputation.

Herrick's first published novel, *The Man Who Wins*, appeared in 1896 though it was written entirely under the aegis of his pre-Chicago life. Here he had turned to a study of personal relations, opposing the creative instinct to the sexual and making his hero, who had suffered a triumph of the latter, seek to prevent a repetition of his tragedy by breaking off relations between his daughter and her artist suitor so the artist might find his true life in his career. Such opposition of an ideal to life was characteristic of the Harvard of the nineties and had, indeed, been the staple conflict of Herrick's unpublished first novel. But Chicago was to force a new statement of the problem upon the young writer.

This, however, made its way into his work only by degrees. *The Gospel of Freedom* of 1898 continued the aesthetic-genteel theme but sought to bring the whole reality of Chicago into relation to it. Adela Anthon, Herrick's protagonist, is shown seeking the good life, using her leisure and means for her quest which, apparently, must result in marriage. Her possibilities narrow to Simon Erard, an expatriate critic and artist, (based upon Herrick's friend, Berenson,) and John Wilbur, a Chicago business man. The values which they represent are diametrically opposed. Erard, almost as a matter of conscience, lives on the gifts of others—at first those of Adela's aunt and those of Adela herself. He paints a bit, but his chief devotion is to taste and appreciation. His fame, as it increases, comes as a result of critical writing rather than creative work. Unlike the merely genteel artist, Erard is an exclusive devotee of beauty. He lives for its sake alone and develops his perception and judgment to an intense degree. To Adela, who seeks the nebulous quantity of self-fulfillment, Erard offers the discipline and the rewards of aestheticism. She must shut herself away from the mundane world and shun its values. In exchange, Erard assures her, she will gain a comprehension of beauty, the one durable and real element.

His judgment of Chicago is Herrick's, without doubt. " 'Superb, superb,' he murmurs to himself, " 'I must have walked five miles, and not a building, not a dog hutch, where there is an idea expressed beyond size, convenience, and either the possession of money or the desire for it.—It is a new race, a new world.' "[1] Erard affects Adela with his awareness of the ugly and the hopeless and so sets the ethical tone to which she reverts in her final separation from Wilbur, the business man. To the aesthete, the dominant forces in American civilization are those of democracy and science, and both represent an abnegation of standards and taste. He declares, " 'They will either smash all the good buildings or pull them down piecemeal in the process of restoration. . . . And science—that refuge for the commonplace mind—will reign supreme in a mighty democracy. Science will then go forth with its tin dinner pail, the emblem of equality, not annoyed by the twaddle of sentimentalists like you and me.' "[2]

The forces which Erard so fears and hates are personified in John Wilbur who, early in the novel, wins Adela away from Erard, marries her, and takes her to Chicago to live. She is finally driven to leave him, however, upon discovering that his vitality, independence, and shrewdness can operate only in a moral and aesthetic vacuum. Moreover, her position as a business man's wife increasingly separates her from her sought-for freedom as she finds it necessary to live in certain places, according to certain habits and in conformance with the taste of people whom she despises. She tries returning to Erard briefly, but cannot in the end accept the passivity and exclusiveness of his situation. Her only hope, and the resolution of the novel can consist only in hope, is in the advice of Jennings, one of Chicago's civil reformers. Unlike Erard, he believes that one must accept the world "as it comes to our hands." Unlike Wilbur, he recommends shaping it "painfully, without regard for self," toward a high destiny.[3] That, he concludes, brings the soul to peace, which is the true freedom.

Herrick's novel had posed a problem without a possible solution. Its concern was simply to define the alternatives that faced its heroine—and its author—whether to retreat from the world into the self, if that course were possible, or to accept the world as it came to hand. The Chicago novels which followed, *The Web of Life* in 1900, *The Common Lot* in 1904, and *The Memoirs of An American Citizen* in 1905 advanced the debate which *The Gospel of Freedom* had begun, and finally resolved it negatively with the wholesale rejection of Chicago and its dominant business culture despite the subjective chaos this invited.

In *The Common Lot* Herrick advanced his dialectic radically by altering the city's condition from that of a positive evil in its own right to that of an enhancer of the evil native to mankind. His hero now was to join the city in its ways and so become a corrupter. As in the first of this series the hero was an aesthete, so Jackson Hart is a young, Paris trained architect. Unlike Erard, however, Hart brings only a half-hearted devotion to his art. He is fond of leisure, happy in the expectation of a large inheritance from his wealthy uncle, and given to congratulating himself that he, at least, will not have to enter the bloody arena of Chicago's business life. He leaves Europe with genuine regrets, but they are more for its lost pleasures than its aesthetic or moral advantages. Upon his return to Chicago, however, he finds that his uncle, dying suddenly, has left him only a small inheritance and that he is to be forced into the dreaded conflict of business life after all. Without a genuine alternative like Erard's, Hart cannot help but yield and comes to a tragic end when a hotel which he and his crooked associate, Graves, have built burns with a great loss of life. Even Chicago is stirred by the tragedy—it is a big one—and both Graves and Hart are brought to trial for violating the building code. Hart cannot be held legally responsible however, and is dismissed. But his wife, feeling that he must face squarely the consequences of his actions, refuses to rejoin him unless he will acknowledge his fault and mend his ways. This, after some struggle, he agrees to do. He accepts a lowly post in an architectural firm and forswears his desire for success.

Hart's reformation is described in Christian terms; he admits a guilt of greed and pride, and seeks salvation in lowly ways. But his conversion comes only when, shaken by the tragedy of the fire, he flees to the country and seeks from nature rather than the Christian God some impulse of correction. After wandering the fields for days and nights he falls exhausted, and only then does a change of the success image into its moral equivalent take place. "Greed, greed! The spirit of greed had eaten him through and through, the lust for money, the desire for the fat things of the world, the ambition to ride high among his fellows. In the world where he had lived, this passion had a dignified name; it was called enterprise and ambition. But now he saw it for what it was—greed and lust, nothing more."[4]

Not only was there the generalized moral insight, but also Hart, and Herrick, see the ubiquitous greed manifested in the hard details of life itself; and when Hart comes to a full reformation he realizes that only by disavowing the world completely can he hope to regain his soul. Greed, he discovers, is not something which exists in the large to be removed by proper social reform. It is the very warp of individual existence and of his own private tragedy. "Now, for the first day since the strength of his manhood, he saw acts, not blurred by his own passions, not shifting with the opinions of the day; but he saw them fixed and hard,—living, human acts, each one of them in its own integrity, with its own irrevocable fate; acts expressed in lowered eyelids of consent, in shrugs, in meaningful broken phrases; acts unprofessional, sharp, dishonest, criminal."[5] The evil was not that of a convenient social scapegoat but of an assemblage of private persons under conditions where the worst in them was not only tolerated but insisted upon. The evil lay in the human seed though it was brought to flower by the hothouse of Chicago life.

In such terms, ethical rather than social, Herrick found the thematic correlative for his version of the realistic method, occupied as it was with the plight of individuals, not masses. Hart, and the other sinners of Herrick's story, were edged on to their vicious actions by the world, but the world held its power over them only because they themselves chose to give a loyalty to the world. The act of rejection was a difficult one, but it was the act which had to be made if virtue and freedom were to result.

How, in modern life, was one to reject the world and still retain the sense of identity which the world conferred? Orthodox Christianity, though Herrick was concerned here with its basic problem and in this novel used its terminology and point of view, held no promise for him because belief had gone out of it. The aestheticism of Erard had proved unworkable in its unrelieved negativism. The high, personal resolves of Dr. Sommers of *The Web of Life*, needed the support of a devoted and wealthy wife. Herrick himself could not accept any part of the bohemia which, during his later career was offering itself increasingly as an anti-world, nor did he make any rebel political or social affiliations despite an irregularly activity in behalf of liberal causes. His difficulty, in large part, grew from the same moral anarchy which embraced both the Chicago he belabored so roundly and the attenuated New England culture of his youth. From the first he drew back in horror while the second, it seemed, offered no useful alternative except that of a basis for radical criticism.

The best possibility was to show precisely and in full the evil which the triumphantly real world could wreak at its largest degree— to detail the destruction of an individual soul caught up wholly in the world's force. By such a course, the world might at least be paid off, the power and evil of its squalor fully revealed, even though the author was still trapped in it. In *The Memoirs of an American Citizen* all this was done by piling irony upon irony. As Van Harrington advances steadily toward overwhelming success in the meat packing business, and finally takes his place, having bought it directly from the Illinois legislature, in the millionaires' Senate of the early 1900's, he is shown to have given up more and more of himself until finally, as he enters the Capitol to take his seat, he is nothing but success; the man has died. His own view of his past is warped and suppressed while his pleasure in the present is one wholly in meaningless triumph. The capability of seeing truly where he is or of comprehending the cost of his attainment is beyond him. Erard and Hart had chosen to reject the world. Harrington, accepting the world without reservation, is destroyed by his success without a trace. The mighty and meaningless structure of his society is left in sole possession of the field.

With the *Memoirs* Herrick's series of Chicago novels came to an end. Though in later stories he occasionally used the city for a setting, it never again became a principal theme. The reason was not far to seek when one considers the intricate and manifold turns which Herrick's four Chicago novels had taken around and within his theme and the limited base of operations from which he began. For him, the subject was exhausted. Throughout he had remained loyal to the genteel standards which he had posed in his earliest work. Chicago was boring. Chicago was vulgar. Chicago was ugly. Chicago was cruel. These were the recurrent complaints made against the city as they had been the complaints Jarvis Thornton made against his predatory wife in *The Man Who Wins* of 1896. Neither that unfortunate lady nor Chicago could suit the passion for the beautiful and the fine which Herrick had generated in his Chicago years and which his first novel had pictured in his own college friends. "Waring felt that deep seated complacency of a Harvard man on seeing Harvard men. They were, all in all, though widely different in type and condition, gentlemen. A conviction of the essential modesty, fine sense of honor, and love of right dealing among the crowded youth returned with its accustomed force."[6] And it was Herrick's own kind of loyalty to modesty, honor, and right dealing which shaped his criticism of Chicago.

In this sense one may say that Herrick's realistic novels all took form in the world of genteel moral standards. In his work the method of realism was but a logical extension of his moral position to make of it a pointed critique of the raw and threatening American life symbolized by Chicago. When he came in 1913 to set down in manuscript his most ambitious autobiographical record, it was to his moral heritage that he pointed first of all in explaining the ideological basis for his fiction. "Literature for the large American public still remains mostly amusement, a pretty cheap and vulgar form of amusement at that. And I was always desperately serious, with the seriousness of the artist, a seriousness fully as deep as the moralist's."[7] For Herrick, indeed, one may doubt that there was ever much difference between the seriousness of the artist and that of the moralist. He frequently expressed his impatience with the problem of style and was quick to reject fiction in which he felt that the aesthetic or imaginative aim of the writer had been separated from his content. The substance of the novelist's work was well summed up in his own view of New England's genteel standards. "First, intellectual interest, next, simplicity of personal life, third, respect, exaggerated no doubt, for the importance of education, and lastly the need for religious expression."[8]

The juxtaposition of such values as these against the reality of

Chicago in terms of individual careers, most of them copied from life, constituted the staple of Herrick's art. Thus, of *The Gospel of Freedom*, "It was in a word the spiritual confrontation of that Puritanism I have been at so much pains to exemplify with my newer experience of the world gained from my residence in the West." It was "ultra-aestheticism" versus "robust commercialism," colored by "the sense of puritan doom."[9] For Herrick, the literary method of realism was not only a way of looking at and writing about life, but also an opportunity for moral judgment utilizing the standards to which Herrick gave the not altogether apt label of "Puritanism." Herrick took from Puritanism no God, no dogmatic moral law, no apparatus of moral logic, and no redemption. There remained only a diffused moral duty to oppose the evil and the ugly. These negative acts, as exemplified in his characters' lives and fates, were the chief accomplishments of his realistic art.

Herrick's life was to end in 1938, only three years after he found for the first time a wholly congenial and stimulating occupation as Governor of the Virgin Islands. At this late date, he wrote to a friend, he felt sure that his true vocation had not been realized. He had misspent a whole lifetime trying to live as an artist and thinker. His nature and abilities all along had been those of a man of action. The varying nature of Herrick's literary production, and the fluctuating quality of it, suggested that his opinion was correct. For of all his many novels, the most durable are those few in which he came closest to dealing with the world of contemporary action, those realistic stories which grew from his early experience of Chicago and his immediate and profound distaste for it.

Assuming such a deep seated negativism in Herrick's attitude, it may have been his professional good fortune to arrive in Chicago when he did even though the city caused him such pain. His talent for criticism was provided with an object worthy of its inclusive power. When, however, even Chicago had yielded up the last drop of juice, Herrick was left without an object. His later work, that which moved away from Chicago, followed one of four directions in its search for new matter, but none of them was to prove of great use. There was one block of five or six novels, particularly *One*

Woman's Life, Clark's Field, and *Homely Lilla* which were openly searching and experimental. Some of these re-turned old material in a new guise and some ranged beyond it, but there was little distinction in any of them. Another direction was that of his "idealistic" writing in which he sought to phrase a positive complement for his negative vision. But, lacking the imagination which Fuller had brought to a similar task, Herrick was only banal. Of these novels, by far the most successful was *Together* of 1908—a story which combined a broadened and complicated realistic narrative with an extended idealistic conclusion. Though he was still close enough to his realistic work to maintain much of the live texture which had distinguished it, he found it too easy to lose himself in the vague and bodiless hopes which were the staple of his idealism. The World War brought to Herrick his third direction, that of a brief but very intense pro-ally feeling, but it was one which gave way speedily to the complete disillusion of his last period, that of *Wanderings, Waste, The End of Desire,* and *Sometime.*

Herrick's work has been singled out for its social enlightenment as the work of a liberal novelist who in the conflicts of a commercialized society was on the side of public interest. Such a judgment had its worth, but it failed too deeply in a perception of the personal force in Herrick's writing and of the essentially negative, a-political nature of his choices to stand unqualified. For Herrick's rejection of Chicago's bankers, meat packers, builders, architects, doctors, lawyers, and manufacturers, though complete and validated, was far from being a social criticism of these types. It was a deeply estranged, personal act made by a confused author who, perhaps envying the man of affairs his active life, could seldom rise to a tragic understanding. On the political and social level, his novels have a muckraking value, but there is a difference between the man who rakes muck out of a formulable conviction, and one who finds himself floundering in it and must register his despair at being trapped.

Part Two

THE LIBERATION

World and Self

DURING the last two decades of the nineteenth century, Chicago scrambled hard to achieve a metropolitan culture. But as the city crossed into the twentieth, though the motives and much of the impetus which occasioned its aspirations continued to operate, old forces under a new guise came into play and all but destroyed the upward movement. The town had grown strong on its strategic location—lake, river, canal, and railroad. Its reason for being was economic, not cultural. And this fundamental fact was to triumph over all efforts, whether of upper or lower class, to change its destiny.

The great men of Chicago, those who had taken the largest immediate part in determining its nineteenth century course, largely disappeared around the turn of the century. George Pullman died in 1897, Phillip Armour in 1901, Potter Palmer in 1902, Gustavus Swift in 1903, Charles Yerkes in 1905. President Harper of the University and Marshall Field died in 1906. Cyrus McCormick, Chicago's first great tycoon, had died in 1884, and the personal interest which his works represented disappeared ultimately into the anonymous combine of the International Harvester Company directed by J. P. Morgan. What was lost in these men was much more than a collection of picturesque figures; it was also a major phase of Chicago's and America's culture. With them went not only the age of the tycoon, of the individual creator of wealth and power through business means, but also much of the pseudo-aristocratic life which the tycoon had begun to create. When Newberry died in 1868, his gift of the library was a tangible gift to the cultural uplift of his community. But when Insull, for example, died in 1938, he left only a small amount in real wealth; the rest was contained in a tissue of bankrupt holding companies with small relation to the community.

By the later thirties the business leaders, when they had not moved wholly away from Chicago, were to be found in the suburbs where privacy and anonymity were possible. In 1938 there were no Fields, Palmers, Pullmans, Ogdens, Armours, or Wentworths left within Chicago or its environs, and of 130 business leaders, seventy-four lived outside the city—the highest ratio in the nation.

The older "Society" fell apart almost before it had defined itself; its span was scarcely that of a generation. As the city, in a new way, began again to elevate monetary standards above all, its impersonality, mobility and overwhelming numbers were to force Society away from the hereditary condition to which it aspired toward mere wealth, youth, cliquishness, and display. In the twentieth century it became almost wholly identified with the new business culture, serving as its department of luxury, entertainment, and fashionable relaxation. Prairie avenue, at its peak as a residential location in 1890, had begun to degenerate by 1910 and turned into near slum by 1930. The north side colony (continuing its prestige up to the present day,) fared better. But it changed steadily from an area of well-known and individualized houses to one of expensive hotels and apartments whose tenants moved in and out at the dictate of their own notions and without a sense of community or establishment.

The process, of course, was neither sudden nor uniform in its workings. The Civic Federation, for example, lasted on into the twentieth century. It was no doubt accidental that one of the aldermanic candidates approved by the Federation in 1900 was William Hale Thompson, who, after becoming Mayor in 1915, was to deliver Chicago into the hands of that new and uninhibited entrepreneur, the racketeer. But, accident or not, the affair symbolized the reduced effectiveness of the Association and the upper class it represented. The inauguration of the Chicago Plan Commission in 1909 seemed an extension of the upward movement, and was so in part. Its guiding spirit was Daniel Burnham, the Chicago architect who had been in general charge of design and construction at the World's Fair of 1893 and who had gone on from there to achieve certain of the more overpowering effects in Washington, D. C. His ideal of the city seemed always to be the classic-baroque vision which he had achieved in Jackson Park: monumentality, harmony, vista. The aims of the Commission established upon his incessant urging were of the same kind. They included, in the order of importance:

> *First, the improvement of the lake-front.*
>
> *Second, the creation of a system of highways outside the city.*
>
> *Third, the improvement of railway terminals and development of a complete traction-system for both freight and passengers.*
>
> *Fourth, the acquisition of an outer park-system, and of parkway circuits.*
>
> *Fifth, the systematic arrangement of the streets and avenues within the city, in order to facilitate the movement to and from the business district.*
>
> *Sixth, the development of centers of intellectual life and of civic administration, so related as to give coherence and unity to the city.*

But, though certain gains were herein suggested, no one seemed to note that Burnham's plan had almost entirely to do with façade. Where were people to live? And what were they to do other than ride from one part of the town to another? Such questions failed to trouble the Chicago planners, one must conclude, because the latter had small concern for people. Their aim, as it had been at the World's Fair, was to make an attractive and impressive place to view. Their improvements were little different from those of a department store or hotel manager who renovates his place of business for business reasons. Burnham and the chief of the Commission, Charles Wacker, stumped endlessly for the adoption of their project, and one of their constant and primary arguments was that of economic utility. But the final irony was that their lengthy and laborious efforts changed Chicago so little. Its lake front, to be sure, gained an impressive monumentality. Twelfth Street was widened to make an artery westward, but its grime and shabbiness went unaltered and, though Wacker Drive brought a degree of coherence to the river-side for a few blocks, it trailed quickly away into an irrepressible wholesale and slum district. Burnham and Wacker labored greatly and in good faith, but they could alter neither the real sources of the city's strength nor its inherent nature.

Behind the façade, and pouring around its southern edge in a wave which stretched from old Park Row through Gary, the real twentieth-century Chicago triumphed without compromise. A large portion was reeking industry. One quarter of the two hundred miles was slum. Behind and mixed in with the slums was the immense, anonymous apartment and rooming house area merging slowly into the ring of single family residences which formed the city's edge. Beyond them lay the fashionable suburbs—the new seats of power, the new home of the city's great. Chicago had been deserted by its builders and leaders, and with them had gone what elements of community and coherence it had ever possessed. Now there were two or three million people living together because they had to.

It was hardly surprising that the higher culture of such a city should find an expression in bohemia, that part of megalopolis which has formally declared its independence of the nameless rest and devoted itself to achieving a maximum of individual expression for itself. There was little occasion for a bohemia in Chicago until the turn of century, or at least there was no bohemia; but during the 1900's two bohemian centers appeared in the city. One was in a little strip of ornate wooden store buildings, built for the 1893 Fair, which still stands on Fifty-Seventh street beside the Illinois Central embankment. The other was on the near north side and lay mainly east of State street, though it was also scattered throughout an area surrounding the Water Tower at Michigan and Chicago avenues within a half-mile radius. Both these settlements allowed for strong assertions of individuality—artiness, intellectuality, radical politics, anti-religion, free love, and homosexuality. But, though Chicago's bohemia fancied itself in violent and solitary opposition to a set and rigid status quo, it had important elements in common with its incongruous north side neighbors, the rooming house and slum dwellers of State, Dearborn, and Clark streets and the high society of Michigan avenue and Lake Shore Drive. All were growing in isolation and alienation. Bohemia's real enemy was not so much the city as the suburbs to which the city's older culture had made a strategic retreat and from which it continued to issue defenses of itself and attacks on the new ways.

If one turns too hastily from the first generation of Chicago writers to the second, it will seem, undoubtedly, that the connections between the two were tenuous and unimportant. Though Harriet Monroe's career spanned both, and was significant in both, and though Henry Fuller could be a confidant of the young Mark Turbyfill of the twenties as well as the rising Hamlin Garland of the nineties, there were few other personal ties; and ties of intellectual, imaginative, or emotional kinship seem still less apparent. Floyd Dell occasionally visited The Little Room, but was not sufficiently impressed to make even an allusion to the group in his autobiography. Of the luminaries of the second generation, Masters, Lindsay, Sandburg, and Anderson, none except Masters showed any awareness of the older generation, and Masters was unfriendly. Indeed, much of what the first generation desired came to be precisely the values against which the newer writers were most loudly to hurl their attack. One must, therefore, disclaim at the outset any of the more patent forms of historical continuity between the two. The generations, though not far separated in years, had distinct characters.

But there is another important if less obvious form of continuity left unexamined, and this does show a strikingly high degree of kinship between the genteel writers on the one hand and the assertively liberated intellectual bohemians of the rising school. The turning point at which one yields a precedence of vitality to the latter must be set between 1910 and 1915. At the beginning of this period one finds Fuller and Garland still active in Chicago, The Little Room flourishing, Robert Herrick still at the University and active as a writer, William Vaughn Moody still living, though in his last illness, and the *Dial* firmly in the hands of Francis Fisher Browne and his son. All but one or two of the salient features of the earlier Chicago literary landscape were in their places. By 1915, however, Garland was leaving for New York, The Little Room was nearly through its spontaneous life, Herrick had departed for York Village, Maine, and his novels of despair, Moody was dead, and the

Dial was on the verge of sale. To these casualties, one may add the sale of H. S. Stone and Co. in 1905, the departure of Will Payne and I. K. Friedman from Chicago journalism in 1907 and 1908, and the earlier columnists' evacuation of the city by 1900. A literary movement, it would seem, had come to an end.

By 1915 another had begun and indeed was well under way. As the older names slid out of sight, the younger ones were nearly all in place. The older group was largely unfamiliar to the newer, and represented a vaguely hostile force, so that the newer men had no hesitation in proclaiming themselves discoverers. Burton Rascoe, literary editor for the *Tribune* during 1918 and 1919, wrote in his *Bookman's Daybook* that Chicago's literary renaissance must be dated from the conception of the *Friday Literary Review* of the *Evening Post* in 1908 and the naming of Francis Hackett as its editor. His judgment seems indisputable if one can allow to the second generation a character *sui generis*. In a less strictly dedicated view, however, there can be little doubt that Chicago's second generation, howbeit forming no obvious continuum with the first, was another branch of the same root that had given the first its life and character—that of romantic and idealistic protest against the doctrine of the good life which the nineteenth and twentieth century world of business preached, the exclusive gospel of work and wealth. Both first generation and second, that is, were engaged in the same ethical action. In the first case the mode was that of uplift and reform. In the second, separation and rebellion. As the second was more radical than the first, it failed to recognize any real kinship. Equally, its more thoroughgoing attack turned up points of antagonism which the first had ignored. Consequently, it tended to identify the earlier effort with the enemy which both of them, actually, held in common. Ironically, and in much the same way, the optimistically romantic and rebellious second generation was in its turn to be criticized and discarded by the programmatically disillusioned group of the twenties, to whom such diverse forms of despair as naturalism, dada, and the Waste Land seemed logical rebels' ends. As the sustenance of aesthetic and moral uplift was to fail the older Chicago group, so was the appeal of transcendent individuality to seem illusive. The progress of the western intellectual world, the American intellectual world, and the Chicago intellectual world, in their literary sectors, was to be measured by an ever widening angle between themselves and the bourgeois culture they opposed. The first Chicago group had begun to generate this angle, and the second was only to push its arm further on around a fixed center. It proclaimed the necessity of liberation from the business culture, to the point at times of preaching outright anarchy, where the older group had proclaimed the necessity of beauty and virtue against the prevailing squalor and viciousness. But the later claim, we may now say, was only a more specific and more deeply penetrating version of the earlier.

For both generations the problem existed as a case of the writer's identity, but where the older group had sought identification through different and inept versions of Arnold's standard of the best that had been thought and said, the newer made a more radical approach by insisting that only in complete freedom from all standards, except those forwarding the most widely spread individual freedom, lay the writer's proper being. The later movement was, if one likes, the romantic revival which the New Humanists declared it to be, and certainly it was an intensification of the romantic spirit which the older group had wished to restrain to proper means. Now, any means which seemed to produce the desired end, became proper. Verse could be recognized by an unjustified right-hand margin. Fiction telescoped into autobiography, and autobiography into the sketch which was in turn brought to life by imagination. The city of Chicago changed its aspect. Where for the genteel group it was a beast to be tamed, for the newer men it had an anarchic force to be taken advantage of in the great struggle for liberation. From an enemy of poetry it was even transformed into a source of poetry, and so one found in the culture of the city itself forces which could be used to destroy the inhibitions it laid upon one. But the writer was not wholly to identify himself with these forces. He was, above all, the freed spirit helping to free other spirits, and his problem of identity was solved by a declaration of independence: the writer had identity as he had individuality. The older group had teetered uneasily on a too narrow fulcrum. The newer, freed from the cultural context of the city, could occupy itself with its own image. Its friends were those engaged in a like occupation; its enemies those who denied its personal reality. Said Floyd Dell as editor of the *Friday Literary Review* to his apprentice writer, Margaret Anderson, "Here is a book about China. Now don't send me an article about China but one about yourself."

The new generation's concern was reflected directly in its habitat and manners. Where the older Chicago group had met in downtown studios among substantially supported foundations like the Art Institute and the orchestra with its Michigan avenue hall, the younger was to find its most congenial surroundings among outlying areas in a group of ramshackle store buildings, in the lofts of abandoned carriage houses, in a temporary warehouse office, in shabby hall bedrooms, in a narrow German restaurant jostled by the El, or even in a tent on the Lake Michigan shore. It could, to be sure, boast apartment dwellings and an occasional house. But as a group it turned to the appurtenances of bohemia for its meetings, and in part its lodgings, and so became individualized in manner as well as in mind. It was in April of 1913 that Floyd Dell and Margery Currey, having then decided upon a companionate separation, moved from their Rodgers Park apartment to separate studios in a group of buildings which lined both sides of the thickly settled 57th street for one block west of Stoney Island avenue, and, on the south, trailed around the corner to run half a block down the avenue itself. This diminutive Latin Quarter had been erected as a series of uniform, one-story frame buildings, properly gingerbreaded, to house stores which had lined a main approach to the World's Fair of 1893. Since that date they had been occupied largely by bohemians, chiefly anonymous but counting among their number Thorstein Veblen. Much could be said in favor of this south side haven. If the Illinois Central trains thundered by on their embankment at one end of the village, they offered convenient transportation to the Loop. The other end fronted on the avenue, which at this point formed the boundary of Jackson Park allowing a tree-filled view to the east capped by the old Fine Arts building of the fair and the lake itself. The university and the parked Midway were within three blocks, while the Chicago South Shore line gave direct access to the dune country, much favored for outings. The buildings, to be sure, were flimsy in the extreme, though they stand today largely unchanged and housing artists still. Each one consisted of a single store room with display windows at the street front and few windows elsewhere. Temporary partitions were erected though they fell far short of reaching the high ceilings. Originally decorated curtains could be hung in the windows to afford some degree of privacy and a capital chance for self-expression. Little could be done about plumbing which consisted of one iron sink per building. As in the case of all bohemias, the crowning glory of this one was its cheapness.

Dell and Margery Currey found congenial neighbors who, like the original settlers of the Greenwich Village colony, were mostly artists. Next door to Dell lived B. J. O. Nordfelt, a painter working under the post-Impressionist influences recently loosed upon the country by New York's Armory Show. He had painted Veblen and was shortly to paint Dell in so discerning a manner that he became the original in one of Dell's short stories for alarming artistic intuition. A sculptress, Mary Randolph, tried a bust of Dell which she could not bring off so satisfactorily. Ernestine Evans lived in another of the store-front studios, and the rest were filled with photographers, etchers, and the like. It was, in direct contrast to the older tenants of the Fine Arts building downtown, a group of whole hearted devotees for whom their art, their mode of life, their thought, and their social and domestic relations were integral parts of a single dedication to the new life.

Dell occupied his studio less than six months. But even this brief time served to point up the basically serious nature of the gesture he made. Its picturesqueness, no doubt, was intriguing but was only part of a larger scheme. During that short period Margery Currey played hostess frequently to gatherings in which Dell saw Theodore Dreiser, whom he had probably met earlier in the year while Dreiser was visiting the city to gather material on Yerkes. From Dreiser, he learned of Edgar Lee Masters but failed to follow up the lead because he found the pre-*Spoon River* verses uninteresting. In turn, he introduced Dreiser to the Chicago group, and as a result Dreiser wrote to Mencken calling his attention to the Chicago writers and urging him to do something about them "right away." Here lay the basis for Mencken's later and famous salutes to Chicago. It was through the Dell-Currey menage, to which he had been introduced by his brother Karl, that Sherwood Anderson made his first acquaintance of the new movement in Chicago, just as it was with Dell's and Dreiser's help that he was to secure publication of his first novel, *Windy McPherson's Son*. It was at Margery Currey's studio that Margaret Anderson made her announcement of the *Little Review* to a multitude of guests, and enthusiastic applause, and it was there she met Dewitt C. Wing who was to be the original angel for her magazine. Though Vachel Lindsay had met Dell earlier when a few of his verses were printed in the *Friday Literary Review*, he met Chicago's renaissance itself through the 57th street bohemia as well as through the *Poetry* lunches held at Victor's, an Italian restaurant on the north side. It would not, indeed, be claiming too much to say that, along with the *Poetry* office, the 57th street bohemia was the catalyst needed to produce a sense of community among the Chicago writers after 1912.

A letter of Dell's to his friend, Arthur Davison Ficke in May of 1913 suggests both the texture of the life, apart from its incessant and important partying, and the hopes that lay in it.

> It is 11:30 P.M. I have just returned from the north side, where I have been seeing the Carys, to my ice cold studio, where I have built a fire with scraps of linoleum, a piece of wainscoting, and the contents of an elaborate filing system of four years' creation. I am writing at a desk spattered with Kalsomine, and lighted by four candles. The room contains one bookcase and nine Fels-Naphtha soap boxes full of books counting the one full of books I am giving away to get rid of them—a typewriter stand, a fireless cooker, a patent coat and trouser hanger, and a couch with a mattress and blanket. In this blanket I roll myself securely, and sleep till 5:30 A.M., when I am awakened by a flood of daylight, also by the fact that my shoulders are cold. I wrap myself tighter, and sleep till 8 o'clock when I get up, take a sketchy bath at a faucet, and go around the corner for

breakfast. *In the window seat, along with my shirts, is a great bundle containing a magnificent and very expensive bolt of beautiful cloth for curtains for the windows. If I am ever able to pay for that and for my new suit, I shall give a party, and you shall come and see the combination of luxury and asceticism which will be the charm of my studio. At present, its only luxury consists in that same asceticism. . . .*

I have been reading [your] sonnets over again, twice in two moods. Leaving my studio, I thought they were an expression of exactly that thought-pallid cast of modernity which I think we agree in thinking a transition stage to something more simple, vigorous and (as Elia Peattie would say) wholesome. On my way back I was startled to find them so completely an expression of my own mood. The latter mood I repudiate, and take the poems, aforetime, as a satire on the masculine idealism with its sick assertiveness of the claims of intellect, its unmanly contempt for the unmanliness of passion, which we are, truly enough, but which, thank God, is not us! Incidentally, it is a noble poem.[1]

It was Dell himself, and Margery Currey with him, who provided the essenital vitality of the 57th street colony, and after his departure for New York the importance of the colony itself became less. Like a seed pod which was broken, however, its force was carried out of 57th street and into half a dozen scattered centers of activity. Some fell on the home ground, to be sure, and about 1915 sprouted into the second 57th street group centering around Maxwell Bodenheim, Lou Wall Moore, Stanislaus Szukalski and "The Questioners." Beginning in 1914 there was the *Little Review* office in the Fine Arts building downtown, flourishing until Margaret Anderson's departure for New York in December of 1916. The same building housed Maurice Browne's Little Theatre which, though organized in 1912 before the 57th street impetus had taken form, was strengthened by it. In the spring of 1915 Sherwood Anderson, soon to be divorced from Cornelia Lane, his first wife, was to move into the rooming house at 735 Cass street, now Wabash avenue, wherein existed a minor bohemia of painters, writers, and musicians, headed by Anderson and called by him "The Little Brothers of the Arts." Here he was to write the *Winesburg* stories. On Wells street, in the Loop, near the old *Daily News* office, lay Schlogl's restaurant which, about 1915, grew into Chicago's best known literary eating and talking place. The Schlogl's group, dominated by men from the *News* staff, reflected the interests of the numerous members of that paper who came, after the 57th street group, to represent the firmest nexus of literary interest in the city. But they had been quickened by the influence of Anderson and Hecht, both of whom had shared in the excitement of the south-side colony. And finally, about 1916, Jack Jones organized a theater and meeting place called the Dill Pickle Club located in Tooker alley off State street just north of Chicago avenue. Here, original plays, lectures, and readings were offered for a fee to whatever audience might appear. The latter certainly included the literati in its number, but increasingly into the twenties the Dill Pickle became a pretentious curiosity seeker's port of call and failed to generate any significant creative impulse. For a decade after 1913, however, Chicago's serious writers, whatever their workaday trades and domiciles, were represented by a series of groups bohemian in manner and liberated in spirit.

Such a survey of the manners and gathering places of Chicago's second generation raises the question of motives: why, within a very few years, should the earlier Chicago writers have been followed by a new generation whose habits and modes were so vastly different from their own? The answer cannot be either positive or exhaustive, but a number of contributing elements suggest themselves. In the first place, though the two groups did overlap each other in time, their centers of vitality lay at least a decade and a half apart, ranging from the late nineties to the early teens. Thus the earlier generation, chronologically, had matured under the aegis of the late nineteenth century. The artist or writer of Chicago's earlier group could and did cry hypocrisy, brutality, or incompleteness against the culture which surrounded him, but he would find it difficult to make the full separation achieved by the later generation since there was little positive dissent he could embrace.

By 1912, however, the Midwest and the country at large had felt the full impact of Populism, Bryan, and the progressive movement against its established economic mores. It had read the muckrakers.

It had studied atheism with Ingersoll. It had produced *The Mysterious Stranger* and *The Education of Henry Adams*. It was coming to know Suffragism with its corollary of woman's independence. Its advanced spirits were learning of the existence in England of a two decades' development of sexual radicalism in the thought of such as Havelock Ellis, Ellen Key, and Edward Carpenter. And it was feeling the widely circulated effect of the American Socialist movement which, at this time, often added agnosticism, women's rights, sexual freedom, self-expression, and an admiration for artistic beauty to its proposals for economic democracy. The writer-intellectual of the nineties, in the Midwest, could scarcely have identified himself with Anarchism, a criminal, unwashed, and totally foreign affair. But to Margaret Anderson in 1914 Anarchism was only a rephrasing of the central Emersonian ideal. As the far-carried seeds of Nietzsche, Freud, and Marx fell on the Midwest during the second decade of the century, they took ready root in the already prepared native ground of dissent and rebellion.

This rebellion, taken in terms broad enough to include political radicalism as only one component, summed up the recurrent mode of Chicago's second generation. It found expression in bohemian thought and life of a variety of sorts because a rationale for such thought and life lay increasingly at hand. Where the earlier generation had largely been reared by urban, genteel, upper-class families to whom a program of inward idealism, outward conformity, and general good taste was central, the majority of Chicago's second generation grew up in small towns under a mixed but none the less real tradition of individual independence. Hamlin Garland is a seeming exception, but Garland's maturity came not in the Dakotas or even Wisconsin, but through a dedicated apprenticeship in Boston and New York under the direct tutelage of Howells, Gilder, and the *Boston Evening Transcript*. Like the second generation, the first had inherited the romantic tradition in literature, but its inheritance had been won only through a probate court of urban gentility. The newer group, in its more loosely organized fresh-water schools, libraries, and colleges, had had a better chance to see Shelley plain, and in its small-town forum of newspaper, livery stable, and general store to know the full flavor of idiosyncrasy. Last, growing up within a generally lower middle-class context, the second generation had felt especially the ground swell of dissent and rebellion which the late nineteenth and early twentieth centuries were turning against themselves. Masters was an ardent Bryan Democrat, Dell and Sandburg active Socialists. Hecht and Bodenheim matured in a lower-class knowledge of poverty. Anderson's first writing, by his account, was entitled "Why I Am a Socialist," though he early lost whatever positive allegiance to the movement itself he may have possessed. And Lindsay took with enthusiastic freedom the millenarian Campbellite Christianity in which he had been trained as a boy.

All these forces, cemented together by a joyous iconoclasm, constituted the "newer spirit" for which critics like Van Wyck Brooks and John Macy were calling—a spirit which was the clearest differentia of Chicago's second literary generation. In a characteristic passage of *America's Coming of Age* Brooks saluted this new hope for American cultural vitality, one he felt to be stirring the desiccated back yard garden which all the transplantings of European thought and writing of the previous three centuries had failed to quicken. After quoting J. B. Yeats' observation that "the fiddles are tuning as it were all over America," he added his own metaphor. "A fresh and more sensitive emotion seems to be running up and down the old Yankee backbone, that rarely blossoming stalk."[2] His words were not unique in the hope they expressed. In 1913, John Macy's revision of his *Spirit of American Literature* had complained against the sterility, or the timidity of native letters. "The poets are thin, moonshiny, meticulous in technique. Novelists are few and feeble, and dramatists are non-existent." The impoverished American spirit, he felt, though it had been given Edith Wharton and Theodore Dreiser as hopeful tokens of a new estate, had still to be figured "as petitioning the Muses for twelve novelists, ten poets, and eight dramatists, to be delivered at the earliest possible moment."[3] The petition was to be filled with a swiftness so astonishing that one is left wondering at Macy's power of incantation.

What the "newer spirit" should be called to distinguish it from its genteel predecessor on the one hand and from the increasingly pessimistic, irrationalist, aesthetically conscious attitude of those who in part inherited it and in part repudiated it later is a question. Within its confines, among other things, lay the critical writing of the "literary radicals," Macy, Brooks, Bourne, and Boyd. But literary radicalism was only a means to a greater end, that of fulfilled individuality. For the newer spirit, as it touched upon politics, morality, psychology, arts, or letters, sought characteristically for a liberation of the individual. It preached a socialist economics, a relativistic morality, and self-fulfillment as the great end, and only if these could all somehow be subsumed under one whole could that whole be called the fruit of the particular new vine. The idea of liberation was the chief fructifying force—a freedom from the old not so much to enjoy the immediately realizable benefits of the new as to search them out from the promising beginnings which had been made, and for this reason, "the Liberation," seems a tag acceptable for naming its faith and its works.

The newer spirit, in turn, was brought to focus by Chicago itself, the city of 1912 and after. Chicago's great difference for the creative imagination from the city of fifteen years earlier lay precisely in the degree to which its own leading classes had lost the urge to imaginative enlargement and moral reform which had been the wellspring of Fuller's upward movement. By 1905 all the institutions which were to give the group of the nineties so much of hope and vitality were completed and passed over to their presidents, boards of directors, and executive committees, cementing thus their relation to the very social classes which the younger group was most ready to distrust. Floyd Dell's autobiography made much of the care taken with the *Evening Post* to keep its owner unaware of how intelligent and iconoclastic a paper he was publishing. The *Daily News* had passed from the adventuresome hands of Melville Stone to those of the cautious and conservative Victor Lawson, and it was not until Henry Justin Smith became its news editor in 1913 that its staff was encouraged to develop a literary interest, or Harry Blackman Sell, in 1916, was allowed to inaugurate its first regular "book page." The creative force of the nineties heaped up its monuments, hired its managers, and then turned back to business. Its impetus had been nurtured by its upper classes. The second generation was collected out of a group of poor but passionate newcomers who took root in the city which business had built only because in the city's fissures, which were its social and intellectual bohemia, lay the soil which could nourish a fully liberated and romantic will. The earlier generation had tried to plant in the middle of an urban ground, but the later felt more surely the barrenness that was there.

Edgar Lee Masters:
The Advent of Liberation

THE general feeling of the later generation toward the earlier was summed up by Edgar Lee Masters describing his first impression of *Poetry*. "I thought the magazine an efflorescence of that group in Chicago which had founded The Little Room whose dilletanti practiced a haughty exclusiveness, and where the lions were Henry Fuller, Hamlin Garland, and some of literary set of The University of Chicago."[1] To Masters, The Little Room was remote, inaccessible, and unfriendly. It spoke with no compelling power to his own interest in poetry, and though he might well have cherished membership in it during his early years in Chicago, he would not suffer the humiliation of truckling. He had, he records, formed a tie with "the Press Club crowd," where perhaps a struggling lawyer of downstate origins, without Chicago connections or entry to genteel circles, could hope for better status. Opie Read, John McGovern, William Lightfoot Visscher, and the other luminaries of the Press Club spoke the language and represented the life of the rural county seat in which Masters had grown up where politics, whiskey, horseplay, lubricity, sentiment, and independence took about equal parts. For the Press Club these were made to suffice. In Opie Read's account, the club was "a distinctive and far-famed institution, organized in 1879 with Mark Twain as one of its promoters. . . . It was a democracy of the mind. It was a primping of the intellect rather than the body."[2] During the Columbian Exposition, however, it entertained distinguished visitors with another kind of contribution. "There at night Egyptian girls would sometimes dance, their faces in dark seclusion, but all else exposed to the glaring light. They would stand to be caressed, fondled in giggling fun, but shuddered back in Mohammedan repulsion if wine were offered. One night," Read recalled, "a ponderous man gazed somewhat in awe upon them," the visitor in this case being President Cleveland who was in Chicago to open the Exposition. In the Press Club, "Field recited some of his poems not indited to children, indeed framed only for men who might find old Rabelais too tame, or the poets of the restoration too much given to prudery."[3] And a part of the Press Club membership spilled over into the gawky diabolism of the Whitechapel group.

Such carryings-on and the attitude which they represented, were in the tradition under which Masters, and indeed many of the later generation, were to mature, though they doubtless represented also an impact of the open city upon a rural upbringing. Still, the classic triad of hard liquor, fast horses, and loose women, reduced to pioneer terms, had been a familiar though disruptable feature of western life since frontier days, and the deliberate drive against respectability represented in the Press Club was little more than a magnification of one kind of life to be found in varying guises across the back country of the Liberation from Clyde, Ohio, to Davenport, Iowa. Later critics tagged the Liberation a "revolt against the village," which it was. But that revolt had begun long before in a host of rural philosophers, village free thinkers, disenchanted paragraphers, corner saloons, and makeshift brothels. Huck Finn's Pap, or Puddinhead Wilson, was as indigenous to Midwestern life as was Aunt Polly. Thus, when the Liberation arrived in its fuller intellectual panoply it found a ready ground in the village rebels. Anarchism, free love, and independence of soul had already been accepted in principle by Masters, the Press Club, and a larger group of dissident spirits.

There is a clue here to the apparent suddenness with which Midwestern writers seized upon the forces of the Liberation in spite of their foreign origins and seeming remoteness. The later generation, for the most part, had grown up in the villages or small cities where the forces of propriety were strong and where, consequently, the urge to rebellion ran high among the dissenters. Davenport, Columbus, Whitewater, Springfield, Lewistown, Galesburg, Clyde, Warsaw.

These were the spots from which the later generation was to recruit itself, and almost without exception, the recruitments were made from those who felt penned in, suppressed by the village mores and village power. The preacher and the banker were familiar and potent enemies. Earlier rebels could become newspapermen in Chicago and join the Press Club. But as the later generation found its way to the city, actuated by much the same drive toward freedom from the village, it was to find an increasingly coherent life of rebellion, the Liberation itself, and to seize upon this new force as its own.

I

Such was the history of Edgar Lee Masters. His life conformed to the curve of transition which dictated so much of the character of the Chicago Liberation, a curve which began in rebellion against the village, at first nurtured by the dissenting forces of the village itself, and proceeded thence through a departure for the city, a new frustration at the potency of the village forces within the city, further rebellion, the advent of Liberation, a brief ride on the crest of its wave, and the long drift after its wave had subsided enlivened only by mixed and often muddled nostalgias. In 1925 Masters wrote to Harriet Monroe, "New York is gay and free and that recommends it; for Chicago is reform cursed and under tyrannies of all sorts, and cliques and spites of the village spire. But I don't like New York with all my heart. These feelings make wanderers, but the writing people are likely to be so. . . . That man is fortunate who lives where his father lived and where he knows everyone. . . . I believe my spiritual home is Petersburg, Illinois: where my grandparents lived. But it is all so changed of course. I couldn't stand it there."[4] Twelve years later, to Eunice Tietjens, "I certainly want to see your autobiography. I'll fall upon it instanter. I hope you make a good picture of Chicago and the old crowd, and indulge yourself in whatever criticisms come to your mind. We were a riotous crowd were we not, Slip Shoe and all of us? All of us headed toward the shades into which Lindsay has gone."[5]

Masters had grown up in Menard and Fulton counties, Illinois, in the neighborhood of Springfield, among people to whom farming, the ministry, and the law were natural occupations. His father's family was of Southern stock, having emigrated from Virginia, while his mother's people were New Englanders. Something of the traditional clash between these regions seems to have been carried into his blood. For, while he was his father's son admiring his father's democratic, free-thinking, and liberal ways, he became increasingly devoted during his youthful years to an idealistic view of literature and education which his father's practical nature could not understand. Little of this latter urge, however, came directly from his mother. It was another New Englander, a teacher at the academy in Lewistown where the family had settled in 1880, that gave Masters his first positive impulse toward literature.

Masters had come up through the public schools of Petersburg and Lewistown in a way little out of the ordinary. His home life had been more unhappy than otherwise, largely because of his father's unsettled condition and his mother's apparent inability to make her family comfortable. Hardin Masters had entered Lewistown without friends or prospects to create a law practice for himself and for a period of several years, had found the going hard. As a consequence, the family lived in poverty, occupied a series of drab and unpleasant houses, and suffered the indignities of the aspiring poor. Masters' great delights during this time were the visits he was able to make to his grandparents' farm in Petersburg which seemed to him a miracle of order and plenty, one from which each return was an ordeal. He disliked the squalor and harshness of the Petersburg school and did poorly there, but following the move to Lewistown and his entry into the grammar and high school his work improved. It was here, during his high school years, that Masters came under Mary Fisher's teaching. She was one of the large number of school teachers New England had exported to the West well supplied with a moral and literary idealism, all too ready to excite the imaginations of her charges with dreams and ambitions unlikely of fulfillment. In Lewistown she had drawn a small group of students around her to whom she recounted the tale of her meeting with Louisa May Alcott and lent books not generally available in the country town. From her library Masters first read Dickens, and Bob Ingersoll's

Mistakes of Moses. It was apparently at her suggestion that Masters began writing although his testimony on this point is confused. However, his first writing was done about this time, 1884 or 1885, verses which were published in newspapers of Quincy and Bushnell and in the Chicago *Inter-Ocean.*

Masters' interest in things literary and intellectual was given a great help forward by his friendship with one Will Winters whose father, a judge, owned a large library. Here Masters read Locke, Hume on miracles, and Scott. But the great galvanizing force came for him from a volume of Shelley which he bought by chance in 1885. This indeed promised a new world to him. More than any of his other reading, it suggested also a link between the new world and the old. It was Shelley who spoke to him with a new glory, and who gave him hope that such glory was within his own reach. "This passion for humanity, this adoration for the beautiful, this celebration of The Awful Shadow of an Unseen Power, this exquisite music in words, this ethereal imagery! I was carried out of myself. I began to see that I, too, had a passion for humanity, and that my father's democracy and integrity were the roots out of which this devotion to Shelley's poetry took immediate nourishment. And to what ends Shelley led me! To more metaphysics, to Plato, to the Greek writers. Poe and Burns fled back out of my own interest."[6] Masters' awakening continued through 1888 during a term of preparation in Lewistown academy for entry to Knox College and throughout his year at Knox in 1889 and 1890. Here he studied Greek and proceeded to the *Anabasis* and Homer. A life long passion for Goethe was created in him at Knox as a result of the study of that poet. He read Huxley, Spencer, and Swinburne, and, like Shelley, acquired for himself the nickname of "Atheist." To harmonize all, he entered simultaneously upon two love affairs, one of which was largely intellectual and the other almost completely physical and emotional.

Masters' progress thus from about 1885 to 1890 was one which led in a spiral curve away from the confinements of Lewistown to the intense delights of a first intellectual awakening and of adolescent love. The end of the path was nowhere to be seen in 1890, but it presumably lay nearer to the exaltations of a Shelley, or the heady scepticisms of a Hume, than to the Spoon River valley on the edge of which Lewistown stood. A gate had been opened and a shining promise given. In the fall of 1890, however, the gate was suddenly slammed shut when his father, disturbed by Masters' lack of practical ability, decided that he could not return to college but should instead come into the law office and begin reading for the bar. Masters had little interest in law and none in becoming a lawyer. Furthermore, the change meant that, condemned to the mundaneity of Lewistown, he would be prevented from ascending his personal Olympus.

He respected his father's views on village issues, and indeed on larger matters, but he could find no comfort in remaining in the village even though he would there inherit some tradition of revolt against the village. His desire was for freedom and fulfillment of the self alone. He attempted school teaching for a few months, but found this lonely and wholly rural life insupportable. He returned then to Lewistown, entered his father's office, and soon passed the bar examination.

Masters' life at home continued to be unpleasant. He attempted briefly to established himself in St. Paul, but no success came, and he soon returned to Lewistown. In 1892, however, he again made a strike for independence, turning down a job his father had obtained for him in Lewistown and setting out, with no prospects except letters to friends of his father and the encouragement of Henry Busbey, editor of the *Inter-Ocean* to whom he had been sending verse contributions, for Chicago and whatever fortune the city might bring. This, within a year, led him to a clerkship in a lawyer's office, and an association with the Press Club obtained largely through the good offices of a fellow contributor to the *Inter-Ocean*, one Maltravers.

The twenty years between 1893 and 1914, the year of *Spoon River's* magazine publication, were for Masters a mixed affair, one which brought into open conflict the strains built up in his earlier experience as well as those created by his Chicago years. There was, first, the dedicated romanticism of his poetry together with his revolt against village mores and taste. These forces, often combined, flourished at least to the time of *Spoon River*, and were written out again and again in the three volumes of poetry preceding that epochal book. Masters' first volume, *A Book of Verses*, published in 1898, gathered together much of the imitative romanticism which was his earliest vein suggested by an *Ode to Autumn* ("Rich fruitful autumn, dear for thine own sake, Through thy most fair disguise/We see Death's eyes,"), an ode to spring, an ode to night, a *Sappho*, and a *Lark*. But there was also a poem on Illinois, one on the White City of the Columbian Exposition, and a poem celebrating Whitman written at the time of that poet's death. Thus, by an occasional choice of subject, Masters had at a very early period begun the turn toward native life from which his more significant writing was to spring. All this early work, however, was the writing of a dedicated epigone, one to whom romantic archaisms of phrase, raptures of feeling, and elaboration of stanza and rhyme came as loving but taxing duties. Masters' reading in Shelley and Goethe greatly excited him. But this earliest volume gave no hint of an ability to transmute excited feelings into a verse of his own. The poems were imitative, but one must also remember their deep seriousness to their author. It was not merely that of exercise.

Though *A Book of Verses* had been accepted by Way and Williams, it was released by them only on the day of their failure, and consequently was never fully published. Most of the printing reverted to Masters himself who sent out a few copies for review. These brought some favorable comment. Otherwise the book occasioned no notice. Though Masters seemed unaware of the fact, his first volume suffered not only from an extreme imitativeness but from a lack of subject. Called forth more by a desire to write poetry than by any real occasion for it, his poems showed little indication of the new focus of interest and conflict which gave his second and third volumes a considerably sharper bite, and which was to make up the chief intellectual fabric of *Spoon River*.

While working as a lawyer's clerk, Masters had been much stirred by the depression of 1893 and 1894, by the American Railroad Union strike of the latter year, and by the use of federal troops to break the strike. His politics, largely learned from his father's Democratic ways, rebelled against what seemed to be a wanton display of power and special interest. Then, in 1896, his father came to Chicago as a Bryan delegate for the Democratic convention of that year and was able to get Masters tickets to the sessions. Here he heard Altgeld, David Bennett Hill, and at last Bryan himself. The experience was a momentous one for him, bringing into focus many of the feelings built up in his earlier years but left largely unarticulated, unrelated except through a fledgling verse, to the realities of American life and his own practical loyalties. Bryan's speech confirmed for him the baptism of his early romanticism into the structure of midwestern life.

> As the vast crowd rose in ecstasy and cheered, and as the delegates marched about yelling and rejoicing for the good part of an hour, I sat there thinking of what I had read in Milton, in Mill, in More, in Bacon's New Atlantis, in Shelley, and resolving that I would throw myself into this new cause, which concerned itself with humanity and left behind ignored and forgotten the monotonous commonplaces of the tariff, and the quarrels of the War Between the States. A new life had come to me as well as to the Democracy. And at night, at the apartment, my father and I talked. Bryan would sweep the country, and it would be reclaimed from the banks and the syndicates who had robbed the people since 1861 and whose course had made it so impossible for a young man to get along in the world, save by allying himself with the financial oligarchs. Andrew Jackson had come back in the person of Bryan.[7]

By 1896 Masters had adopted a political and social creed, progressivism, and this was to influence his writing for at least twenty years and, with a decreasing intensity, for a decade after that. He was to revolt strongly against Wilson, both in 1912 and 1916, for abandoning true Bryanism in favor of Eastern, prudential, and Presbyterian ways. Republicanism he saw as an extension and tremendous magnification of the money power of the village banker, the more potent member of his King Charles' head of a team of villains. In 1900 he was to write his first play, *Maximilian*, which was intended as an allegory against post-Spanish War imperialism, McKinley, and Hearst;

and in 1904 came his first volume of prose, *The New Star Chamber*, a collection of essays directed against the same reactionary forces. Thus by the time his second volume of poems, *The Blood of the Prophets*, was published in 1905, Masters advanced far beyond the academic and self-sufficient romanticism which had predominated in *A Book of Verses*. Contrary to a frequently expressed opinion, *Spoon River* marked no abrupt change in Masters' poetic interest. The poems of 1905 moved in full panoply onto the ground from which his later scathing analysis of village life was to be launched. The *Anthology* lay at the end of a consistent series of steps.

The Blood of the Prophets contained two poems of unusual length for Masters. The first, "A Ballad of Jesus of Nazareth," stretching out to 126 stanzas, presented Jesus as a humane and liberal philosopher who consorted with publicans and sinners out of a taste for their essential humanity and superior liveliness, and who preached a gospel of human love and human fulfillment. Because he was successful in stirring up his hearers, he was attacked by the priests and bankers of his day who protested to Rome that he was a dangerous social agitator.

> But at last the argument
> They killed him with was that he stirred
> The people's discontent.

That such sentiments reflected an influence upon Masters from the social-gospel preachers and writers of his day seems doubtful, though he did record a friendship with the "liberal" Chicago preacher who headed his wife's church until he was dismissed for engaging in a love affair with a young member of his congregation. Masters nowhere records reading or hearing Walter Rauschenbusch or any like-minded ministers, and his use of the Christ as a social reformer in this poem and a number of later ones was frequently compounded with an open paganism. Masters' views, in a word, would seem to have been much more nearly out of Bob Ingersoll than the social gospel.

Another poem in the same volume took Satan as its hero and

"The World Saver" as its title. The devil, in this Shelleyan view, became saviour by giving the supreme example of independence, rebellion against God himself. Even though he was crushed in defeat, his banner still flew and still proclaimed the chief necessity —that of each individual's seeking his own fulfillment in his own freedom. Other poems in the volume continued with a reiteration of the same theme and a more specific application of it to contemporary America. "A Ballade of Dead Republics" chronicled those nations which had fallen through greed and repression. "America" noted the same destiny in store for the United States.

> But thou hast hearkened to guile, to
> the cunning words of shame,
> To the tempter with pieces of gold
> and the praise of the drunken throng.

"On a Picture of John D. Rockefeller," made capital of "a condor beak and python eyes" while "Filipinos Remember Us," urged the people of that land to heed in time the warning which America gave by the bad use of its freedom. Masters' dedication to Shelley was not a limited one.

The second long poem of the book, "Samson and Delilah," took up a second theme which Masters' Chicago years supplied him through the time of his separation from his wife in 1919, that of the passions, rapturous or agonizing as the case might be, of his numerous love affairs, both the adulterous ones and those occurring before his marriage in 1898. These were detailed in his autobiography though he shielded the women under such romantic pseudonyms as Julia, Cecile, Deirdre, Virginia, and, for his wife, The Golden Aura. The number of affairs did not argue any great variety. They began with varying degrees of attachment, proceeded into a period of relative bliss, and ended with recriminations and self-pity. Masters, like Samson, was forever the strong man caught by the wiles of faithless woman. He had married Helen Jenkins, he said, out of physical lust and a desire for the professional advantages which a union with her supposedly wealthy and influential family would give him. The marriage, however, disappointed him on both the personal and prudential counts, and Masters seized upon his bad fortune as a warrant for whatever licentiousness he desired. This, almost from the time of his marriage, became a staple of his life and of his poetry as well, and provided the moral and personal equivalent of his political liberalism. Only one link was needed for complete freedom, the cutting away completely of the shell of conventionality which still held his verse form in check.

The chief impulse for this last was to come after 1905 and Masters' meeting with William Marion Reedy. Until then, his chief literary associates had been his friend Maltravers and his acquaintances of the Press Club, and neither of these were likely sources for any very radical advances in literary technique. His meeting with Reedy, however, led to the publication of some of his work in the *Mirror*, that significant and neglected journal of midwestern intellectuality, and here Masters came under the scrutiny of an able and informed editor. He entered, indeed, into professional literary circles. Reedy had praised Pater, recommended Mark Twain as "a rich and many sided personality" rather than as the humorist he was commonly conceded to be, made perceptive criticism of Henry James, expressed his delight with James Huneker, and printed de Maupassant, Edith Wharton, W. B. Yeats, and John Donne. All this before the meeting with Masters in 1905. It was Reedy, according to Masters, who opened his eyes to the conventionality of his style and who suggested that the new paths he was cutting in subject and attitude should be matched by a commensurate form. The fruit of this suggestion was not fully realized until *Spoon River*, but Masters' volume of 1910, *Songs and Sonnets*, at least revealed a willingness to harmonize more fully his themes and forms. As *The Blood of the Prophets* had been dominated by Masters' political and social interests, so *Songs and Sonnets* was to be filled largely with poems made out of his engrossing love life. And these, for the most part, were carried off with a directness and straightforward passion that marked a definite advance in his art from the mixed purposes and methods of his earlier volume. Thus, in "The Thanksgiving," the rejected lover takes a cold comfort from the end of an affair in appropriately raucous Skeltonics.

> *Your future lover*
> *Can never discover*
> *The hours which cover*
> *Joys gone before.*
> *And none so wise is*
> *As he who prizes*
> *Love while it rises*
> *And love that is o'er.*

Or William Blake is made to sum up his life in an epigram.

> *For life I do not grudge the price.*
> *I who took heaven can suffer hell.*

The tendency of the earlier work to go soft or awkward at important spots was partly eliminated. Verbosity remained. Self pity was too frequent. But Masters, by 1910, was well on the way to finding a voice, one in which intellect bolstered lyric feeling.

Meanwhile, a third aspect of his life lay largely cut off from his political or amatory adventures. This was his career as a Chicago lawyer, husband, and father. In 1893 he had made a first foothold upon Chicago's professional world. His place was humble, his duties largely clerical. But he had made a start upon what was to be a reasonably successful career. Within a year of his marriage in 1898 Masters was financially independent and had reached a point where, during the lingering period of his father-in-law's last illness, he could undertake a number of important professional responsibilities for him. But his entry into politics was perhaps the chief element determining his legal career. The essays he collected in *The New Star Chamber* he had published first in the Chicago *Chronicle* and in the pro-Bryan *Jeffersonian Magazine*. These gave him a name as a liberal lawyer and brought to his office a number of causes from labor groups. In 1903, Clarence Darrow, who was reorganizing John Altgeld's law firm in Chicago after Altgeld's death, proposed a partnership to Masters which was accepted and maintained for eight years.

The kind of practice attracted to the Darrow-Masters firm was not that cherished by corporation lawyers. Many of their clients were laboring people and labor groups, and the remainder were largely attracted by Darrow's growing reputation as a criminal lawyer. But the firm, through ups and downs, prospered sufficiently to enable Masters to buy a house on Kenwood avenue and to take his wife for a trip through the West in 1905 and to Europe in 1906. For about five years his association with Darrow seems to have been a satisfactory one, but by 1908 or 1909 friction had developed between the two, and the last two or three years of their partnership were troubled. There were quarrels over the division of fees, and over Darrow's increasing preoccupation with lecturing which brought an income to him but not to the firm. Further, Darrow, according to Masters, was attempting to use the firm's political connections for his own purposes rather than the furtherance of Bryan's cause. In 1908 Darrow refused to support Bryan unless he was guaranteed the Illinois patronage. In 1908 or 1909 Darrow returned from an extended trial in the West, where he had made a fee of $50,000, and begged off turning the money into the firm because of an expensive illness. Masters' share was to have been $9,000, and this money, Masters claimed, was never paid him. By 1911 relations between the two had broken into open hostility and their partnership was dissolved.

Masters' independent practice continued in part along the same lines as that of the Darrow-Masters firm, although he had in addition cases coming to him through family connections and an increasing number of cases involving wills. In 1914 he undertook what was to be an involved matter, a defense of Chicago hotel and restaurant waitresses against an employers' association charge of conspiracy, and this was to occupy him for some months including the period during which the earlier part of *Spoon River* was written. In 1916, a very long and important will case was settled which netted Masters a fee of $20,000. The money gave him some leisure, enabled him to buy a house at Spring Lake, Michigan, for summer occupancy and to hope for permanence of location in the Grand Haven area to which he had been attracted for years.

In the fall of 1917, however, he entered into a violent crisis, one which uprooted him from Chicago permanently and marked a distinct turn in his life. It began when he walked out on his family at the end of a trying summer during which he and his wife had quarreled over what friends their children should be allowed to see. The break was not surprising since Masters and his wife for some years had lived in a state of neutral hostility, but in this case it led to another love, identified only as "Pamela," presumably Masters' second wife. Mrs. Masters, however, blocked his hope for divorce and held him in an estranged and bitter relationship which lasted until 1923. She engaged Darrow as her attorney and the earlier enmity between the two men flared into violent activity, so much so that Masters felt he had been blackened beyond the possibility of ever settling in Chicago again. In 1923 he married for the second time and settled in New York which was to be his home for another two decades.

Here, then, lay the provenance of *Spoon River*: an atmosphere mixed of perennial romanticism, revolt against the village, Bryan democracy, a long series of illicit love affairs, the experience of an urban law practice, and an unhappy marriage. These were the forces which at one time in Masters' life were to be brought into a working relation and given expression in what was essentially a single dialectical poem. The achievement was not to be repeated. Though Masters wrote interesting verse before and after *Spoon River*, it was only on rare occasion that he could speak with the same convincing integrity. *Spoon River* stands as the highest literary achievement of that complex attitude to which the Liberation called and which, in this case, it precipitated into poetic being—the force of indigenous dissent.

II

The details of *Spoon River*'s beginnings are muddled by conflicting testimony of a kind which obscures a number of the critical points in Masters' life. In the poet's own account, his work grew into being from an impulse he had felt as early as 1906 when he conceived the idea of treating "the macrocosm in microcosm." No specific writing was done on this idea until May of 1914. During that month, Masters recorded, his mother visited him and the talk between the two turned much toward the old days in Lewistown. There had been a recalling of particular individuals and events of a kind which suddenly suggested to Masters a way of carrying out his original plan. Lewistown had in it the seeds of America. If characters who had been typical of it, imagined and real, could be made to speak from their graves giving the various sides of conflicts and causes in which they had been opposed, the forces at work in American life might be given a full and dramatic treatment. On May 20, after returning to his house from seeing his mother onto the train, Masters sat down, he said, and wrote out the introductory poem, "The Hill," and several of the individual portraits. His first publication then came nine days later in Reedy's *Mirror* and the anthology was launched upon its serial publication.

There are, however, several details which mar this story and which suggest Masters' anxiety to have it understood that *Spoon River* was launched without any kind of poetic influence, except a generalized one from his earlier reading. His date for the beginning of composition is clearly in error since on April 20 of 1914 he wrote Dreiser, with whom he now had a friendship, that Dreiser was in *Spoon River* as "Theodore the Poet," a poem which was the thirty-eighth of the series. And since the order of printing generally paralleled the order of composition, there is the likelihood that the beginning of the series must be pushed back ahead of April 20th. Such precise dating has some significance since it was in April, or possibly March, of 1914 that Masters first met Sandburg who came to see him as a reporter in connection with the waitresses' conspiracy case and so began an association which was to continue for some years. And it was in March of 1914 that Sandburg's first "Chicago Poems" appeared in *Poetry*. Masters' later insistences, repeated and vehement, that Sandburg had no influence upon the conception or style of the poem and that he, Masters, had no use for Sandburg or his poetry are thus brought into question, and the question is made larger by Harriet Monroe's remark in her "Comments and Reviews" for *Poetry* of March, 1915, that, "Mr. Edgar

Lee Masters . . . told how *Spoon River Anthology* was conceived nearly a year ago when his mind, already shaken out of certain literary prejudices by the reading in *Poetry* of much free verse, especially that of Mr. Carl Sandburg, was spurred to a more active radicalism through a friendship with that iconoclastic champion of free speech, free form, free art—freedom of the soul."[8]

Despite Masters' claims to the contrary, it thus seems likely that Sandburg was a precipitating force in the composition of his masterpiece. To what extent Sandburg's influence may have been operative, or in what ways, remains obscure however. The first of the writers of the Liberation with whom Masters had come into contact had been Theodore Dreiser. He had written the novelist in November of 1912 to express his pleasure in *The Financier*, and had thus launched a correspondence which led to a friendly association with Dreiser when he came to Chicago in January and February of 1913 to collect material on Yerkes. It was during this visit that Dreiser tried unsuccessfully to interest Floyd Dell in Masters. From Dreiser, or through his association with him, Masters felt an impact of ideas and attitude which was the first influence of a major literary figure upon him since that of Reedy and one which tended to push further ajar the door Reedy already had opened. He wrote of Dreiser's work in his first letter, "I believe no American writer understands the facts of modern American life as well as you do. And your 'sceptical daring' is immense. Your treatment of evil, and sin and such things is such an unmasking of the passing show. You make it like the tawdry chariots and the be-spangled equestriennes of the circus parade, as they appear to us in adult life."[9] The tone of these remarks, concerned with *The Financier*, caught up Masters' pleasure in simple exposé—the true story of an American financier. Dreiser seems, for Masters, to have provided largely a reenforcement of his dissenting views rather than an altering or initiating force. Such reenforcement, however, was of the first significance because of Dreiser's stature. Masters, the provincial poet, was in touch with and in agreement with America's chief inconoclastic novelist, and such a connection could not fail to lend status to his own view of himself. Dreiser had lavished praise on Masters' poetry. It was to Dreiser that Masters wrote protesting an essay on *Spoon River* by Willard Huntington Wright which charged that the poem derived from Edwin Arlington Robinson; and again it was to Dreiser that Masters sent for approval a suggested protest against "the huge Boetia called America."

> *What would you think about preparing a manifesto, calling it the Artists' Manifesto, and get ten to twenty leading men and women to sign it, on the general subject of the state of the country?*
> *What I have in mind is that something should be done to counteract the influence and the insistent labors of these people—preachers, professors and suburban minds who are really running the country. . . . We could lay down a program with reference to liberty of speech and of the press, marriage, ethics, art, or anything else, and all other things important. Make it forthright and direct, revolutionary if that word be applicable.*[10]

During the whole period of the composition of *Spoon River* Masters was receiving from his association with Dreiser a strong impetus toward the kind of dissent for which that poem spoke. When it was to be brought out in book form in 1915, Masters sent the proofs to Dreiser for his approval and correction just as he himself had read the proofs a few months earlier for Dreiser's *Titan*. This relationship, like so much else in Masters' career, served as a prototype for the Chicago Liberation. The drawing of aid and comfort from the achievements and views of the pioneering midwestern liberator, shown in Masters' case, can be duplicated in those of Dell, Anderson and others of the Chicago group. Dreiser's visits to Chicago were always major events, and when the Chicago writers drifted eastward it was Dreiser more often than not who received them, introduced them, and in general acted as impresario for them. It was Dreiser, one will recall, who turned Mencken's attention toward Chicago, and it was with Dreiser that Masters and Anderson retained a friendship lasting long beyond the time of the Chicago bubble.

Spoon River thus may be said to have emerged from the totality of Masters' background under the immediate impetus of Dreiser's and Sandburg's friendship. But immediate recognition of the poem, launched by Reedy on May 29 of 1914, plunged Masters into the midst of a going literary movement in Chicago itself. His acquaintance was suddenly extended to include the whole of the *Poetry* group of which he had been so scornful two years before when the magazine began, and of the Chicago bohemian world which, until his friendship with Sandburg, had been unknown to him. He was away from Chicago, at Spring Lake, during the summer of 1914, but his walks and talks with Sandburg in the spring and his introduction to the *Poetry* office in the fall launched a new kind of life for him. "The ideas of Ibsen, of Shaw, of the Irish Theatre, of advancing science, of a re-arisen liberty were blossoming everywhere, and nowhere more than in Chicago, where vitality and youth, almost abandoned in its assertion of freedom and delight, streamed along Michigan avenue carrying the new books under their arms, or congregated at bohemian restaurants to talk poetry and the drama. All this came to my eyes as though I had been confined in darkness and had suddenly come into the sunlight. Kenwood Avenue with its tinkling church bell, my law office and my study at home were not all of Chicago. I became cognizant of the Little Theatre of Maurice Browne, of various theatrical ventures, of new Latin Quarter restaurants."[11]

A particularly strategic confluence of events occurred here for Masters as it did for many other members of the Chicago renaissance. There was first, the coming together of his feelings about past experience with a present and ready mode for their expression—a mode which suited their dissenting nature. Second, there was the acquaintance with other writers of like mind and background. And, third, the congruent intellectual forces of the Liberation, heretofore largely foreign or unknown, were suddenly made relevant to his own desires and needs thus lifting him from a provincial backwater into what seemed a revolutionary world current. The result was the production of *Spoon River* at a kind of sustained white heat quite different from the lonelier situations in which the earlier writing had grown. "Often after writing," Masters said, "during which I became unconscious of the passing time and would suddenly realize that it was twilight, I would experience a sensation of lightness of body, as though I were about to float to the ceiling or could drift out the window without falling. Then I would rush out of the room and catch up one of the children to get hold of reality again; or I would descend for a beer and a sandwich. These nights I was playing on the victrola the fifth symphony of Beethoven, out of which came the poem, "Isaiah Beethoven" in *Spoon River Anthology*. Truly I was in a hypersensitive state of clairvoyance and clairaudience."[12] From March or April until January of 1915 this concentration continued. The last poem, in which Masters wrote an epitaph for himself as "Webster Ford," appeared on January 15, 1915, and the task was done. Within a few days, to mark the occasion, the poet was in bed with a severe case of pneumonia which kept him immobilized for the rest of the winter.

The impetus which drove *Spoon River* toward completion had some effect upon the nature of the poem. Masters' original too-symmetrical plan of opposed personages broadened to become a whole dialectical chorus. There were, indeed, many direct oppositions within the work, but these by no means dominated it. Much of the poem's charm grew directly from the strong sense of individuality which each of the portraits conveyed. Some of them gave way too easily to programmatic handling, but for the most part they had a particular quality which was balanced and given unity by the underlying conflict of the work—a unity expressed directly only in a postscript poem, "The Spooniad," attributed to Jonathan Swift Somers, "the laureate of Spoon River." Masters' portrait of Somers suggested the frustration which was to limit the *Spooniad*, planned as an epic, to the fragment of a single book.

> After you have enriched your soul
> To the highest point,
> With books, thought, suffering, the understanding
>   of many personalities,
> The power to interpret glances, silences,
> The pauses in momentous transformations,
> The genius of divination and prophecy;
> So that you feel able at times to hold the world
> In the hollow of your hand;

> Then, if, by the crowding of so many powers
> Into the compass of your soul,
> Your soul takes fire,
> And in the conflagration of your soul
> The evil of the world is lighted up and made clear—
> Be thankful if in that hour of supreme vision
> Life does not fiddle.

Though a clumsy fragment, "The Spooniad" was nevertheless sufficient to provide an argument for *Spoon River Anthology*, a plot within which most of the characters took their places. The dialectical nature of the poem went beyond the ironic and mixed relationship of the individual portraits to include the division of the town of Spoon River into its opposed camps, the liberal and the conservative. The issue was drawn in a meeting of the dissenters called to support John Cabanis for mayor against the perennial incumbent, A. D. Blood. The meeting, chaired by Harmon Whitney, lately come to Spoon River in flight from a wife whose "cold, white bosom, treasonous, pure and hard" had denied him the love which might have made him a happy man, was attended by a large number of the Spoon River rebels. These included Jefferson Howard who, inheriting the valiant spirit of his Virginia-bred father,

> Hating slavery, but no less war,
> I full of spirit, audacity, courage,
> Thrown into life here in Spoon River
> With its dominant forces drawn from New England,
> Republican, Calvinist, merchants, bankers,

> .   .   .

> Foe of the church with its charnel darkness,
> Friend of the human touch of the tavern;
> Tangled with fates all alien to me,
> Deserted by hands I called my own.

Howard was highly suggestive of the poet's father, Hardin Masters, as also was the occasion which had precipitated John Cabanis into making his run for the mayor's chair. An elaborate ball given for his daughter brought strong condemnation from the forces dominant in Spoon River just as elaborate parties and a dashing courtship had brought the condemnation of Lewistown upon Masters' sister and her family, though without the same consequences as those portrayed in the poem.

Also present at the liberals' meeting were Wendell Bloyd, the free-thinker.

> *The reason I believe God crucified His Own Son*
> *To get out of the wretched tangle is, because it*
> *   sounds just like him.*

Immanuel Ehrenhardt, the philosopher who borrowed his books from Judge Somers, the laureate's father, even as Masters' had borrowed books from Judge Winters in Lewistown; Seth Compton, who had built a private circulating library for Spoon River, but failed in his larger interest.

> *For I could never make you see*
> *That no one knows what is good*
> *Who knows not what is evil;*
> *And no one knows what is true*
> *Who knows not what is false.*

The compromised George Trimble espoused the single-tax and Bryan but, upon his wife's advice, also supported prohibition to keep in favor with the respectable party.

> *Well, she ruined me:*
> *For the radicals grew suspicious of me,*
> *And the conservatives were never sure of me—*
> *And here I lie unwept of all.*

There were Penniwit the artist who brought his talent and integrity to work as the town photographer but so lost the patronage of Spoon River; Daisy Fraser, the town whore; and Hiram Scates, who sold out his liberal followers in a school board election for the crumbs from the conservative table. These and others. On the same night the opposition held a meeting of its own heads attended by Judge Somers, Thomas Rhodes the banker, Editor Whedon, and their more important followers.

Masters did well to attach the *Spooniad* to the anthology since it supplied lines of conflict and structure which the poem would otherwise, except by inference, have lacked. But he was also wise to place it at the end of the anthology. In such a position his argument took its place as a support for the whole poem but left sufficient room for the play of irony and suggestion which gave the work its highest quality. Here there was both agreement and contradiction balancing each other off in a constant lively dialogue of five voices. There were, first, that of the aspiring but frustrated souls like Minerva the poetess. Then, largest in number, came the victims, or sometimes the benefactees of life's irony—the pawns of a complex and predictable destiny. Most of them, like Adam Weirauch the butcher had proceeded from hope through frustration to utter confusion.

> *I was crushed between Altgeld and Armour.*
> *I lost many friends, much time and money*
> *Fighting for Altgeld whom Editor Whedon*
> *Denounced as the candidate of gamblers*
> > *anarchists.*
> *Then Armour started to ship dressed meat*
> > *to Spoon River,*
> *Forcing me to shut down my slaughter-house,*
> *And my butcher shops went all to pieces.*
> *The new forces of Altgeld and Armour caught*
> > *me*
> *At the same time.*
> *I thought it due me, to recoup the money I lost*
> *And to make good the friends that left me,*
> *For the Governor to appoint me Canal Commissioner*
> *Instead he appointed Whedon of the Spoon River*
> > *Argus,*
> *So I ran for the legislature and was elected.*
> *I said to hell with principle and sold my vote*
> *On Charles T. Yerkes' street-car franchise.*

> Of course I was one of the fellows they caught.
> Who was it, Armour, Altgeld or myself
> That ruined me?

Those whose lot in life was simply to suffer without comprehension or hope were figured in the portrait of "Indignation" Jones, while a fourth group was made up of the secret sinners, the hypocrites. Last of all, and lending a flavor to the total work which has often been slighted by its critics, came the records of those who found a share of happiness and fulfillment. Their portraits ran to a similarity of pattern, one of a life lived without pretension, in conformity with natural impulses and free of effort to constrain or use others. There was Conrad Siever,

> Not in that wasted garden
> Where bodies are drawn into grass
> That feeds no flocks, and into evergreens
> That bear no fruit—
> There where along the shaded walks
> Vain sighs are heard,
> And vainer dreams are dreamed
> Of close communion with departed souls—
> But here under the apple tree
> I loved and watched and pruned
> With gnarled hands
> In the long, long years;
> Here under the roots of this northern-spy
> To move in the chemic change and circle of life,
> Into the soil and into the flesh of the tree,
> And into the living epitaphs
> Of redder apples!

or Lois Spears,

> Here lies the body of Lois Spears,
> Born Lois Fluke, daughter of Willard Fluke,
> Wife of Cyrus Spears,
> Mother of Myrtle and Virgil Spears,

Children with clear eyes and sound limbs—
(I was born blind)
I was the happiest of women
As wife, mother and housekeeper,
Caring for my loved ones,
And making my home
A place of order and bounteous hospitality:
For I went about the rooms,
And about the garden
With an instinct as sure as sight,
As though there were eyes in my
Finger tips—
Glory be to God in the highest.

Such a classification of the figures of the poem suggests some reasons for both its popularity and its essential quality. These may be summed up in the honest conformity of *Spoon River* to the warp and woof of its subject. There can be no doubt that much of the work's initial appeal lay in its ripping the veil of seeming propriety from American life, rural or urban. The curious or titillated reader could find here confirmation for what he might long have known, that there was more to American life than was allowed to exist officially. He could eavesdrop at the confessional. *Spoon River* was an exposé published during the full summer of exposé writing which, beginning with the earlier realists and continuing in the muckrakers, had been brought to a forced-draft of heat by the writers of the Liberation. Such a move, regarded in its purely literary aspect, was indeed a reaction against genteel inhibitions, but more important was the degree to which it returned truth to American literature as a basic ingredient. However, Masters' accomplishment in *Spoon River* did not rest in exposé. Assuming the realist's attitude, the poem proceeded to a view which allowed a genuinely tragic stability and penetration. This came not so much in any of the individual portraits as in the totality of the work—a totality in which complexity and balance stood as the leading features.

Though *Spoon River* was first an exposé, it finished as dramatic reality. It began as a series of depositions in the cause of the People vs. Respectability, but it ended as literature. Its status does not depend on an agreement with the rightness of Masters' cause but upon the rightness of his kind of imaginative participation in small-town life. In its wholeness, the elements in it of sentimentality and special pleading sink into place and are largely transformed to become, themselves, part of the dramatic whole. The town of Spoon River was, in part, what it was because of sentimentality and special pleading. These, in their dramatic use, were authentic parts of an integrated whole; and Masters, in this poem, achieved drama.

III

Masters' long career after *Spoon River* remains to be dealt with, but an account of it need not be extensive. Only one thread has pertinence to our present interests. Masters' publication between 1915 and 1950 was numerous and diverse. The thirty-five years were to see thirty-nine volumes from his hand, a number which suggests accurately enough his habit of easy composition and his almost total lack of self-criticism. The general level of those books did not vary widely. Until his last three collections of verse, where he turned to sentimental recollection of the Spoon River country, his argument remained what it had been in *Spoon River* itself—the evils of inhibition, the virtues of freedom and self-fulfillment, and the villainous roles of banker and preacher in American life. But with the exception of a few individual poems, perhaps a dozen in all, Masters' work was dull, tremendously garrulous, and wholly unenlightened by the imaginative and dramatic resilience which had marked *Spoon River*. The difference between these later works and the *Anthology* itself was almost entirely one of literary achievement as such, but this difference seems to have been of a kind for which Masters had no interest and no comprehension.

His writing throughout had only to pass the test of self-expression to satisfy its author. Did a given work state his feelings, prejudices, desires? Then it was, by an automatic process, literature. In 1938, he wrote Eunice Tietjens listing fifty poems written in the ten years between *Spoon River* and the publication of his *Selected Poems* in 1925 which he was willing to match against any written during that period, by any other poet, for quality. The list is fatally revealing. There are in it perhaps five or six poems like "The Loop" or "Steam

Shovel Cut" which have wholeness, independence, and excitement
in them, but the bulk consists of diffuse, inward, and formless
maundering of which a portion of "In Michigan" is representative.

> *And that day I said:*
> *There are wild places, blue water, pine forests,*
> *There are apple orchards, and wonderful roads*
> *Around Elk Lake—shall we go?*
> *And we went, for your desire was mine.*
> *And there we climbed hills,*
> *And ate apples along the shaded ways,*
> *And rolled great boulders down the steeps*
> *To watch them splash in the water.*
> *And we stood and wondered what was beyond*
> *The farther shore two miles away.*
> *And we came to a place on the shore*
> *Where four great pine trees stood,*
> *And underneath them wild flowers to the edge*
> *Of sand so soft for naked feet.*
> *And here, for not a soul was near,*
> *We stripped and swam far out, laughing, rejoicing,*
> *Rolling and diving in those great depths*
> *Of bracing water under a glittering sun.*
> *There were farm houses enough for food and shelter.*
> *But something urged us on.*
> *One knows the end and dreads the end,*
> *Yet seeks the end.*
> *And you asked, "Is there a town near?*
> *Let's see a town."*
> *So we walked to Traverse City*
> *Through cut-over land and blasted*
> *Trunks and stumps of pine,*
> *And by the side of the desolate hills.*
> *You were not content, nor was I.*
> *Something urged us on.*
> *Then you thought of Northport*
> *And of its Norse and German fishermen,*
> *And its quaint piers where they smoke fish.*[18]

This hodge-podge of random recollection, true confession, and bathos can scarcely be said to have even poetic existence, much less poetic quality. But for Masters, because the poem dealt with an amorous expedition conducted with his most absorbing love, Deirdre, "In Michigan" stood among his best work.

Such a subjective test was by no means peculiar to Masters among the midwestern romantics. It represented the preoccupation of the whole group with the melodramatized self. Poetry existed subjectively. Whatever was felt to be poetical was poetry. Such a view, of course, was wholly consistent with the general devotion of the group to free verse. Even Imagism, except in some of Sandburg's earlier work, was not attractive to the midwestern writers. They had little interest of any kind in literary form as such. Their desire, generally, was for a sense of immediate, emotional communication between poet and reader—a communication in which a withering away of the poem to allow for total sublimation would have stood as the ideal achievement.

How did the group then succeed in producing any significant literature? The case of *Spoon River* is typical and enlightening. The writer of the Liberation, and Masters like the rest, needed a strong formal element in his subject itself if his work was to achieve imaginative coherence. He was grounded in the same art as that of the earlier realists. The village of Lewistown did in fact provide Masters with the dramatic and even tragic elements which lifted *Spoon River* above the rest of his writing. By resting wholly upon its reality, by abandoning any more purely literary concern, the poet could here achieve something beyond a clumsy and repetitious pouring out of himself on paper. The problem, of course, lay in the rarity with which such subjects came to hand and the difficulty of letting-go the self sufficiently to achieve an imaginative identity with the subject. Though Masters claimed the presence of a subtle verse form in the first third of the *Spoon River* portraits, the most careful analysis fails to reveal any difference between these and the remaining poems, and one is forced to conclude that their "form" was as subjective as all else in Masters' writing. In this case, as it happened, Masters turned to a subject which he understood and sympathized with. He allowed it to emerge in a way which made its own formal lines clear, and so drew the authentic being of his poem from the shape, general and detailed, of the town, Spoon River, itself. If the process was more akin to midwifery than to creative labor, it was all the more congruent with a dedicatedly romantic view of the poetic art.

The process, for Masters, could not be often repeated. There was in him no real power of imagination once he departed from the familiar ground of Lewistown. As the years drew on, his letters were given over increasingly to a criticism and abuse which bordered on paranoia. Self-pity, fear, and hatred became his own ruling passions and these, perforce, were the ruling passions of his later work. His avowed subjects, too often, were only nominal—excuses for a display of his own bitterness and frustration, and the substance of poetry itself had little reality or interest for him. It is, perhaps, misleading to speak of this later work as a decline. The more nearly correct picture is that of *Spoon River*, together with a handful of other poems, standing, like rock chimneys, above the rather dreary tableland of the rest of Masters' work. His successes, one may say, were accidents—the fortuitous coalescence of author and subject in what turned out to be a poem. His failures were the more deliberate achievements of what Masters felt poetry ought to be.

Three Voices
of the Liberation

EDGAR LEE MASTERS, during the *Spoon River* years, had felt an influential charge not only from new ideas and new ways of feeling but also from the re-emergence in Chicago of a living community of intellect and the arts. But, though the Liberation did quicken his writing for a time, it had not drastically altered his career. The participation of most of the Chicago literary community in the renaissance, however, was a generally quickening experience. They came by its means to know the Liberation not only as a set of ideas and influences but as a whole cultural envelope—one whose effect was to be measured in their lives as much as in their works. In many cases, like Masters, they brought with them to Chicago ideas and manners which were to contribute to the Liberation. They were in part pre-formed even as Masters had been. But what the Chicago of the second decade gave them was precisely a new definition of community and identity in which their ideas and their lives could take on the achieved reality of liberation. Their writing, thus, proceeded out of a new experience as a part of the experience itself, and much of its authentic nature will be missed if this fact is neglected.

The Chicago Liberation linked them to new centers of energy—its own dominant personalities, its editors, its hosts and hostesses, its publishers, and its critics. Many of these in turn derived their own vitality from outside. The *Friday Literary Review*, first published in 1909, was its earliest spokesman, and the *Review* was nurtured into being by a direct impact from British and Fabian intellectuality in the person of Francis Hackett. Maurice Browne, the founder and director of the Little Theatre, likewise brought a British background to his Chicago activities. Pascal Covici, despite an American upbringing, retained a continental superiority to Midwestern inhibitions. The spirit of the Liberation proper, the source of community which Masters, so deeply rooted in indigenous dissent, had missed, was typically that generated by a discovery that dissent could have an international and so a reputable or even glamorous standing. Harriet Monroe was wholly native, but her magazine, the forum which the *Poetry* office became, and the *Poetry* lunches staged at Victor's restaurant in Erie Street provided a steady influence from Europe through the pipe line provided by Ezra Pound. Margaret Anderson's *Little Review* was deeply indigenous—but most of all so in the wide-eyed naiveté with which it reacted to European forces. Ben Hecht's *Literary Times* was born into a cheerful and multi-colored raucousness most suggestive of Balaban and Katz, but it had been first conceived in the penetration of Hecht's fancy by Huysmans, a feat achieved in the city room of the *Daily News* where Vincent Starrett acted as the Chicago translator and guide to the European decadence, Huysmans and Machen especially, for a whole sub-section of the renaissance. Chicago's second literary generation was thus one brought into community by the presence of a newer spirit, so named by Van Wyck Brooks, acting to confirm and validate a native urge. Though diverse in its origins, the newer spirit was single in effect—that of bolstering the Chicago group with a force massive enough to break the bounds of convention and deliver native dissent from its provincial swamps.

I

The newer spirit could be felt and enjoyed by all, but its substance needed explaining and documenting, and this was first made available in the pages of the *Friday Literary Review*. Its founder was Francis Hackett, a lively, intelligent, and personable young Irishman whose wanderings in search of journalistic employment since his arrival in the United States in 1901 had led him to Chicago, Hull House, and the *Evening Post* by 1905. He brought with him an admiration and competence for British literary journalism. As a Fabian Socialist and a participant in the Irish literary renaissance he could rightly claim an international literary sophistication. He had begun as a reporter on the *Post* under the editorship of Julian Mason, but within a few months was writing book reviews and editorials. By 1908 he was deemed competent to take over the new literary supplement planned for the paper's Friday edition and so became the editor of the *Literary Review* itself. Hackett's training and interest made possible a new kind of journalism for the city. He was an intellectual and a cosmopolite. Further, he had acquaintance among British literary circles, determined in large part by his Fabian leanings, upon which he could draw for both ideas and style. The result was an incisive and perceptive writing, prose in the Shavian manner, of a kind and quality quite different from that which the *Post*, even with such distinguished reviewers as Tiffany Blake and Henry Fuller, had heretofore displayed. Hackett's *forte* was the swift movement of a shaped and informed mind over its material. What he found to be good, like the feeling for the complex human relations shown in such an otherwise murky performance as Robert Herrick's *Together* of 1908, he separated from its inept context. What he found to be bad, the obdurate mediocrity of Winston Churchill perhaps, he labelled as such and attacked with a clear and vigorous rationale. His admirations, and indeed the admirations of the *Friday Review* throughout its seminal years, were Shaw, Wells, Galsworthy, Bennett, and whatever other writers might be shown to have their kind of quality. These were the spokesmen for an enlightened and humane point of view. Where criticism was made, it was apt to be directed against such phenomena as the sense of weariness in Maeterlinck's *Blue Bird* or the waste represented by the able trivialities of E. F. Benson.

His medium was well chosen. The *Post* was a newspaper of small but qualitatively high circulation. Its journalistic policies were conservative, based upon able reporting and editing, and were directed toward the intelligent and informed, a world apart from the sensationalisms of a Medill or a Hearst. Its circulation was largely in the loftier reaches of the business and professional community, a seemingly strange place for a Socialist literary reviewer. But, through the *Post*, Hackett might hope for an acceptance of at least the quality of his argument. Like the Fabians in general, the *Friday Review* looked for readers who, though their assumptions might be hostile, could still ponder the proposals made to them. Hackett's rise in Chicago, further, had come about very largely through his contact with the members of The Little Room in whom he found a genuine friendliness and sympathy. Small wonder that he addressed himself with some confidence to a larger readership which he might well conceive to be an extension of The Little Room and which he knew would contain members of the Civic Federation and of Chicago's other self-improvement societies. How better might a literary critic exercise his intelligence and benefit his art than by addressing himself to the dominant, and generally friendly leaders of his community— the seeming source of its best hopes?

Address himself he did, from March 5, 1909, until Floyd Dell's accession to the editor's desk in July of 1911. There were storms at times. Hackett's radicalism needed a prudential eye lest it break the bounds of safety and offend the paper's owner, as it almost did on one occasion when he advocated inter-racial marriage. Here a timely stroke by Dell saved publication of the offensive bit though Hackett was upset by the censorship. But Hackett himself had contemplated no permanent stay with the *Literary Review* and, when he felt he had enough of enlightening Chicago and was ready to resume his travels, he left his authority to Dell, then twenty-four years old and with less than three years experience of the *Post* and of Chicago. The *Literary Review* was not to suffer. In place of Hackett's British Socialist interests came Dell's American Socialist interests, but otherwise little was changed. Dell had learned something of his critic's style from Hackett. His interests varied only by a somewhat lesser intellectuality and a rather greater range of sympathies.

Dell had come to his new job from a lively few years in Davenport, Iowa, where he had learned his reporter's trade and had embraced the doctrines of Socialism as he found them preached by the local party (largely Germanic in origin and character). Here he had rebelled against the party's endless involvement with parliamentary routine and begun his writing as poet, novelist, and critic. Like Hackett, his was a quick and genial intellect with considerable drive and a wholehearted joy in the forces of the Liberation. In Chicago he had met and married Margery Currey in a Jewish ceremony, chosen for its picturesqueness and conducted by his Davenport friend, Rabbi Fine-shriber, and had settled in a Rogers Park apartment which became the scene of much youthful gaiety. His wife continued her work as a school-teacher, and Dell rejoiced in so independent a mate. Another Davenport friend, George Cram Cook, arrived in Chicago after a time to work on a dictionary and make Dell's apartment the scene of his characteristically earthy-mystical-erotic lucubrations. Dell's position on the *Review* gave him an enormous satisfaction reflected directly in the confident and precocious ability of its pages.

His perennial concern was defined in an editorial essay labeled, capaciously, "Literature and Life" directed against the deadly bel-letrism which the Liberation saw as the most pernicious legacy of the genteel order to it. The writers for the *Literary Review*, under Dell, were encouraged to develop their interest in extra-literary matters the better to aid his opposition to what Gilder called "beauty" in literature and what Howells had attacked under the name of "romanticism." For Dell, these terms had little to do with the case. The genteelists were actually defending a thin prettiness coupled with sentiment and a proper melodrama, all of them being fixed in the amber of a narrowly conventional style. The question that Dell raised in his editorial was that of reality. How could literature free itself from a convention which denied it importance or relevance? The answer, he concluded, lay in its innate liberating power. "Science has its own purpose, and so has philosophy; but literature exists to encourage human beings to be human. The masters of prose fiction and of poetry in every age have been those who, while having the highest conception of order afforded by their generation, have nevertheless exalted the individual with his follies, his crimes, and his intractable aspirations above that conception of order. The poets have always preached the gospel of disorder. The novelists from Fielding to Galsworthy have spoken in behalf of the man at odds with society."[1]

This was a clear blast on the horn of liberation, but its note was one which had worth as it penetrated the simpers of genteel taste not for iconoclasm's sake alone, but to herald one more re-discovery of literary integrity and identity. The literature of the newer spirit sought a truth to which the new taste might resort for refreshment and assurance, and in an editorial answer to Stuart Sherman, Dell took up a defense of Rousseau which revealed plainly where that center lay. The natural impulses of humanity, he declared, were good. They formed a basis for conduct and judgment which had "never been successfully impugned." Pragmatism, along with Rousseau, was another source of freedom, this time from logical rather than social restraints. "The real meaning of pragmatism," declared Dell, "is to be found in its denial of the finality of logic, its insistence on the existence of values in life not to be captured and confined within the terms of the syllogism."[2] Here, in one of the earliest explicit links between the newer spirit in literature and James' philosophy, Dell anticipated much of the drift of later critical thought which might have had small use for the *Literary Review* but which, like it, sought in a philosophy of existence for the identity of literature. In Dell's words, "The Idea is not the play. It is the reality in the play which gives potency to the Idea."[3] The supreme concept, whether in literature or life, was that of reality, and the critics who voiced the newer spirit for the *Friday Review* were concerned for those works which seemed to them real.

The *Review's* list of "best books" for 1913 gave a clear notion of its editorial concern. The fiction section included Constance Garnett's translation of *The Idiot*, Lawrence's *Sons and Lovers*, Galsworthy's *The Dark Flower*, H. G. Wells' *The Passionate Friends*, Ethel Sidgwick's *Succession*, Edith Wharton's *The Custom of The Country*, Coningsby Dawson's *The Garden Without Walls*, Louis Joseph Vance's *Joan Thursday*, Compton Mackenzie's *Youth's Encounter*, Hugh Walpole's *Fortitude*, and Hardy's *A Changed Man and Other Tales*. Though the variety of kind and quality contained in such a tabulation may suggest a contemporary reviewer's statistical average of best-selling and most talked about books, there can be little doubt that for the Friday reviewers such variety had center and purport. For the deep irrationalism of Dostoievsky, the exacerbated decadence of Mackenzie, the brittle realism of Vance, and Hardy's somber refusals of comfort, despite their conflicting natures, could be used as blows in the war of liberation. They were separate but related individual actions. The Liberation itself appeared most coherent as one kept its enemies in view. It would first of all demolish the conventional inhibitions, whether political, economic, literary, or moral. These once gone, the reality which they had hidden, and the fear of which they generated, were to become inescapably and benevolently apparent as guide and goal.

The local bearings of this general strategy were given in the *Review* through a series of articles by Dell on the general subject, "Chicago in Fiction" whose point was to strike another blow for the Liberation within and upon the city which housed so enormous an enemy potential. Chicago had been the home of an earnest and fitfully successful upward movement, but that movement needed direction and criticism if it was not to lose itself in the vast unpredictability of its tasks and its often vague methods. Such leadership, Dell claimed, must come from modern literature, for modern literature was the vital advance guard. It summed up and motivated the new aspirations, disseminating them among what hearers it could find and turning their minds to the great task at hand. "Since Norris wrote *The Pit*," Dell argued, "the city's soul has changed. And what has changed it? Books. . . . Everybody reads the newspapers and some of the men who write the newspapers have absorbed Shaw, Ibsen, Nietzsche, Veblen, Weininger, Havelock Ellis. . . . Chicago has been clay in the hands of the potter, and the potter has been twentieth-century literature, a literature imbued with two new things—socialism and the new, truer individualism, its complement and corrective."[4]

Some books, of course, had been more helpful than others. Robert Herrick had condemned the city and its works, but he had shown little hope of dealing with its evil except for a few "clear souled men and women who attempt to free themselves, to get out and away from it all."[5] Finley Dunne, in the person of Mr. Dooley, had been too tolerant of the city's gas storage tanks. "A man ought to hate a gas tank. Chicago has been growing, partly by virtue of that hatred, out of the gas-tank stage. Mr. Dooley has not noticed it."[6] Fuller's Chicago, somewhat like Herrick's, was "hopelessly sordid and drab."[7] It allowed no possibility for the aspiration which, in the case of the liberated intellectual, was the breath of life. "I wish," declared Dell of Fuller, "he would give us a great talker, a philosopher after his own heart, an American Bergerat—it were worth a dozen Chicago novels."⁸ Here, Fuller would be exercising his full talent instead of blunting and wasting it against an unsuitable foil. Only in Dreiser, and particularly in *Sister Carrie*, did Dell see a fully realized, liberated handling of Chicago. In Dreiser he found criticism and hope wedded. The individual had here set himself apart enough from the city, had sufficiently achieved the liberating which he advocated, to give in the substance of his work itself the fruits of victory. He was neither a sufferer licking his wounds nor a slave habituated to his shackles but a true creative spirit. "Mr. Dreiser has not looked to see the badness of the city, nor its goodness; he has looked to see its beauty and ugliness, and he has seen a beauty even in its ugliness. And, in doing that, he has given us, there is little doubt, the Chicago of the whole middle west—a beacon across the prairies, a place of splendor and joy and triumph, the place toward which the young faces turn and the end of the road along which young feet yearn to tread."⁹ This, of course, was a liberated vision, and, one may think, it reflected an essential rather than existential reality. But essential reality, rightly considered, had to be the force of the Liberation. Unless there were something evermore about to be, of what use the battle?

Right minds were making their appearance in increasing numbers and vehemence. The *Literary Review* itself caught up a number of them, and it lent strength and encouragement to others. Along with *Poetry* magazine, it assisted Vachel Lindsay in his search for a hearing. Two weeks later it was in receipt of a letter from Sara Teasdale in appreciation of an article on Shakespeare's sonnets. The young poet wrote further, "I have many times before wanted to thank you for the charm of your critiques, for their unfailing freshness of spirit, and for the great amount that they have taught me."¹⁰ The *Review* had noticed the advent of *Poetry* in the fall of 1912, though it could not resist an air of patronage in so doing. However, the death of Francis Fisher Browne in 1913 gave it an opportunity for a more generous estimate. Browne's *Dial* had never become a spokesman for the newer spirit and indeed had often attacked it. Dell, however, could give Browne an accolade in keeping with the rebel's essential virtue. "*The Dial* has not succeeded in being always right; but it has succeeded in being always sincere. . . . It has not failed to take account of the irruption of new forces into our literature, as into our life. . . . Francis Fisher Browne believed in order, but he did not believe in tyranny."[11] And when that flaming jacobin of the Liberation, Margaret Anderson, published the first number of her *Little Review* in 1914, the *Friday Review*, now under the editorship of Dell's successor and friend, Lucian Cary, expressed its highest approval.

So it ran, from 1909 until May of 1914 and the advent of Llewellyn Jones as editor. Dell's joyous hand had been replaced by that of Cary in October of 1913, but, as in the case of the earlier change from Hackett to Dell, no fundamental change was made in the policy of the *Review*. Mrs. Humphrey Ward continued to be dealt with most severely while the heroes of the Liberation steadfastly received honor after honor. It was only with Jones that the *Review* gave a new impression, that of a putting on of brakes if not an actual change of direction. Jones criticized Stanton Coit's *Soul of America* for its "psychic socialism," actually an effort to convert Bergsonian metaphysics into a politics, and this occasion was probably the first in the *Review's* five-year history where the word socialism had appeared in a pejorative context. Dreiser, heretofore capable of no wrong, was criticized for an exclusive use of economic and sexual motives in *The Titan*. And when Wyndham Lewis' and Ezra Pound's *Blast* arrived in Chicago for review, Jones attacked it in terms which differed little from those of its most deeply conservative enemies ". . . the deciphering of [its] significance will be about as painful and tedious a task as the deciphering of the partly outworn hieroglyphic description of some forgotten mystic, obscene cult of old." However, "*Blast* contains at least a laugh or two."[12] This was the work of that same Ezra Pound which had been rhapsodized by Dell, "Ezra Pound we salute you! You are the most enchanting poet alive. Your poems in the April *Poetry* are so mockingly, so delicately, so unblushingly beautiful, that you seem to have brought into the world a grace which (probably) never existed." Even allowing for the difference between *Blast* and Pound's earlier poetry, this was an abrupt shift of tenor from that of the Liberation.

If it was Francis Hackett who first brought the new light to Chicago, it was Dell who made plain the creative power of its rays, and his task by no means ended with its departure for New York in 1913. He moved on to Greenwich Village, the *Masses*, and a larger theater of operations, but the force he had acquired in Chicago and the Midwest remained fresh in his memory and operative in his life. In 1920 and 1921 he published two important novels, *The Moon Calf* and *The Briary Bush*, and wrote into them what must remain the classic account of the Chicago experience. The novels, written with the same lively and intelligent imagination Dell brought to all his work, caught up not only the details of his adventure but enlivened them with a high and dramatic sense of the whole movement.

The adventures of Felix Fay, Dell's hero, were of course the author's own. They began in a lower-class, not quite respectable family and continued through a dramatic discovery that respectability, the Presbyterian Church, and the town's business leaders were hostile and repressive of youthful dissenters. Felix thence stumbles upon Laurence Gronlund and Robert Ingersoll in the town library, enters into newspaper work, love affairs, and further intellectual enlightenment, and finally makes the critical decision that life can be fully realized only in the big city where he may hope to find the freedom denied by the smaller town. Quincy, or Davenport where Dell had lived for some years before his move to Chicago, could supply some books, a few congenial friends, and an opportunity for hope. But the full and real life of the desired liberation had to be sought in roomier places. "The shadow world of echoes, of theories, of poetic fancies amidst which [Felix] had moved all his life, was not enough. He must live in the real world. It was no longer a place of refuge—it was a task, a challenge. He would go there not as a moonstruck dreamer, but as a realist, able to face the hard facts of life."

For Felix Fay, as for many another, the Chicago years were those of working out in actual life the glimpses and hypotheses of liberation which had been vouchsafed earlier but which needed a metropolitan community to give them actuality. And for Felix there was a special destiny, that not only of sharing in the liberation but of helping to create it. Clive Bangs of the "*Chronicle*" staff, who conformed to the portrait of Charles Hallinan, book reviewer of the *Evening*

Post, gave Felix his basic lesson in the art of shaping minds through literary criticism. "He repudiated any preoccupation with literature as an art. It was to him a kind of social dynamics. It had been used to build up through the ages a vast system of 'taboos'—and it was being used to break them down again."[13] The task of the critic was to break taboos. He was a culture-hero—one who had achieved first the new patterns into which all eventually must fall. However, upon his first arrival in Chicago, the culture-hero was still a novice; he had yet to learn the sacrifice required if his own liberation was to be achieved. It was no less an act than a slaying of himself, a complete immolation of his residual scruples upon the altar of the new freedom and the achievement of moral anonymity. Such an oblation was difficult and, for Felix, not to be made without the assisting power of love. This was extended to him through Rose-Ann whom he came to know in Chicago and who was to be not only his wife but the avatar of a new existence. Thus, when Felix is repelled and confused by his discovery that the stage director with whom he works at a settlement house falls under the most rigid of his own taboos, that against homosexuality, Rose-Ann informs him that if he is to break with respectability he must acknowledge the goodness of all deviation since only by deviation is the break to be made.

> "Don't blame him," she said. "We're all a little like that—
> I mean queer. I'm sure I seem quite as queer as that to my
> family down in Springfield. If you live in Arkansas and want
> to make lovely stage pictures, you are a freak; you become one
> trying to keep from being dull like everybody else. It's
> inevitable."
> "You frighten me," Felix said soberly. "Am I a freak?
> I suppose I am—but somehow I don't like the idea."
> "Do you want to make a million dollars?"
> "No, not at all."
> "Then of course you're a freak." She laughed cheerfully.[14]

Not only the acknowledgment of freakishness but the embracing of it with joy and pride were essential to the new life and the characteristic affirmation of the Liberation. As Dell discovered its importance in his Chicago experience, so he voiced it for Chicago in the

Literary Review. But consistently with his own teachings, it was the experience values of his Chicago years that emerged with a final importance for him. The five years' participation in the life of the Liberation was the difference between boyhood and manhood. He had, in accepting its wisdom, accepted maturity. It was not the slogans or battle cries of the Liberation which Dell had learned but rather the truth to which they pointed—that men and women must be respected for themselves or not at all. He wrote of this to Rabbi Fineshriber from the train which was taking him to New York in 1913.

> It is then, if I have succeeded in showing you what I mean, a rather different person going to New York than came to Chicago five years ago. I am not so much of an idealist. I would not hurt anybody's feelings to prove the most beautiful theory ever invented. I care a great deal for people, and damned little for ideas. I know a great deal more than I did about how to go about making other people happy.
>
> It may be that I shall not get along so well as I might by reason of these very changes, which are by way of making me an ordinary person. But in any case, I have no fear of life, which has always displayed the utmost generosity toward me, and whose favor I shall always continue to expect. My experiences in marriage and in love have left me believing in them more thoroughly than ever I did before.[15]

This was not an epitaph of the Liberation, but a confirming of its own kind of reality.

II

Such existence values as Chicago had given Dell, though different in their nature, paralleled in direction its gift to many. As the Chicago group was truly a community, making available to its members a sense of place and importance, so it may be said that the gains they drew from it were much more than those usually indicated in the term "literary influence." And of the centers from which such an intangible but crucially important creative force spread, none was more important than *Poetry* magazine. Its story has been told often, best and most accurately by Harriet Monroe herself, who never forgot that she was helping to inaugurate an era in American cultural life. She herself took no stand in the battle of the books which raged around her except that of keeping the lines of communication open— to wherever they might lead. She defended her poets, all of them alike, on the grounds that they were poets and so needed defending. Among them she had pronounced likes and dislikes: with some she could agree while others seemed fools. No matter. So long as they wrote successful verse, they might claim her interest and sympathy. And successful verse was whatever proved to be living verse.

She was scolded by Ezra Pound, abused behind her back by Masters, and patronized by her avant-gard contributors; but these reactions left her admiration for the poetry of Pound, Masters, or the avant-gard unaffected. She printed and praised what she thought good, and returned the rest with polite refusals. Such deeply muddled persons as Maxwell Bodenheim or Emmanuel Carnevali were accommodated with amazing reaches of charity while a gentlemanly poet like Arthur Davison Ficke was valued as a gentleman. But in all three cases, it was the poetry of the man that counted where the magazine was concerned. Harriet Monroe gave comfort to bohemians and gentlemen alike, but for *Poetry* she maintained the inviolability of a dedicated schoolmistress. She had brought her magazine to life in the first place by an extended campaign among the Chicago gentry to establish a sound financial basis for it. Following the suggestion of Hobart Chatfield-Taylor, to whom she had proposed her problem, she spent the spring and summer of 1912 building up by personal calls a group of one hundred guarantors from each of whom she exacted a promise of fifty dollars a year for five years. Many of these were friends or acquaintances who could receive her on equal terms and who could be persuaded to support *Poetry* in much the same way as they contributed to the Art Institute or the orchestra. Her supporters included Daniel Burnham, Mrs. William Vaughn Moody, Charles L. Hutchinson, President of the Art Institute, Charles Deering of the McCormick Deering harvester company, Charles and Rufus Dawes, Victor Lawson, Samuel Insull, and the two sons of Potter Palmer. *Poetry's* maintenance was drawn directly out of the same genteel circles which had supported and patronized Chicago's earlier literary groups.

In August of 1912, however, she circularized as nearly as she could the whole world of living British and American poets announcing the forthcoming magazine and inviting their interest and contributions. "In order that this effort may be recognized as just and necessary, and may develop for this art a responsive public, we ask the poets to send us their best verse. We promise to refuse nothing because it is too good, whatever be the nature of its excellence. We shall read with special interest poems of modern significance, but the most classic subject will not be declined if it reaches a high standard of quality."[16] The same inclusive taste was shown in the choice of poets to which Harriet made her first approach. These included advanced practitioners such as Pound and Yeats, equally with more conservative masters like John Masefield and Edwin Arlington Robinson. Her method was systematic and responsible, and at all points she was herself in charge, without reference to schools or cliques. It took a very short time, however, for the forces of the Liberation to sweep in and threaten to alter drastically her procedure. The situation was met, in characteristic fashion, by Harriet Monroe's decision that the new and revolutionary work must be given a precedence in her pages not because she wished in any way to reject the past but because, in accordance with her original plan, poetry must be treated as a developing rather than a static art. Once such a decision was made, the Liberation had perforce found another point of rest and refreshment. It was the vanguard of poetry that Harriet Monroe would serve, and the Liberation was the vanguard.

The going was not therefore unruffled. Ezra Pound, admitted as *Poetry's* "foreign correspondent" before the publication of its second issue, was a lively and insistent critic whose approval of the new American writing was couched in terms completely foreign to the standards of the native poets—a difference of attitude which was to flare into heated disagreement within a few years. For the time being, Pound could give hearty approval to Masters and a modified acquiescence to Sandburg, but the basis of his judgment was as radically opposed to the real nature of these poets' work as it well could be.

"Can you teach the American poet that poetry *is* an art?" he asked. "Can you teach him that it is not a pentametric echo of the sociological dogma printed in last year's magazines?"[17] Harriet Monroe was, herself, to teach very little. But she opened *Poetry* to Pound and the Imagists, defended them against attack from the *Dial,* and so gave them their first regular publication and their primary outlet until the founding of the *Glebe* in 1913 and the *Egoist* in 1914. Harriet Monroe had persuaded a Lake Bluff friend, Alice Corbin Henderson, to act as her assistant and was supported by an advisory board composed of Henry Fuller, Edith Wyatt, and Hobart Chatfield-Taylor. With the unpredictable support of society folk, dedicated artists, suburbanites, impresarios, bohemians, and dilettantes she established for a time the center of modern poetry in Chicago.

In 1913 another one of Pound's epistolary explosions reached her. "Good God! Isn't there one of them that can write natural speech without copying clichés out of every Eighteenth Century poet still in the public libraries!"[18] His reference was to the American contributors to *Poetry,* here considered *en bloc* and opposed to the Imagists whom Ezra thought should take over the magazine. Harriet Monroe would not hear of his exclusiveness however. If she had not exactly discovered Lindsay she was the first to cast the mantle of greatness upon him. "General William Booth Enters Into Heaven" appeared in January of 1913 and was immediately hailed as the first appearance of a major poet, was given *Poetry's* Guarantors' Prize, and became the subject of a special accolade from W. B. Yeats when he visited Chicago in March of 1914. Sandburg's "Chicago Poems," like the work of the Imagists, again brought an attack from the *Dial,* and Harriet Monroe defended them as ardently as she had Pound's friends despite Pound's lack of enthusiasm for Sandburg.

Poetry had become in less than a year the liveliest center of new verse in the English-speaking world. The midwesterners, after years of frustration, suddenly found themselves hailed by Yeats, argued over by the stormy dictator of the new movement in London, and defended in terms of poetic greatness—all in the same magazine. No wonder that Masters could write to Harriet Monroe, "You see what you've done. You've started a cultus and it's moving fast. Hold on to the magazine. It has done more for Chicago authors than any-thing we've had."[19] Mrs. Sandburg told Harriet Monroe that *Poetry* had brought her husband back to creative life after years of rejection slips. And Lindsay formed an attachment to her that was to be a main-stay in his unhappy life. *Poetry* encouraged the midwesterners' inde-pendence, printed and praised their work, and brought them directly into the only center of revolutionary poetic activity which either Eng-land or America could boast in 1912 and 1913. It was, in the deepest sense, their professional home. They could turn to the *Friday Review* for ideas, or to the 57th street colony or Scholgl's round table for a bolstering sense of companionship, but *Poetry's* contribution to the Chicago renaissance was unique. It was for a crucial time the nexus of all twentieth-century poetic life, and, in admitting the Chicago poets to that life, it brought them full into the twentieth century world. They could consider themselves provincials no longer.

Even a partial list of those who appeared for the first time, or for the first time in America, in the pages of *Poetry* is sufficient to indicate the company into which the midwestern poets were admitted. Poems by Anderson, Masters, Sandburg, and Lindsay were printed along with the early work of Pound, Richard Aldington, T. S. Eliot, Marianne Moore, Wallace Stevens, Robert Frost, D. H. Lawrence, and William Carlos Williams. Of the older poets, Edwin Arling-ton Robinson and W. B. Yeats made appearances as, posthumously, did William Vaughn Moody. Rabindranath Tagore was printed for the first time in America a year before his reception of the Nobel prize and indeed found in Chicago so congenial an atmosphere that he made a residence there of some months in 1913. American readers heard not only about Imagism, but about a whole new objective and aesthetic view of poetry through Pound's letters, and were upset by his classification of them as "that mass of dolts" for their failure to understand Whistler. Ford Madox Hueffer defined his theory of literary "impressionism" which was to be one of the important roots of the new criticism as it developed through Pound and Eliot. Some semblance of a theory justifying and explaining *vers libre* was pro-vided by Amy Lowell who in turn took up Masters and Sandburg as two trail blazers in her own *Tendencies* in *Modern American*

Poetry of 1917. Pound persuaded Harriet Monroe to publish Ernest Fenellosa's translations from the Japanese in 1914 and so gave impetus to the fashion of Hokku writing and the more generally oriental interest which spread among some of the midwesterners. Remy de Gourmont's *Epigrammes* brought a further exotic and international note to one issue of the magazine.

Poetry, as it developed through its first decade, continued to function as a chief outlet and spokesman for modern verse, but after 1918 or thereabouts its importance for local writers altered somewhat and diminished. As it took on the character of an established fixture of the American literary landscape, and as the Chicago renaissance itself lost creative impetus, *Poetry*'s Chicago location became more incidental to its significance. Itself to a large degree a product of the literary community which it had helped to build, it survived that community by finding its ultimate strength in breadth of connections. Her discovery and publishing of the midwesterners, Harriet Monroe declared, remained her proudest achievement. But she refused to tie *Poetry* to that discovery any more than she had to any other group represented in its pages. She had contributed enormously to the midwestern success, and perhaps it was only fair that it should take a place as contributor to hers.

Lindsay, Masters, and Sandburg apart, *Poetry* printed the work of Chicago poets numerous enough to be counted by the dozen. They included Sara Teasdale, Alice Corbin Henderson, Arthur Davison Ficke, Maurice Browne, Edith Wyatt, Helen Hoyt, Mary Aldis, Maxwell Bodenheim, Alice Gerstenberg, Eunice Tietjens, Mark Turbyfill, Emmanuel Carnevali, Roger Sergel, Floyd Dell, Jun Fujita, Lew Sarett, Marion Strobel, John V. A. Weaver, Maurice Leseman, Florence Kiper Frank, Harriet Monroe herself, Louis Grudin, Mitchell Dawson, and such members of the University of Chicago's Poetry Club as Yvor Winters and Glenway Wescott. Even this long list cannot be taken as an exhaustive one, and to it must be added the novelists of the Liberation. The lyrical urge which produced the bulk of the poetry lay also at the roots of the personalized and self-expressive fiction characteristic of its mood.

As in the case of Masters, the concept of self-expression, explicit or implied, formed a chief rationale for much of the minor verse-writing. Consequently, the poet had to do little to secure interest beyond satisfying himself and his editor of his own sincerity, and of the presence of a vague quantity most often known as "magic" or "charm" in his style. Such ease of judgment, however, was wholly consistent. By 1912 the realistic vein which had supplied the earlier Chicago writers with a chance for personal expression had largely been exhausted. After a series of novelists, often through a series of books, had had their way with Chicago there was little left to mine. Poetry, meanwhile, had been largely neglected by the older Chicago generation, and consequently, in a strictly formalistic view, there was, at the advent of the later generation, a new genre to be explored. The whole spirit of the Liberation, moreover, suited this genre. As it emphasized and eulogized the personal, so it gave strong approval to the romantic and lyric urge.

The Liberation, in its poetry as in its pragmatic and libertarian philosophy, its voluntaristic psychology, its progressive politics, and its bohemian manners and morals centered in the self. Earlier generations, it felt, had censored this charismatic image almost beyond recognition. As one now discovered and released himself, so he attained his fullest human possibility. And the romantic lyric was a direct means of such discovery and release. It was at once a refuge from the constraining world and an achievement of the essential qualities of personal love, inner truth, and inner beauty. The poets' voices, and their particular concerns, differed, but common to them all was the narcissistic force of Sara Teasdale's *Wisdom*.

> *Oh to relinquish, with no more of sound*
> *Than the bent boughs when the bright apples fall;*
> *Oh to let go, without a cry or call*
> *That can be heard by any above ground;*
> *Let the dead know, but not the living see.*
> *The dead who loved me will not suffer, knowing*
> *It is all one, the coming or the going,*
> *If I have kept the last, essential me.*
> *If that is safe, then I am safe indeed,*
> *It is my citadel, my church, my home,*
> *My mother and my child, my constant friend;*

> *It is my music, making for my need*
> *A paean like the cymbals of the foam,*
> *Or silence, level, spacious, without end.*[20]

In *Poetry* their bleeding hearts, high hopes, or poignant regrets emerged from the chrysalis of silence to speak and be known in the great world.

III

If *Poetry* marked for the Liberation an achievement of status; and the *Friday Literary Review* supplied a rationale for it, the *Little Review* may be said to have held up a mirror to its soul. Margaret Anderson, having broken with her family in Columbus, Indiana, had proceeded to Chicago in 1911 fervently dedicated to the life of the Liberation and convinced that self-expression was the heart of all right belief. For a time she found her opportunities limited. She reviewed books for the religious magazine, *Interior*, and lived at the Y.W.C.A.—a destiny far from that she had pictured for herself. Within a few months, however, she had taken a step forward in securing a book reviewer's connection with the *Friday Review* and so was brought face to face with the new movement itself. In 1912 she became a clerk in Francis Fisher Browne's book store in the Fine Arts building, which had been opened as a center for Chicago's intellectual life. Through the *Friday Review* she came to know Floyd Dell who for her as for others served as a personal introduction to the world of the Liberation. At the Dells she met Dreiser, Anderson, George Cram Cook, Susan Glaspel, Arthur Davison Ficke, DeWitt Wing, and John Cooper Powys. In 1913 she heard Powys lecture on Arnold and Pater, and it was from this lecture, she said later, that the first definite impulse toward founding the *Little Review* had come.

The immediate preparation for the magazine consisted largely of talk which went on during the spring and summer of 1914 and embraced all who could be persuaded to listen. They were a numerous company and gave enthusiastic moral support to her plans, but it was not until she met Wing at the 57th street colony that she found someone "who really 'saw' the *Little Review*." Wing and Margaret talked excitedly of the whole world of new ideas and agreed that it must have expression in a magazine. Wing, who had little money except his salary earned on the staff of an agricultural paper, agreed to underwrite the expense of printing and of an office. Room 917 in the Fine Arts building was taken for the magazine, Dell and Lucian Cary gave the new venture advance publicity in the *Friday Review*, and its career was under way.

From March, 1914, until December of 1916 the *Little Review* served as the unpredictable but inclusive expression of Chicago's community of the Liberation. Frank Lloyd Wright donated $100 to it. Vachel Lindsay, according to Masters, gave his *Poetry* prize money as well as his poems to it. Anderson, Masters, Sandburg, Ficke, Bodenheim, Hecht, Dell, George Soule, Margery Currey, Cornelia Anderson, Llewellyn Jones, Eunice Tietjens, Sara Teasdale, Harry Blackman Sell, William Saphier, DeWitt Wing, Edith Wyatt, Helen Hoyt, Clarence Darrow, Mary Aldis, Mark Turbyfill, and Florence Kiper Frank were all contributors of money or manuscripts or both. More than either *Poetry* or the *Friday Review*, the first limited by its concentration upon verse, the other to what could be smuggled into book reviewers' columns, the *Little Review* embraced the whole of the renaissance. Margaret set no limits to the magazine. Each issue, filled with contributions uneven in quality and assembled purely on the principle of inspiration, was printed more or less accurately on wood pulp, rag, or glossy paper depending on the condition of the month's finances and Margaret's mood. After the advent of Jane Heap in 1916, the *Little Review* took on a larger aspect of order and regularity, but her influence was not greatly felt during the Chicago period.

The magazine's characteristic note was struck definitively by Sherwood Anderson in the second number. "It is the most delicate and the most unbelievably difficult task to catch, understand, and record your own mood. The thing must be done simply and without pretense or vindictiveness, for the moment these creep in your mind is no longer a record but a mere mass of words meaning nothing."[21] As Anderson was to be, perhaps, the most fully characteristic writer of the Liberation, so his testimony here in the *Little Review* had a peculiar authenticity both for the journal and literary movement which it expressed. He stated the premises, which he was himself completely to fulfill, for the whole Chicago movement.

The first number, except for a letter of greeting from John Galsworthy, was made up entirely of contributions from the Chicago group, and such a preponderance, though lessened in degree, continued through all the Chicago years of the magazine. Margaret Anderson, unlike either Dell or Harriet Monroe, was without wide acquaintance and, indeed, except for her enthusiasms, was neither a systematic reader nor greatly devoted to the life of books. She turned for her contributions to the familiar group in Chicago who had heard and applauded her plans for the *Little Review*, and they responded in abundance. Arthur Ficke, reflecting a constant passion of his, sent a poem entitled "Five Japanese Prints." Margaret herself defended Galsworthy against his moralistic critics and explained that Paderewski was a great pianist because of eternal striving. Floyd Dell preached a sermon on the joy of independent work and its moral value, especially, for women. George Soule, to be known later as an economist, printed a sonnet, "The Major Symphony," in which the true greatness of music was declared to lie in the eagerness of will it expressed,

> *In passion striving to surmount the world,*
> *Growing in sensuous dalliance, sudden whirled*
> *To ecstasies of shivering joy, and still*
> *Marching and mastering, singing mightily,*
> *Consummate when the silence makes it free.*[22]

Professor George Burman Foster of the University of Chicago Divinity School began what was to be a long series of articles on Nietzsche as the gospeler of a new and radically benevolent ethic. Lindsay printed a poem. Sherwood Anderson contributed "The New Note," his first literary item to be published. Cornelia Anderson reviewed contemporary opinions of Rahel Vernhagen. Llewellyn Jones wrote on the meaning of Bergsonism, and Eunice Tietjens printed a poem, "To a Lost Friend." The remainder of the magazine was made up of book reviews and notices.

The tone of the magazine was established at once as a radical voice of the Chicago Liberation making a constant reiteration of the value of absolute freedom. "Whim" was indeed written on its door sill. Its subsequent issues simply amplified and compounded its one idea. Scarcely a number appeared which did not carry a note from Margaret Anderson in furtherance of the great cause. The magazine had been launched with a manifesto from her hand, and this was followed by editorial after editorial designed to strike all shackles of whatever kind from all people. In October of 1914 humanity was relieved of its interdependence. "That human being is of most use to other people who has first become of most use to himself. . . . Only on such a basis is built up that intensity of inner life which is the sole compensation one can wrest from a world of mysterious terrors . . . and of ecstasies too dazzling to be shared."[23] Shortly after, humanity was freed from the necessity of liberation itself—if its home-life was satisfactory. Margaret had spent a week with her family and was moved to rhapsody. "The wonder and comfort of a week at home with Mother and Dad, and Bertha bringing in cider and doughnuts, and the house like a Nutting print. Oh you people who have homes! Why *don't* you realize what they might yield you."[24] But in February, 1915, she declared that the *Little Review* "existed to create some attitude which so far is absolutely alien to the American tradition,"[25] and the next month Mrs. Havelock Ellis was criticized for her failure in a recently given Chicago lecture to include explicit approval of "free love, free divorce, social motherhood, birth control, and the 'sex' morality of the future." "She knows," declared Margaret, "of boys and girls, men and women, tortured and crucified every day *for their love*,"[26] but was silent concerning them. Two numbers later Margaret was in a humble mood, ". . . we haven't gone to any real *lengths*—and that is just what is the matter with us,"[27] but in the June-July issue a length, though a familiar one, seemed to have been reached. "It really all comes to one end: Life for Art's sake. We believe in that because it is the only way to get more life . . . It means more intensity, in short, it means the *New* Hellenism."[28] By August of 1916, however, she was again disappointed. The *Little Review* had fallen far short of its aim. "Now, we shall have Art in this magazine or we shall stop publishing it. . . . If there is only one really beautiful thing for the September number it shall go in and the other pages will be left blank."[29] The result, in September, was the famous empty issue of the *Little Review*, which was not really blank but from which all imaginative writing had been excluded leaving a number of empty pages. As if to confirm her disappointment, Margaret, in the December number announced the impending move of the magazine to New York, and after January Chicago had seen the last of her.

Her stay, however, had been decisive in importance. For the first time the full force and scope of the Chicago movement was made apparent to those who were living in it. It was revolutionary; it was inclusive, and it had the stature of a genuine intellectual adventure. The bulk of the *Review's* contents were expository and hortatory rather than imaginative, but its function in Chicago was primarily that of defining the nature of the new movement and arousing enthusiasm for it. The literature of the Liberation was largely printed elsewhere. For Margaret Anderson, it was the spirit of her undertaking that was most important. She talked much about art and herself produced none. She did however help to a substantial degree in creating a climate of feeling and opinion in which art, of a certain kind, was almost inevitable.

The Struggle for Affirmation—
Anderson, Sandburg, Lindsay

THE cause and ground of the later Chicago renaissance, the solvent which made of it a homogenous entity, was a struggle against withering restraint. Many in the movement were dedicated to the struggle itself and satisfied by its negative aims. But of the major writers, three at least owed their distinction to the efforts they made, while accepting the Liberation as a beneficent first step, to proceed thence to affirmation, to make their writing speak the Yea which a fulfillment of the Liberation required. Sherwood Anderson, Carl Sandburg, and Vachel Lindsay were wholly of the Liberation. Each of them lived in it and, in part, from it. But each felt the need of a world-view in which one need not always be a rebel. What, after freedom had been achieved, should be the realization? This was the question which they sought to answer.

I

Sherwood Anderson's history was one of affirmation made through a process of denial and torturous re-learning, a case of conversion in which the lines ran one way until suddenly they broke into confusion and indecision, and then, after a sorting period, gradually reasserted themselves in a new direction. He was born in Camden, Ohio, in 1876, but grew up largely in the near-by town of Clyde where his father had established himself as a house painter and odd-job man. He worked briefly in Chicago as a laborer, served in the Spanish-American War, spent a year at Wittenberg Academy in Ohio, and, in 1900, came again to Chicago to work as an advertising copy writer and begin what seemed an ordinarily promising business career. He not only wrote copy for the Frank B. White Co., but for a time conducted columns in *Agricultural Advertising* in which he expressed optimistic and go-getting sentiments appropriate to his calling. In 1904 he married Cornelia Lane, and in 1906 moved to Cleveland into the nominal presidency of a merchandising organization. This venture, however, proved disappointing, and in 1907 he settled in Elyria to the management of a paint-sales business. Then, in 1912, he experienced what was his great crisis, the turning of his back upon the business world and a deliberate estrangement from the only life and values he had known.

His business, increasingly, had seemed sheer involvement without interest or satisfaction; his acquaintance in the city meant less and less; and his home life gave him little satisfaction. With a motive which was in the beginning perhaps purely one of flight he turned to writing, but the positive direction of his work was made clear even in his first effort. This work, he recorded, was called "Why I Am a Socialist," and, although the manuscript itself he later destroyed, the title remained significant. In this instance the primary aim was that of self-definition. As the conflicts of the Elyria years sharpened, Anderson's experience was stretched more and more threateningly between the poles of his business career and his growing sense of literary dedication. In the first he felt increasingly little reality while the second exerted a stronger and stronger pull. These years of strain saw the writing of his first two published novels, *Windy McPherson's Son* and *Marching Men*. He had read Whitman and indulged in literary conversations with professors from a nearby college, perhaps Oberlin, against whose taste he attacked Howells. He neglected his business increasingly for writing and for conversation upon art and life with congenial cronies. The inevitable break came in the fall of 1912 when Anderson walked out of his office under considerable nervous strain, made his way to Cleveland where he spent a mysterious few days from which he recovered in a hospital of that city, and then returned to Elyria convinced that he must scuttle his business commitments and adopt a new life. This aim he realized when in December he left Elyria for Chicago.

Though its ultimate importance has been brought into question by later writers, Anderson's action had always a major significance for himself. It is correct to suggest that he exaggerated, that his accounts of his departure from his paint warehouse grew more dramatic and more distorted with the telling, that actually he was as much running away from a shaky business enterprise as he was projecting himself into a life of mind and imagination. But such qualifications are more easily made after the fact by too detached observers than the whole truth may require. As Anderson was a man always profoundly stirred by his own image of himself, so one must understand and accept that image if one is to understand the causes of his behavior and the forces conditioning his writing. There was, moreover, an objective reality in his choice. Born and reared in a lower class family, from his earliest years he had worked within the structure and values of a mobile world. As a youngster he acquired for himself the nickname "Jobby" because of his eagerness and skill in making money through scraped-up opportunities. He had always clung to such main chances as came his way and used them bit by bit to make of himself a case of that classic and accepted American type, the man who has risen. He was far from achieving success in his business ventures by the time of the Elyria period, but in turning his back upon them, in shaking off as much as he could of his old character, he did not so much slide down the rungs of American life as cast off his hold upon the very ladder itself. His earlier efforts had been mixed, but they had been in character; his successes and failures had been definable to himself and his world. Upon his arrival in Chicago, however, in December of 1912, he was for the time a man without place or identity.

The Elyria episode was no doubt a flight. Because Anderson wrote again and again of flights, because his style and structure were deliberately fugitive and elusive in character, because of his many marriages, because in a genuine sense his life for the nearly thirty years after 1912 hinged around repeated flights, it is easy to see in his work nothing but flight—that, of course, being one from reality. Such a judgment is not wholly false, but it is partial. And what it leaves out is best suggested by a contrast between the whole career of Anderson and of another member of the Liberation, like Margaret Anderson, to whom rejection and rebellion were in fact the only cogent modes of belief and action. Anderson, for his part, was more seeker than fugitive. What he found was without doubt nebulous, but his search was none the less genuine. In his writing there was little to suggest that he ever came upon a body of finally satisfying ideas or experiences, but, if one look at his work rather than through it, the achievement of Anderson's search can be defined. It was nothing less than a sense of self, to be achieved in the craft of writing, which the world of business and middle class propriety had destroyed. He, in a radical sense, had rejected that world, but having done so he turned to the creation of another world which could be put in its place. His effort, no doubt, was quixotic, but in one way it accomplished its end. Anderson did in a genuine sense, define himself in his best work. Stories of the quality of "Death in the Woods," "The Man Who Became a Woman," or "The Egg," gave to him what he sought, and they conveyed an act of fulfillment to the reader. They were realizations of what, potentially, Anderson could be—the imaginatively honest and acute narrator of his own bewildering quest. His achievement was lyrical, but, within that limit, one of occasional high success.

Windy McPherson's Son and *Marching Men*, however, had been largely written before Anderson's fulfillment, in Elyria, though one cannot be sure how much they may have been altered between 1912 and their publication in 1916 and 1917. In 1915, for example, Anderson wrote Dell, who had carried *Marching Men* to New York with him, "Send Marching Men to me, I am ready to do some patient sustained work on it."[1] As early work, his novels partook of his earlier sense of tension rather than his later fulfillment. They spelled out a shaky but revealing pattern. Sam McPherson, the hero of the first, was precisely Anderson, the business man in self-discovery and revolt, with a good deal of autobiography thrown in for good measure. Beaut McGregor, hero of the second, was all this plus Anderson's early vision of himself as he might be, the idealist, visionary leader of men who, was perhaps the self-envisaged author of "Why I Am a Socialist." Neither book succeeded as literature or as self-fulfillment. Anderson the rebel was to find ends and means wholly different from Sam McPherson's while Anderson the visionary was to realize his hopes as a writer rather than a leader. But both stories were marking-wands along the path of a liberated midwesterner in search of affirmation.

They shared equally a sense of strain caused by their uneasy balance between objective and inner narrative. Sam McPherson's story was that of a small town boy who, like Anderson, had grown up under a double heritage and double loyalty. He absorbed the standard of success which his world put faith in and, indeed, excelled in its pursuit. Like his author he bore the nickname, Jobby, but he retained also a deep hunger for self-realization unrelated to worldly success. After exhausting the business possibilities of the home town of his story, he proceeds to Chicago and there rises rapidly by a ruthless dedication to business and a total denial of his instinctive self. In becoming a millionaire, however, Sam retains his sense of himself as seeker, and when his business success is shown to involve his father-in-law's suicide, and his own estrangement from his wife, he decides with reason that his personal being must now be given its play. His achievement has turned to ashes, business holds no further lure for him, and on the spur of the moment he makes an about face. Disposing of his business affairs and packing a bag, he strikes alone into the country determined to find out what in life he has missed.

The story, of course, was to be Anderson's own. He plotted out for himself in this novel the course which he himself was to follow except for the bumbling way in which the last third of the book attempted to find a solution for Sam. That hero suffers from the persecutions of a corrupt and driving boss. He joins with laborers and leads a strike for them. He communes with nature. He sinks into dissipation. These experiences all have a redemptive value, but none of them is satisfying. Finally he chances on a drunken and dissolute mother who wants to abandon her children. Sam adopts them, brings them home to his wife, who has lost several children through miscarriages, and reconcilement takes place.

The tale is a wandering and indecisive one entirely congruent with Anderson's frame of mind before the 1912 break. His state of indecision in regard to the story was indicated by his dissatisfaction with the original ending and his plan of writing a new one for the book's republication by Ben Huebsch in 1922. He wished then to take the children back to their own mother, apparently in an effort to show finally that Sam realizes the evils he has turned away from cannot be overcome by a sentimental gesture, even as Anderson's own plight was not to be solved simply by leaving his paint business. One might guess, however, that the real failure in the ending of *Windy* was not that of lighting upon the wrong kind of event, but just that of trying to solve Sam's problem by events at all. This, of course, was also Anderson's problem, and Anderson himself had not in these early years found the consummate experience which he needed to bring Sam's troubles to a convincing end.

The book, as a result, was only the beginning of a search, or the postulation of its necessity, rather than any substantial advance toward ending it. It had value as it gave definition to the dilemma upon which Anderson's consciousness was hung—that lying between the meaninglessness of life for the aspiring individual in the middle-class world and the elusiveness of fulfillment in the pure act of rebellion. *Marching Men* explored the third choice which was necessary if the matter was to be resolved. Though its hope, that of a natural and mystical brotherhood of the men who had been made strangers to each other by an urban and industrial civilization, was rejected in the end, it came from deep in Anderson's feelings and remained in changed form and emphasis a chief element in much of his later work. Sanity, and perhaps survival, depended upon the re-establishment of instinctive human contact. The world in Anderson's view could be made habitable only by love. Individuals could be redeemed only by the same force.

Such for Anderson was the great goal of human life. In 1931, on grounds that Communism was institutional and puritanical, he rejected Dreiser's proposal that he enter the Communist Party. At best it was irrelevant to the deepest human needs and at worst it was a tyranny. Four years later, a letter to Dreiser summed up much of what nearly twenty years of Anderson's writing had been saying. "Now what I have been thinking is that we need here among us some kind of new building up of relationship between man and man.[2] Such too was the theme of *Marching Men*, the deep need for human solidarity and the hopes that lay in such a fulfillment. The book ended, however, with the collapse of Beaut McGregor's vision—that of organizing bodies of workmen and training them to march in disciplined silence so to produce a sense of unity among them deeper and more instinctive than any political scheme. His failure came when, on the brink of success, he found it necessary to relapse into talk, to explain and justify. Anderson, not yet prepared with a concept of natural talk, could not yet prevail against divisive artificialities of civilization.

Unlike *Windy*, *Marching Men* was content to record a failure. It did not make an effort to patch up. And here lay great hope for Anderson's later work. With the many faults which weakened these two earliest novels, they possessed one solid quality. In them Anderson, as he had one of his characters say of all worthy writers, did seek to reach that point of complete devotion to the demands of his craft summed up by the phrase, imaginative honesty. Janet Eberly, in *Windy McPherson's Son*, chides Sam, "Books are not full of pretense and lies; you business men are . . . What do you know of books? They are the most wonderful things in the world. Men sit writing them and forget to lie, but you business men never forget." For Anderson, the telling of truth could never become a matter of writing in such a way that his work would correspond to whole and objective situations. The dramatic imagination was not his. But he could, in his best work, rise to the point where he did not delude himself. *Windy* had had an element of self-delusion in it, for Sam McPherson was a heroic, a melodramatized, and finally a fulfilled Sherwood Anderson—but only by power of fancy. *Marching Men* moved on a step. Anderson's hope for himself and for mankind was there considered and rejected because it was stretched over too broad a field. His chief Chicago writing, *Mid-American Chants*, *Winesburg*, and a number of the stories collected in *The Triumph of the Egg*, was first to reduce that field and then re-define it. In this way a victory became possible.

Chicago presented Anderson with two major gifts. First, through an encounter with Gertrude Stein's *Tender Buttons* he found the possibilities of expressive style. His first novels, he felt later, suffered from imitativeness. They were not sufficiently himself, and the fulfilled Anderson was to be in his own writing his own man. But this new turn came largely through a second gift of Chicago to him, the chance he found, particularly in the 57th street colony, to live as an explorer of the Liberation. Both his introduction to Gertrude Stein and to the 57th street group were brought about by his brother, the painter Karl Anderson, and it was in correspondence with Karl that he defined his theory of art as successful intuition, the basic apologia of his developed work. "What we have got to do," he wrote, "is to feel into things. To do that we only need learn from people that what they say and think isn't of very much importance."[3] And after *Marching Men* had been published in 1917, Anderson emphasized to Karl his lack of sympathy with any merely intellectual view of his writing. "It is very amusing to see our American intellectuals taking me so seriously."[4] They could not know that Anderson was discovering not ideas but a whole person, himself.

The effect of the Liberation was to focus new lights in a brightening sense of self-discovery, and it was thus that Anderson recorded a shock of recognition caused by Dell's praise in the *Friday Literary Review*. "Why how exciting," he exclaimed. "There I was, as Dell was saying in print, in a newspaper read as I presumed by thousands, an unknown man (I do not now remember whether or not he mentioned my name) doing, in obscurity, this wonderful thing. And with what eagerness I read. If he had not printed my name at least he had given an outline of my novel. There could be no mistake. 'It's me. It's me.' "[5] By March of 1914 Anderson could contribute to the first number of the *Little Review* an essay on the contemporary movement, expressed now in terms precisely of what were to be the two chief attainments in his own work. There was, first, the discovery of a sense of craft, of the writer's identity as writer rather than as advertiser, reformer or self-instructor. And, second, the necessary condition to this discovery, the freeing of the writer from any responsibilities except those he took upon himself. "In the trade of writing," as Anderson put it, "the so-called new note is as old as the world. Simply stated, it is a cry for the reinjection of truth and honesty into the craft; it is an appeal from standards set up by money-making magazines and book publishers in Europe and America to the older, sweeter standards of the craft itself; it is the voice of the new man come into a new world, proclaiming his right to speak out of the body and soul of youth rather than through the bodies and souls of the craftsmen who are gone."[6] Anderson was no youth when he wrote these words, but he was indeed a new man. No longer was he writing out a substitute for an unsatisfactory world as he had in *Windy* or *Marching Men*. His work now became an end in itself by which the writer participated in real life—that of his fulfilled individuality.

In 1933 he wrote to a friend, "My first conception of literature was through Margaret Anderson who started the *Little Review* in Chicago,"[7] and, though Anderson wrote many things to many people, there is reason to seize upon this remark as a significant one. Taken in conjunction with his declaration in "More About the New Note" appearing in the second number of the *Little Review* it points revealingly to the discovery Anderson's Chicago experience was to give him. He remained devoted to his concept of love as a saving force, but he found that love was not to be obtained by constructing a fanciful simulacrum of it in his novels. Rather, the writer must lavish love upon his creations themselves. He must become a lover to satisfy his need for love. His craft, and a devotion to it, was the indispensable link between mankind and himself, and love lay in a preservation and exploitation of such links. Thus, for Anderson, came a crucial change, that from writing vitalistic propaganda to himself, or of plotting his course in his writing, to imaginative creation for its own sake. This was the essential difference between the two early novels and the great stories of *Winesburg, The Triumph of the Egg,* and *Horses and Men*, and it remained throughout his career the difference between all his work of the first rate and that below first rate. Literature was a creating of persons, a respecting of them, and a realizing by the writer's imagination of their truth. Anderson as craftsman, his key word in this regard, was to be two things simultaneously. He was the artist of language and the artist of life. In discerning and arranging one, he arranged and so discerned the other.

In realizing one he realized the other. The two could not in his view be separated without destroying the very nature of literature. Thus Anderson had no hesitance in founding his critical thought upon a concept of craft despite the latter's seeming incongruity with his passion for life. "The writer is but the workman whose materials are human lives," he wrote in 1925. "It is as true as there is a sun in the sky that men cannot live in the end without love of craft. It is to the man what love of children is to the woman."[8] Later, "The real reward, I fancy, lies just in the work itself, nowhere else. If you cannot get it there, you will not get it at all."[9] Craft, in Anderson's view was not formalistic and not vitalistic, it was both. It was the element common to life and to art. "The imagination must constantly feed upon reality or starve. Separate yourself too much from life and you may at moments be a lyrical poet, but you are not an artist. Something within dries up, starves for the want of food." But it was equally true that, "the life of the imagination will always remain separated from the life of reality. It feeds upon the life of reality, but it is not that life—cannot be."[10] The heart of the matter lay in the inescapable duality of the writer's task.

One more direction was to be tried however before Anderson achieved his first clear success in the new, double vein. That was the composition of his free-verse poems which were collected and published under the title *Mid-American Chants* in 1918. In these, as it were, he abruptly cut the gordian knot of mixed purpose which had been so debilitating a weight on the early novels to launch himself upon outright and unrestrained lyricism—pure expression and undivided feeling. The literary results for the most part were atrocious, perhaps as bad a case of maundering and abortive work as the whole Chicago Liberation, so ready in formless effusion, was to produce. The poems were written during the early years in Chicago. In Anderson's own chronology they followed *Marching Men* and "led into *Winesburg, Poor White*, and *The Triumph*," which, though there is no other positive evidence for so early a date, would put their composition previous to late 1915. Whatever their lack of quality, they were unquestionably of first-rate importance for their author. They marked, first of all, an end to personal rebellion as the great prop of his work. They were testaments of affirmation. *Windy* and *Marching Men*, he wrote to Paul Rosenfeld, had been "the effects of a reaction from business men back to my former associates, the workers. I believe now it was a false reaction. . . . That went. A break came. You will see it in *Mid-American Chants*."[11] The poems declared, in effect, their author's acceptance of Anderson's own region and its characteristic life. The change, of course, was not a simple flip of the mind to uncritical acceptance. But it was a deep conversion from fear and bewilderment at the Midwest and its ways to a sympathetic concern for it. There was, in the *Chants*, a deliberate effort to say yea, not to all Anderson had formerly denied, but to the inevitable essence of his own development and his work. His new acceptance depended on hope and imagination: new perceptions, that is, of qualities in Midwestern people and their lives which not only gave a different tone to the region than he had formerly recorded but also and more important made it available for imaginative and sympathetic scrutiny. The early Anderson had been, as much as he could, a pessimistic rebel crying to himself the news of doom. After *Mid-American Chants* with their broad acceptance, he could pick up the pieces of what he still regarded as a spoiled and broken life for detailed and genuinely loving treatment. *Winesburg* and the *Triumph* stories were not acts of judgment but of commiseration and understanding.

> *Back of Chicago the open fields—were you ever there?*
> *Trains coming toward you out of the West—*
> *Streaks of light on the long gray plains?—many a song—*
> *Aching to sing.*
>
> *I've got a grey and ragged brother in my breast—*
> *That's a fact.*
>
> *Back of Chicago the open fields—were you ever there?*
> *Trains going from you into the West—*
> *Clouds of dust on the long grey plain.*
> *Long trains go West, too—in the silence*
> *Always the song—*
> *Waiting to sing.*[12]

Anderson's new approach to the Midwest drew its strength from humility and love. There was also the unabashed lyricism which, though it was to be transmuted in the later work by sympathy, here cut loose from the clogs of realistic convention. But particularly, the *Chants* revealed a concentrated effort to make poetry out of Anderson's own language. This was simple and limited, frequently not sufficient to the demands he put upon it. In the *Chants*, for the first time, he came down upon his language, not to prune and order, but to let come from it whatever was, in nature, there. This was a part of his acceptance. He had felt in Gertrude Stein the achievement of poetry in the aggressively simple. And that, in a literary way, was where his own work must begin and end. He wrote to Paul Rosenfeld, "Being as I have said slow in my nature, I do have to come to words slowly. I do not want to make them rattle. And well enough I know that you, Waldo [Frank], [Van Wyck] Brooks might do in a flash what I will never be able to do. You may get to heights I can never reach. That isn't quite the point. I'm not competitive. I want if I can to save myself."[13]

Such imaginative fulfillment was not conducted in a social vacuum. The change from Elyria to the metropolis had served not only as a change of place, but more deeply as a change in the texture and direction of Anderson's whole life. He left an existence which had been divided among office, home, and country club for a re-alliance with his Chicago advertising firm as a free-lance copywriter, rooms in a boarding house on 57th street, and an intimacy with his artist-brother, Karl, with Floyd Dell and other members of the 57th street group. He could, once again, gratify his taste for flamboyant clothes. He replaced his necktie by a scarf drawn close around his throat with a ring. In the winter of 1913 Anderson and his wife spent some weeks in a cabin in the Ozarks, he with the double purpose of concentration upon his writing and an effort to cement a failing marriage. In the Spring of 1914 he returned to the agency where he wrote furiously at his stories while supposedly turning out advertising copy. During 1914 he also met Tennessee Mitchell, sculptress and suffragette who, Edgar Lee Masters later claimed, had been the great love of Masters' life and was portrayed as Deirdre in his autobiography. He spent the summer of 1915 with her at Lake Chateaugay in the Adirondacks. Here he met Trigant Burrow, one of the early American psychoanalysts, with whom he formed a close friendship. Burrow the medical man and Anderson the writer found an absorbing common ground in their psychological interests.

After this summer Mrs. Cornelia Anderson was to obtain a divorce from the author so that he returned to Chicago in the fall a single man. He took an attic room at 735 Cass Street where he had as neighbors a group of artistically minded and bohemian friends. Chief among them was George Daugherty, a fellow copy writer with Anderson at the Critchfield agency and one of the early admirers of his work. There were also Jerry Lane, a pianist and a writer, Bill Hollingsworth, a painter, and Max Wald, a musician. This group surrounded him during the composition of the bulk of the Winesburg stories in late 1915 and early 1916.

In August of 1916 he married Tennessee Mitchell. By that time also he had met Waldo Frank and through Frank was made known to the staff of *The Seven Arts*, particularly Van Wyck Brooks. These acquaintances led on to a friendship with Paul Rosenfeld which was to last for a number of years and which sealed his acceptance by the New York intellectual circle of the Liberation. This, though like the Chicago group in important particulars, was possessed of greater literary and intellectual sophistication—attainments which attracted and repelled Anderson alternately until his eventual drift away from the New Yorkers during the twenties. In 1918 Anderson spent much of the year in New York and so continued a movement away from Chicago which had begun with his summers at Lake Chateaugay in 1915 and 1916. In 1920 he was in Alabama where he wrote *Poor White*. His first visit to Europe came in 1921 with Rosenfeld, and in 1922 he made his final break with Chicago, moving to New York, to Reno for a divorce from Tennessee, to New Orleans, and finally to Virginia.

The new attitude expressed by Anderson in *Mid-American Chants* was contemporary with the early links in this chain of events. The first two novels, having been finished substantially before Anderson's move to Chicago, were dominated by a tone of solitary plotting against a hostile and unlovely world. The writing which grew subsequently from an achieved freedom and a steadily widening acceptance by the midwestern and eastern literary groups reflected equally a new self-confidence and a new hope. Anderson's ability, by the time of writing *Mid-American Chants* in 1914 or early 1915, to conceive of himself as a loving artist rather than an alienated and confused prophet must have been greatly heightened by the marked enthusiasm of his new friends for his work. Dell, soon after meeting Anderson in 1913, warmed to his writing and undertook to find publishers for *Windy* and *Marching Men*. Margaret Anderson invited him to write for the *Little Review*. George Daugherty was excited by his stories, and his new love, Tennessee Mitchell, thought highly of his achievement. Anderson the unsuccessful and rebellious salesman had been adopted into the liberated community of the arts in Chicago. It was natural that he should in his first years there have gained a new view of himself as artist, that which he summed up in his ruling idea of craft and expressed first in the achievement of the *Winesburg* and *Triumph* stories. Having been baptized into the community of the Liberation, Anderson received the fruits of its spirit.

The first harmonizing of Anderson's new-found sympathy and newly implemented lyricism in an appropriate form was to come in the narrative sketches of the *Winesburg* volume where he based his characters upon originals of his own acquaintance, an exercise of imaginative sympathy quite foreign to the early work in which he alone had been the focus. As in the case of Masters' *Spoon River*, the achievement of literary identity here followed upon the discovery of a proper subject and the granting to that subject an ultimate control over the whole work. The great bulk of the characters in *Winesburg*, like the town itself, grew from Anderson's own experience. By his own account, his fellow lodgers at 735 Cass street served as models, but much also came from his years in Clyde. The layout of Winesburg was markedly similar to that of Clyde. In both towns, the imaginary and the real, were a Heffner block of store buildings and a Sinning's Hardware Store. In Winesburg stood Ransom Surbeck's Pool Room while Clyde included a Ransom Surbeck's Cigar Store. A nurseryman, French, in Clyde became a nurseryman, Spaniard, in Winesburg. Jesse Benton, the original settler in Clyde emerged as the Jesse Bentley, of Anderson's story. A Skinner Letson of Clyde had his name changed to Leason only by an afterthought when the original name in the *Winesburg* manuscript was crossed out and the new inserted. Correspondences with Elyria also appeared. Dr. Reefy of "Paper Pills" had the same name as a newspaper-editor friend of Anderson's in Elyria. And Anderson himself made a partial identification of Joe Welling, hero of "A Man of Ideas" with an Elyria printer whom he had found a congenial conversation partner.

The figures of his stories were fully realized, unlike each other, and different from Anderson himself. This set them apart from Sam McPherson and Beaut McGregor who, in character, were nearly interchangeable with their author or with one another. However, in Wing Biddlebaum, the inhibited lover; Doctor Parcival, discoverer of the great truth that "everyone in the world is Christ and they are all crucified;" Jesse Bentley, convinced of a divine vocation to patriarchy; or the Reverend Curtis Hartman, who perceived the strength of God working upon him through the naked body of Kate Swift, enabling him to put her aside—in these was a collection of persons with whom Anderson could sympathize, but who were far from being just puppets or mouthpieces for their author. Each had identity and individual existence. Neither here nor elsewhere did Anderson achieve dramatic validity. Each of his figures sustained a narrative sketch entirely from his own nature without an independent or complicating structure of its own. But each was moving and real.

The resulting literary achievement was curiously ambiguous but also wholly authentic in its impact. It made Anderson a master of the revealing glimpse. Though interested in Freud, Anderson had rejected the idea of clinical Freudianism. Such practice, he felt, tampered too dangerously because too ineptly with the private and inviolable sources of individuality. These yielded up their secrets only to intuition; the artist's sympathy and craft could perhaps suggest something of their nature and importance. In this way literature came to grips with actuality by its own means. It yielded news of the human situation in its own way. And, by its attainments, it gave distinction and identity to its creator.

Anderson's later years brought no drastic change from the discovery and the achievement which Chicago had given him. His writing was an extension with variations of the *Winesburg* pattern. The relative lack of success of his novels bespoke no failure of his powers but rather the basic and obvious inconsistency of his particular method with the demands of the novel. He found happiness in his last marriage, achieved a degree of settlement at Ripshin Farm in Virginia, and continued to produce work of distinction. His later life, at the same time, had its share of troubles. But it did not, in any case, precipitate a further crisis of the kind which had sent him to Chicago in 1912 or offer any discoveries as significant as that which had led him to *Winesburg*. As a writer he had been perfected so far as it lay within him, and the pattern which had brought him fulfillment continued without basic change. "Artists," he said in a summary of his own discovery, "do not want to cut down trees, root stumps out of the ground, build towns and railroads. The artist wants to sit with a strip of canvas before him, face an open space on a wall, carve a bit of wood, make combinations of words and sentences as I am doing now—and try to express to others some thought or feeling of his own. He wants to dream of color, to lay hold of form, free the sensual in himself, live more fully and freely in this contact with the materials before him than he can possibly live in life."[14] These sentiments, for Anderson, were the creed which Chicago had given him. They marked his way of accepting the universe through his own literary vocation.

II

In the work of Carl Sandburg, the struggle for affirmation began from a base much like that of Anderson's, though its direction was soon shown to be a different one. Both writers grew to their crafts from lower-class beginnings of a kind unlikely to produce literary flowering. The elder Sandburg, an immigrant from Sweden, was a hard working, thrifty, and reasonably successful machinist's blacksmith who throughout his days looked first to establishing his family in something like reasonable comfort and security and thought little of other attainments. Nor did the town of Galesburg, any more than Sherwood Anderson's Clyde, hold particular encouragement for latent talent. It was the county seat and the home of Knox and Lombard colleges. But even these rural advantages meant little to the son of an immigrant who, in his own turn, set to work early earning money for his family. At no time during his earlier Galesburg years had he opportunity for any degree of literary culture.

Sandburg had been born in Galesburg in 1878. He studied in the public schools and, during the summer, in Lutheran parochial schools. This and more informal learning gave him a taste for Gray's "Elegy" and Ingersoll's oration at his brother's grave, but few other literary predilections showed themselves. He left school after the eighth grade to work at a number of the nondescript labors open to boys and came in time to hold a fixed place as porter in Humphrey's barber shop, an elite establishment of the county seat. This job possessed some significance. Though his place in the barber shop was of the humblest, it provided a point of contact with a social class which had heretofore been largely unfamiliar and, for Sandburg, incommunicado. A close acquaintance with the boots of county officers, lawyers, editors, and visiting congressmen was not the same thing as a close acquaintance with the gentlemen themselves, but it was more than had come Sandburg's way earlier. His clients spoke of politics, gossiped of personalities and situations, and weighed their own and the country's fortunes.

From these adjuncts to his bootblack's work, Sandburg formed a first impression of what was to be his great theme—the character of American life—and to his theme, at the age of sixteen, he added a characteristic color. True politics, he decided, were summed up in Bryan Democracy; Sandburg in his first major choice confirmed his own origins and his own character in an act of loyalty to the peoples' cause. Like Anderson and Masters, he began a literary career with a political choice in which much more than politics was at stake. Hardly was it made, and Bryan defeated for the presidency, than Sandburg turned away from his menial work to strike out upon a three year period of vagabondage, throwing himself thus upon the people he had chosen. His wanderings took him to Keokuk, Iowa, to Hannibal and Bean Lake, Kansas, and to Kansas City. He worked at a number of jobs including those of railroad section hand and

farm laborer, and in these seemingly insignificant vocations most
certainly began laying in the store of images and feelings, deeply
populistic in their character, out of which his poetry was to be
generated.

By 1898 he was back in Galesburg in time to enlist there for the
Spanish-American War and serve several months in the army, an
experience which seemed completely consistent in his own mind
with his political loyalties. He apparently felt no anti-imperialist
scruples and perhaps was gratified at the opportunity to strike a
blow against the decadent Spanish tyranny. At any rate the war, or
more properly his own part in it, gave him his first literary opportunity, that of special correspondent to the home town paper, and a
series of letters to the Galesburg *Evening Mail* followed in due
course. Soldiering was so much to his taste that after returning home
he made application for entry to the United States Military Academy
and for a period of two weeks, before the limits of his eighth grade
education were made apparent, was a classmate of Douglas Mac-
Arthur and Ulysses Grant III. Came the judgment upon him however, and he returned to Galesburg in September.

He immediately entered Lombard College, which was offering a
year's tuition to returned veterans, and here began his literary work
in earnest. During the Lombard years, 1898 to 1902, Sandburg was
an intimate of Professor Philip Green Wright and, in turn, a member
of a small group of students who called themselves the poor writers'
club and met at Wright's house on Sunday afternoons. Sandburg's
work, turned instinctively toward poetry, was first given its character by the tutorship of Wright and the student group. It took its
original character, in a word, from the same sort of native influences
which had provided its first impetus and which were to govern it
throughout its course. But Sandburg's exposure to writing at Lombard was not wholly confined to belles lettres. He was a paragrapher
for the student paper, serving for a time as its editor also, and became
editor of his class year book in 1902.

His first volume of verses, published in 1904 under the auspices
of Wright, marked clearly enough the poetic direction which he
followed throughout his career. This was, first of all, romantic—the
identification of vision-making with poetry. The title of his book,

In Reckless Ecstasy, was taken unabashedly from a sentence of Marie Corelli's, "Ideas which cannot be stated in direct words may be brought home by reckless ecstasies of thought," and this sort of poetic commitment, one which exceeded by definition the possibilities of thought and language, determined both the strength and the weakness of all Sandburg's verse. There was also, even in this intense romanticism, an element of the imaginative populism which was to grow larger and more dominant as time passed.

> *For the hovels shall pass and the shackles*
>   *shall drop,*
> *The Gods shall tumble and the systems fall,*
> *And the things they will make with their loves*
>   *at stake*
> *Shall be for the gladness of each and all.*[15]

And if these halting anapests bespoke the impact of Kipling on the young poet, his work included also some examples of free verse, which might well have been imitated from Whitman, to suggest his later development.

Like Masters, who had also been a student in Galesburg, though some ten years earlier and at Knox rather than Lombard College, Sandburg indicated no perception of any poetic possibilities other than the romantic one. It, along with Whitman, Kipling, and Marie Corelli, constituted the living classics: to be a poet was to be romantic, to adopt an attitude before anything else. In this loose jointed and idealistic view, poetry was a thing to be poured out of persons who had it naturally within them, and needed only a paper to spill itself onto. To the unliterate but aspiring writer, Romanticism gave an image of his calling, one which, through its emphasis upon self, promised identity to his otherwise nondescript person.

The similarities between Sandburg's and Anderson's course had been close to this point, but now in Sandburg's early and wholesale commitment to the romantic vision rather than the ambiguities of mixed loyalties and aims lay a decisive difference between them. The poet was to make his affirmation from the beginning and hold to it throughout his career. Where Anderson's fulfillment came as a harmonizing of contradictions, Sandburg's followed rather as a steadily developing grasp of the nature and possibilities of his art. He had, to be sure, elements in his experience which needed fusing before they could assume poetic status. But the solvent of a native midwestern romanticism was to prove sufficient for all his later literary activities as poet, biographer, troubadour, writer of children's tales, and historian, and to make consistent with them his non-literary labors as Socialist, reporter and researcher.

At Lombard College Sandburg read much in Universalist theology and, he said, "got perfect in all the arguments that God is good and will not send us to hell."[16] The interest was a congruent one. Sandburg left school without a degree because of a new rise in his wanderlust and once again took to the road, this time as a salesman of stereopticon views, gratifying his taste for the broadest kind of experience. It is difficult to imagine how deeply he felt his Universalism, but surely this generous religious scheme, comprehensive in its act of acceptance if, perhaps, imperceptive of the real difficulties with which it professed to deal, was exactly the kind congruent with Sandburg's character and interests. He, like Whitman, aspired to be universal, to know and to accept the fullest possible canvas of thoughts and experiences. His wanderings were interrupted from time to time by itinerant newspaper work, but casual jobs were only a way of earning a living while he pursued his developing career as experiencer and writer. Sandburg, perhaps, would not have argued with Ulysses that he was a part of all he had met, but he could have agreed that he was a man in pursuit of a double fulfillment, that of the visionary and the real, in the single harmony which Universalism summed up for him.

In 1907 he settled in Chicago as an associate editor of *The Lyceumite*, the magazine of the International Lyceum and Chautauqua Association. The organization which he had joined descended in a straight line from the New England Lyceum of the early century and so continued in its way that optimistic and liberal effort toward moral uplift and the establishment of vision as an essential. He addressed the convention of the association in 1908 on Whitman and made

Lyceum dates speaking on the same subject. How far his poetry had progressed by this time is not known, but with these explicit references to Whitman one can guess that its final ingredient, a commitment to the free verse as well as the free thought and sympathy of the older poet, was completed.

During 1907 or 1908 Sandburg met Winfield R. Gaylord, a state organizer for the Social Democratic party, and in the latter year he became a professional party worker. This connection, which he maintained until his second move to Chicago in 1912, represented a sudden but thorough focusing of all his earlier interests. The hitherto diffused lines of his life were drawn together in what was far more a vocation than a job. He had his living, in part, from the Socialists, he took his wife, Lillian Steichen, from their ranks in 1908, and he performed the work they gave him to do. As he had become part of a dedicated and idealistic group, these qualities could not help but affect his own life at its roots.

The Socialism he espoused was, among members of the left generally, regarded as a conservative variety. It had been born in 1897 out of a union between the remnants of Eugene Debs' American Railway Union and the Cooperative Commonwealth and was headed by Debs and the Milwaukee Socialist leader, Victor Berger—the only man ever to be elected to Congress by any Socialist group. Much of its strength lay in the Chicago and Milwaukee areas. In 1910 it elected Emil Seidel as mayor of Milwaukee, and during his term, 1910 to 1912, Sandburg served as his private secretary. Derived largely from European and especially German groups in the Midwest and representing a continuation in the United States of German Social Democracy, it was gradualist in its methods, committed to parliamentary means (the same Floyd Dell had revolted against in Davenport) and was sufficiently intellectualized and liberalized to include many a populist romantic of Sandburg's own kind. Its German origins were those of Marx, but it was far from strict in its application of them and included much of the diffused form of German romanticism in its regard for individual human beings, their nature and needs. It was, in a word, a wholly natural place for Sandburg to arrive. As it knew the proletariat, recognized something of the substantial and real conditions of economic life, and spoke especially for the victims of that life like those Sandburg had known at first hand, it was far more congruent with his natural self than the vaguely idealistic Lyceum organization he had worked for earlier. At the same time it was not possessed of the narrow and violent dogmatisms which, in other radical groups, left Sandburg untouched. Many of its tenets appeared directly in his work, and the urban interests of *Chicago Poems* and *Smoke and Steel* were largely defined by its force. Its thought cast a shaping light over all his early work.

Concurrently with Sandburg's Socialist activities began also his regular work as a newspaper writer which was to continue without major interruption until 1932. Its general tone echoed his political interests. Indeed, two of the papers for which he worked were avowedly Socialist, and his writing for the others was apt to be on subjects connected with labor and industry. After moving to Chicago in 1912 he had an odd lot of alliances including E. W. Scripps' *Day Book*, an early experiment in tabloid journalism without advertising, a business efficiency paper called *System*, and the *National Hardware Journal*. But in 1918 he made a connection with the *Daily News* which lasted until 1932 and which confirmed his place in the Chicago renaissance.

His first introduction to that force had come in 1914 with *Poetry's* publication of his "Chicago Poems," which was also his first appearance in a major literary magazine. He had mailed a group of his verses headed by the famous "Chicago," to the *Poetry* office where they were opened by Harriet Monroe's assistant, Alice Henderson, and thence passed on to the editor herself. For Harriet the poem's first impression was that of shock, but she recovered in time to give the group the lead position in her March issue projecting Sandburg thus into the midst of the Chicago renaissance. He was from his first appearance a cynosure of admiration and, thanks to his deliberate and inward personal manner, of some awe. Edgar Lee Masters wrote excitedly to Dreiser in April, "Next Monday I am going for a tramp to the sand dunes with a Swede bard. He is a new find and I think has the right fire."[17] And Sandburg's importance to the Liberation, if it needed confirming, was sealed by an attack from the *Dial* upon him and upon *Poetry* in its subsequent issue. "We have always sympathized with Ruskin," wrote its critic, "for the splenetic words about Whistler that were the occasion of the famous suit for libel, and we think that such an effusion as the one now under consideration is nothing less than an impudent affront to the poetry-loving public."[18] By this last phrase the *Dial* perhaps had in mind such a public as that constituted by The Little Room. If so, its conclusions were correct. "Chicago" was an act of war.

By 1916 Sandburg had accumulated enough verse to make a volume, *Chicago Poems*, and again it was Alice Corbin Henderson who served as mediatrix. She interested Alfred Harcourt, then representing Henry Holt and Co., in Sandburg, and Harcourt in turn persuaded his firm to take on publication of the book. What *Chicago Poems* achieved was of a double kind, success and failure, but the two poles were not absolute in particular poems. These latter ranged over every possible level of the romantic spectrum, from the concreteness of imagism to avowedly cosmic affirmations without vestige of concreteness. Such a range was to be characteristic of Sandburg's whole poetic output, and an analysis of *Chicago Poems*, consequently, would serve to point out some of the differing kinds and levels in his seemingly undifferentiated achievement. Despite this range, however, *Chicago Poems* held firmly to two elements and strove continually to make a harmony of them.

He was later to fashion a series of definitions for poetry, most famous among which was his image of the art as a fusion of hyacinths and biscuits. Here indeed lay figures for two extremes, the two elements out of which Sandburg's verse was compounded. On the one hand, ineffable beauty, and on the other, mundane reality. It was the tension between these romantic and realistic elements, the pattern of their relationship like those of Whitman's before him, out of which Sandburg created his verse.

In all of his poetry a single effort was represented—that of refounding his derived romanticism, its vision and imaginative ecstasy upon the common realities of a labor and populist experience. This latter remained for him a fixed element, one he would not place in perspective and seemingly could not alter. It was a datum which the poet by his own temperament and experience was fastened to. Consequently, the only mobile or adaptable part of his work lay in its other half—the essentially rhetorical and willful exercise of fancy to embellish and stage impressively his obdurate poetic matter. Like the other midwesterners, Sandburg was a poet of subject. Where his subject was in itself arresting, moving, and satisfying, his poem likewise could achieve these qualities. "Chicago," thus, was a striking and shocking poem because its subject, highlighted by Sandburg's rhetoric, was striking and shocking. "Who Am I?" on the other hand, remained as diffuse and pointless as the generality itself of truth unrealized.

> My head knocks against the stars.
> My feet are on the hilltops.
> My finger tips are in the valleys and shores
>   of universal life.
> Down in the sounding foam of primal things
>   I reach
> My hands and play with pebbles of destiny.
> I have been to hell and back many times.
> I know all about heaven, for I have talked with God.
> I dabble in the blood and guts of the terrible.
> I know the passionate seizure of beauty
> And the marvelous rebellion of man at all signs
>   reading, "Keep Off."
> My name is Truth, and I am the most elusive
>   captive in the universe.[17a]

His verse as a rule functioned without interpenetration of form and content; his imagination too often lacked deep wit or sympathy—or any of those esemplastic qualities which Coleridge found to be its essential faculties. As a result, the romanticism of his poetry was refounded upon the common stuff of midwestern life only by an act of will and in an essentially mechanical fashion.

With no real bond between his romantic imagination and the substance of his poetry, Sandburg was in constant danger of breaking loose, of driving toward an exhilarating but vacuous empyrean of the general assertion and the amorphous feeling, of leaving his subject inert, without benefit of insight or handling. Such a separating out was, indeed, common in his work and perhaps could have been avoided apart from accident only by his reliance upon a sufficiently engrossing subject, one which by itself was able to achieve a hold on the reader's imagination and so speak with some authority to it, while the poet simultaneously confined his own fancy to clean-cut presentational modes of action. He did, occasionally, perform this double act, as in *The People, Yes* of 1936. But even here Sandburg's vision, so early given color by an ideal hostility to middle-class ways, still drew upon general concepts and sympathies. His faith in the people came off in the poem as an act of romantic fancy instead of being an affirmation generated out of the stuff of the poem itself and dissolved in the end in a vague though earnestly affirmed hope.

So long as he hewed to essential poetry, his work had life and validity. Where real people at their poetic best were allowed to speak for themselves they achieved Sandburg's poetry for him. But as soon as the poet tried to include them in his own vision the lines of his picture snapped and the reader was left with clouds which floated, however serenely, far above the landscape they purported to hold. A Kansas farmer could speak a shrewd truth.

> Drove up a newcomer in a covered wagon: "What kind of folks live around Here?" "Well, stranger, what kind of folks was there in the country you come from?" "Well, they was mostly a lowdown, lying, thieving, gossiping, backbiting lot of people." "Well, I guess, stranger, that's about the kind of folks you'll find around here."

But when the poet ceased to report and began to poetize, his farmer vanished with all else into an amorphous opalescence.

> The people know the salt of the sea
> and the strength of the winds
> lashing the corners of the earth.
> The people take the earth
> as a tomb of rest and a cradle of hope.

Who else speaks for the Family of Man?
They are in tune and step
with constellations of universal law.

The people is a polychrome,
a spectrum and a prism
held in a moving monolith,
a console organ of changing themes,
a clavilux of color poems
wherein the sea offers fog
and the fog moves off in rain
and the Labrador sunset shortens
to a nocturne of clear stars
serene over the shot spray
of northern lights

The steel mill sky is alive.
The fire breaks white and zigzag
shot on a gun-metal gloaming.
Man is a long time coming.
Man will yet win.
Brother may yet line up with brother.

A subject sufficiently commanding to hold the poet's imagination, and sufficiently friable to allow working and cultivation, seemed clearly to be needed. This came only when Sandburg began serious work on his biography of Lincoln. Here, beginning in 1919, he struck what was for him the natural subject. Lincoln, the native midwesterner, epitome of the people, who in his own life had begun as a raw frontier boy, had known hard labor, kept store, studied to raise himself, wrestled and played, piloted river boats, suffered racking sorrow, practiced law in an intimate and homely community, immersed himself in its politics, and taken on character ultimately by a native streak of high poetry compounded of wit and tragedy in often intense ironies of experience, such a man was in concrete fact the poetry Sandburg had for years been trying to write. He was popular substance, and myth at once. The hitherto discrete elements of Sandburg's verse came together in a subject who, by careful and sympathetic reporting, could speak for himself the word which the poet had never been able to pronounce finally—that word which was the accumulated poetry of midwestern American life.

If Sandburg's knowledge of smoke and steel had seemingly little part in Lincoln's life, all the forces which were to produce them were present, for Lincoln was a Whig and a Republican who began his political career opposing Jackson and the Democrats, supporting a national bank and internal improvements in accord with the dictates of his party leader, Henry Clay. He was the embodiment, as President, of the current in American life which found its impetus in the northern cities and directed itself cruelly and destructively against both the agrarian West and the corrupt, aristocratic South. His administrators, however divided their loyalties, were Seward, Chase, and Stanton, and his battle was won by that behemoth of unenlightened force, Ulysses Grant. Lincoln was the President who fought the Civil War to preserve the Union—and to deliver it into the hands of the pillaging and gutting capitalism of the seventies, eighties, and nineties against which Sandburg himself stood in angry opposition. But Lincoln was also the scrupulous and committed democrat, the man of the people whose origins were wholly himself, or he them, raised to a poignant degree of compassion, perspicuity, and reality. His task lay always with the next step ahead; his wisdom was most often that shrewdness about doing what had to be done which was also the common wisdom of his people. "If I could save the Union without freeing any slaves, I would do it; and if I could save it by freeing some and leaving others alone, I would also do that." But to his task and to his wisdom he gave himself in utmost measure and so achieved for the people from whom he sprang and for himself a dignity which could never have been theirs or his in mere success. Lincoln's life was the mixed stuff of Sandburg's verse, but his compassion, wit, eloquence, devotion, and suffering gave a heightening and point to that life which turned it into poetry and so brought its uncritical but comprehending biographer into high literary distinction.

Sandburg's *Lincoln* was the fulfillment of a singularly homogeneous intellectual and emotional development which cast meaning upon the poems by revealing at last what they had been driving at, by

completing the task they had begun. And the completion, furthermore, was made by the same talents which had created the poetry—
those of an articulate devotion to the common but commanding and
moving elements in midwestern life and of a romantic imagination
which stood ready to transmute those elements into high significance.
In the case of Lincoln that significance could become one of
true and tragic insight rather than willful rhetoric which it had been
too often and too centrally in the poems; the poetry of the *Lincoln*,
consequently, could have both substance and stature. Lincoln was a
man for anecdote and vision both; he was at once hyacinth and bis-
cuit. They were of his nature inextricably, and they made of him
Carl Sandburg's greatest poem.

Sandburg's work on the six volume biography formed the greatest
part of his creative life from 1919 until the publication of *The War
Years* in 1939. Like Masters' *Spoon River* and Anderson's *Winesburg,
Ohio*, the work stood as the cumulated result of its author's long training in the school of native dissent and liberated affirmation. He was
not to pass this point. During his Chicago years, from his joining of the
Daily News in 1918 until his move to Harbert, Michigan, in 1932,
Sandburg was to be in the midst of Chicago's literary life. His colleagues in the *News* office included Vincent Starrett and Ben Hecht,
Henry B. Sell and Harry Hansen among others. But he showed little
if any effect from these more exotic blooms of the Liberation. His
nearest affinity was Lloyd Lewis, whose interest in midwestern history
may well have been a contributing factor in the formation of the
Lincoln, and with whom he held himself at something of a distance
from the more esoterically literary members of the *News* group. His
Imagist period lay behind him and his growing absorption with
Lincoln ahead. The Liberation had done its work for him by recognizing him as a poet and so helping him to recognize himself as a
poet. This had been the office of *Poetry's* acclaim and continued to
be the office of the *Daily News'* liberal attitude toward his staff duties.
To the extent that he had become a free and personal agent, the
Liberation had made him its greatest gift, that of the freed and creative personality itself.

After 1932 he retired from regular journalistic work, and his time
since then has been spent first on his Michigan farm and later in

North Carolina with frequent and long visits to Chicago. His *Lincoln*, by 1941, had sold nearly half a million copies. His reputation as an American folk-singer and folk-song collector spread, and his career issued into a fulfilled maturity. Sandburg's novel, *Remembrance Rock*, published in 1948, added little to his reputation and detracted little. It was essentially a return from the triumph of the *Lincoln* to the mixed achievement of the poetry. If its great length can be accepted, its fault again lay in the author's failure to harmonize fact and vision. Where it was history, *Remembrance Rock* spoke with some authenticity and power, but where it was fiction the failure was the familiar one of vaporousness, of good visionary intentions doing duty for imagined reality. But the author had sufficiently established the validity of his method, imagination, and attitude in his twenty-year labor on the *Lincoln*. It, taken alone, affirmed his life and literary way.

III

Vachel Lindsay's connection with Chicago and with the forces of the Liberation was perhaps more tenuous and more accidental than that of any other important figure of the renaissance. His surest affirmation had been made at the outset of his career, long before his acquaintance with the Chicago group, but the city was eventually to have an importance for him both striking and tragic which brought him within its fold. He learned little from Chicago, and what he did learn worked perhaps more to his undoing than his making. Equally, the Chicago of the Liberation contributed only a little to his own break from middle-western conventionality. This he had achieved largely without its help by the time he came to know the renaissance. But the Liberation did give him Harriet Monroe and *Poetry* and, by their office, his reputation. The process began with the publication of "General William Booth Enters Into Heaven" in *Poetry* of January, 1913, and continued with the appearance of "The Santa Fe Trail," "The Congo," "The Chinese Nightingale," and the rest of the dozen or so poems upon which Lindsay's reputation has largely rested. All of these were much of a type—self-consciously abandoned and broad in their effect with a corresponding light-headed quality. Though they led their author to a great popularity as reciter of his own works, they also sickened him with repetition and convinced him that they had perverted his true imaginative destiny. In Lindsay's own terms, these poems which brought so much of fame and fatigue were "Vaudevilles," perhaps an appropriate gift for Chicago to have bestowed.

Springfield, rather than Chicago, was his spiritual home and, for much of his life, his physical home as well. He had been born in 1879 and, after a few years of private schooling, entered a local grammar school in 1890. In 1893 he passed into the Springfield High School and there, under the teaching of Susan Wilcox, head of the English department, attempted his first disciplined writing of verse. Like both Masters and Sandburg, Lindsay was thus brought to his first serious literary work by professional academics. After graduation in 1896 he entered Hiram College in Ohio, a school of the Disciples of Christ, of which denomination his family, and Lindsay himself, were ardent members and so began his first extended period away from Springfield. He left Hiram without a degree in 1900 for the Chicago Art Institute. Here, in great poverty but with a spirit of high dedication, he became an art student in order to prepare for a Christ-like mission of redemption which was to begin on January 1, 1901. Lindsay had felt this vocation while at Hiram, and, though it was to be much modified and altered, it remained an important part of his understanding of himself and his work throughout his life. He proceeded to New York in 1905, and there for three years, interrupted by his first and second vagabonding expeditions and a trip to Europe with his parents, he continued as an art student, though with little encouragement from his teachers, and as a poet.

In 1909 he returned to Springfield to live beginning officially his career as a crusader and reformer. His first book of poems, *The Tramp's Excuse*, was published privately in that year along with the five *War Bulletins* and *The Sangamon County Peace Advocate*. In 1910 came *The Village Magazine*. In the spring of 1912 he set out on his third walking tour, this time to the far West, and, late in the year after his return, heard that "General Booth" had been accepted by *Poetry*. His Springfield residence, though much broken, continued until 1922 when he taught for two years at Gulf Park College in Mississippi, and it was not resumed until 1927. Once re-established in Springfield, however, Lindsay continued there until his death in 1931.

His family had most of its roots in southern life, though not of the aristocratic variety: rather a tradition of pioneers and farmers, of Democratic politics, plain living, and high thinking. His father, a hawk faced, dark-bearded man, filled a traditional role as town physician. His mother, he recounted, was an imaginative and emotional woman whose tenderness for her son included the preservation of his curls uncut long into his school days. She was a writer, a creator of pageants for church occasions, and a woman of infinite care and anxiety for her children. Lindsay's life, in some aspects a prolonged and irresponsible adolescence, must in part be accounted for by his mother's partiality and willingness to indulge him. In 1917, the year before his father's death, he wrote to Harriet Monroe, "My parents and I are really a triumvirate, and you and I will be much better acquainted after you know them."[19] This was in his thirty-eighth year.

But most important was the devout Campbellite Christianity which ruled his family's life. Lindsay, a docile rather than a rebellious child, was received into the church (by immersion according to Campbell's teaching) at the age of eleven and marked the occasion by the composition of a poem, his earliest preserved work, whose solemn literalness bespoke well enough the feelings which moved the child and which, mutatis mutandis, continued to move the man.. The verse concluded,

> You may not live through the coming night,
> Why do you waver this battle to fight?
> The Master calls you with pitying voice
> You'll choose Heaven, or Hell, which is your
> choice?
>
> If you obey his voice and follow him today,
> Then with a joyful heart he will say:
> Come blessed servant come to me,
> Inherit the kingdom prepared for thee.

That these lines were no mere formality urged upon the young catechumen by his pious parents may be argued from his earliest private records in a series of notebooks he kept while at Hiram College. Each of these was headed, "This book belongs to Christ."

The theology which formed Lindsay was one of the several American additions to Christian sectarianism. Alexander Campbell's original effort, inherited in large part from his father, Thomas Campbell, had been to restore Christian unity by accepting only the New Testament as binding upon the conscience and rejecting all creeds, Protestant and Catholic alike, together with the theology developed from those creeds or any other source, as man-made additions to Holy Gospel. The result, however, was to found a new denomination, The Disciples of Christ, or The Christians. This group was not, as has been claimed in an effort to explain Lindsay's apocalyptic poetry, emotional or ecstatic in its faith. Indeed, it had a standing quarrel with Methodism on just these grounds. The Disciples were sober, firm, given to a common-sense logic, and traditional in ways where they felt the Bible sanctified tradition. Above all, they were devoted to their faith and staunch in its behalf.

On two grounds, however, Campbell may have given Lindsay material for his own visionary religion. He had pictured the earth as the field of struggle between good and evil forces, divided and centered according to a mystical geography. The Kingdom had been instituted by the Holy Spirit at Pentecost, and, since its inception, had been the citadel of a holy war in which all Christians were soldiers. "Their expenses, their rations, are allowed, the arms and munitions of war are supplied them from the magazines in Mount Zion, the stronghold and fortress of the kingdom; where the King, the heads of departments, and all of the legion of angels are resident."[20] This sense of perpetual crusade dominated Lindsay's thought as did also Campbell's vigorous distrust of earthly powers. "Christians have nothing to expect from them except liberty of conscience and protection from violence, while leading peaceable and quiet lives, in all godliness and beauty, till Jesus take to himself his great power, and hurl all those potentates from their thrones and make his cause triumphant—a consummation devoutly to be wished, and which cannot now be regarded as far distant."[21]

Lindsay also inherited from Campbell his strongly developed

awareness of prophecy, of the importance of the Spirit to religion. Like St. Paul, Campbell put prophets next to Apostles in rank, included angels as active administrators of divine affairs, and made the Holy Spirit the activating and vitalizing force of the universe. Though Lindsay lost any specific theological sense of the Spirit as sanctifier, he retained a strong sense of prophetic inspiration.

Lindsay's Hiram notebooks suggested better than anything else the deep penetration of his consciousness by Campbell's teaching. Though he made extensive notes of his reading, especially in Poe and Blake, whom he was to echo frequently in the poetry of his pre-Chicago years, there was more extensive reference to a basic religious vocation—that of establishing the Christian gospel as a vitalizing source of American life. He had as early as his undergraduate days embarked upon the making of a testimony which was to be almost a personal revelation itself and combine self-assertion and religious conviction in a tangled but highly invigorating whole. At the time of his leaving Hiram, Lindsay summarized his nature and basic convictions in its terms.

> My first essays of ten or eleven show I am for generalization rather than a power for doing it accurately. 2, A tendency to fly off at many tangents of thought that confuses the discussion and makes paragraphs impossible. 3, A sense of climax, and strong sense of dogmatic epigram (labor rules the world). 4, A sense that the world is a balanced bundle of laws. 5, A sense of the individuality and strong personal oversight of the Creator. 6, A sense that the laws of the soul of man and the soul of God, and the laws of the roots of the trees are all in common. 7, A sense of the principle of disappointment, decay as a part of the natural order, not to be feared but to be understood. 8, A sense that all honest work ought to be respected. 9, A sense that the only social tie, and the only social motive between citizen and citizen is to be respected. God has provided others. But this is all I have recorded here. 10, Comparison of city and country. A sense that man is fundamentally educated by the phenomena of nature, and that man is the divinely appointed ruler of nature throughout the universe. 11, A fundamental and disastrous irreverence for the paraphernalia of this world, the wrappings and

mannerisms. 12, A reverence for wholesale ruggedness. 13, A mistaken tendency to see indifference in the souls of men, consequent upon their environment and deeds. Now all above I must never expect to understand and get away from. They are a part of me, the essential self. Any of these old opinions I may hope well to defend, and may never feel lost and doctrineless. I can defend them all with a whole heart, and a perfect faith, which will keep me strong.[22]

Lindsay's particular revolt against the village, consummated here in an assertion of self, grew not from atheism or other non-conformity, but, paradoxically, from the very tenets which the village orthodoxy professed but which in practice it so largely ignored. Indeed, the heart of Lindsay's whole prophetic endeavor lay in an intense though often misdirected and wasted effort to awaken the village to the glory which he felt was inherent in its own religious and democratic faith. He came not to add anything to Springfield nor to destroy. He wished rather to awaken and manifest its own soul to itself in a glorious epiphany created by a descent of the Spirit upon the whole world. His artistic endeavors, his reading, his writing, his speaking, his tramping, and even his prolonged bachelorhood—all these were parts of a whole and dedicated career. He did not describe himself as an artist or poet primarily but as a visionary and a prophet. The climax of his career in his own eyes was not "General Booth," but rather the jumbled revelation contained in *The Golden Book of Springfield.*

Lindsay summed up his matured creed in 1912 in "The Gospel of Beauty," written for the pamphlet which he was distributing during his western tour, and therein made his central position plain.

The things most worth while are one's own hearth and neighborhood. We should make our own home and neighborhood the most democratic, the most beautiful and the holiest in the world. The children now growing up should become devout gardeners or architects or park architects or teachers of dancing in the Greek spirit or musicians or novelists or poets or story writers or craftsmen or wood carvers or dramatists or actors or singers. They should find

*their talent and nurse it industriously. They should believe
in every possible application to art-theory of the thoughts of
the Declaration of Independence and Lincoln's Gettysburg
Address. They should, if led by the spirit, wander over the
whole nation in search of democratic beauty with their
hearts at the same time filled to overflowing with the right-
eousness of God.*[23]

Lindsay's people had long known and preached the beauty of holiness; now Lindsay, without at all abandoning that earlier text, added
to it the holiness of beauty.

But his vision ran far outside the strict limits of Christian orthodoxy
to fasten during his New York years, upon the great image of his
life—his "Map of the Universe," which he printed as a frontispiece
to his collected poems. This, he claimed, had come to him in a series
of visions, revelations, not only to give him images for his poetry,
but also to set the stage upon which the great cosmic drama was to
be worked out. The similarity in function of Lindsay's vision to
Yeats' was striking. Both poets found in their revelations a resource
for their art, and also a somewhat ambiguously received but fascinating suggestion of ultimate reality. Lindsay's cosmography provided
him with the setting in which the fall had taken place and upon
which redemption was to be visited. Its chief features, the thrones
and jungles of heaven, the mystical amaranth vine, the harp of
Lucifer, the palace of Eve, the tree of the laughing bells, the boats
of the prophets, the butterfly and the spider, and the caves of
Thule all had place and significance for him and gave place and
significance to much of his poetry. There was one disadvantage for
the poet however. The action in this theater either had taken place
in the past or was to come in the future. For the present, the
universe could only groan in travail, yearning for its great day.

> *Ah, in the night, all music haunts us here. . . .*
> *Is it for naught high Heaven cracks and yawns*
> *And the tremendous Amaranth descends*
> *Sweet with the glory of ten thousand dawns?*

Does it not mean my God would have me say:—
"Whether you will or no, O city young,
Heaven will bloom like one great flower for you
Flash and loom greatly all your marts among"?

Friends, I will not cease hoping though you weep.
Such things I see, and some of them shall come,
Though now our streets are harsh or ashen-gray,
Friends, that sweet town, that wonder town shall rise.
Naught can delay it. Though it may not be
Just as I dream, it comes at last I know,
With streets like channels of an incense sea.

The amaranth vine was for Lindsay the link between heaven and earth, and its flowers were the flowers of the spirit. Those who on earth chose to eat of these flowers could gain the gift of the spirit, and, like Campbell's Christian soldiers, count themselves as arrayed against the enemy—the sloth, cupidity, and ugliness of human life. Heaven, in Lindsay's map, stood far above earth on a tremendous abutment which supported three mountains, the thrones of God, now deserted. The cliffs of heaven were fringed around at their lower levels by the jungles of heaven, originally the home of the angels. The jungles also lay deserted because the angels had gone out to redeem the stars through a shedding of their angelic blood in crucifixion. This blood, transmuted into wine, would someday be poured out to redeem hell. Meanwhile, it created the purple gleam which drew men to high destinies. Below the sun, which stood at the center of the universe, lay the harp of Lucifer. His beautiful song of sorrow at pain and sin had awakened the angels' compassion and sent them out on their redemptive errand while the memory of that song leaped like a flame from hell to heaven. Spotted at various points on Lindsay's map were the more individually related parts of his cosmos. South and west of the sun was the planet of the laughing bells upon which grew the tree of the laughing bells. The genii of Aladdin's lamp would someday carry the laughing bells to each individual while the lamp itself would be used to re-make creation. The tomb of Lucifer was at the bottom of the map. The palace of Eve, from which all beautiful women came, stood at the east of the sun. North and east was the realm of the Queen of the Bubbles. Beside the amaranth vine, between heaven and earth, was the soul of a butterfly named "Beauty," while below earth, in the direction of outer chaos, stood the soul of a spider, the spirit of evil, whose name was Mammon. Around the thrones of heaven, and throughout the cosmos, were boats in which angels and prophets rode, and there were other boats, one for each soul to ride in when its time came.

Out of this system grew some twenty of Lindsay's most effective verses. Like "The Amaranth," they contained awkward or strained lines, and few of them could be ranked as the highest poetry. But here as nowhere else Lindsay achieved power and authenticity of utterance.

> *I went down into the desert*
> *To meet Elijah—*
> *Arisen from the dead.*
> *I thought to find him in an echoing cave;*
> *For so my dreams had said.*
>
> *I went down into the desert*
> *To meet John the Baptist.*
> *I walked with feet that bled,*
> *Seeking that prophet lean and brown*
>   *and bold.*
> *I spied foul fiends instead.*
>
> *I went down into the desert*
> *To meet my God.*
> *By him be comforted.*
> *I went down into the desert*
> *I went down into the desert*
> *To meet my God.*
> *And I met the devil in red.*
>
> *I went down into the desert*
> *To meet my God.*

O Lord my God, awaken from the dead!
I see you there, your thorn-crown on
    the ground,
I see you there, half-buried in the sand.
I see you there, your white bones glisten-
    ing bare
The carrion birds a-wheeling round your
    head.

"Johnny Appleseed's Hymn To the Sun," too long for full quotation, carried even in its parts the majesty of a genuine mysticism.

Christ the dew in the clod,
    Christ the sap of the trees,
Christ the light in the waterfall,
    Christ the soul of the sun,
Innermost blood of the sun,
    Grant I may touch the fringes
Of the outermost robe of the sun;
    Let me store your rays till my ribs
Carry the breath of lightning,
    Till my lips speak the fullness of thunder
To waken world-weary men:
    Till my whisper engenders lions
Out of the desert weeds.

        .   .   .   .

Give me your strength, O sun!
    Give me your hidden wings,
Till I climb to the holiest place,
    That highest plain of all,

With its glassy shallow pools,
    That desert of level fear
Where three great thrones stand high
    Hewn from three ancient mountains,
Blind thrones of a fair, lost land.
    You have left your thrones for the suns,

Great God, O Trinity,
  With all your marvellous hosts,
Cherubim, Seraphim.
  You blaze in our eyes by day.
They gleam from the stars by night.

Give us your life, O sun!
  Body and blood of Christ,
Wafer of awful fire
  Give us the contrite heart,
Take out the death from us.

Lindsay's map had been completed by 1904, and much of the poetry which grew from it followed before 1909. By that date, however, the poet had already allowed a great deal to creep into his awareness which was to go far toward obfuscating the strength and relative purity of his original vision. 1909 was the year in which Lindsay returned to Springfield from New York, and he had scarcely returned before he began issuing his War Bulletin, both a release and a dissipation of his original interest. There were five numbers appearing through the late summer and fall, the first of which began with a lead article, "Why a War Bulletin?" where the author made plain the great extent to which he had achieved freedom of spirit and the degree to which he would exercise his freedom. By the third number, August 30, 1909, Lindsay was prepared to admit anyone to his ranks who in whatever way had seen the purple gleam of the angels' wine. Scarcely had he worked his cosmographic system into being and brought it to fruitful use than his irretrievably syncretic mind began to make additions to it. His mysticism may well have been of a genuine sort, but it was scarcely enough dedicated to a via negativa to achieve poise. He now declared that as he believed in God so he saw Christianity, Judaism, Buddhism, and all the rest of the world's religions as created equally by God, but each with an exclusive and unique quality. He believed further in all institutions that had resulted from a reading of the word of Christ. He declared himself to be, still, a follower of Alexander Campbell, but he accepted also the Mass, the Virgin Mary, Mary Baker Eddy, Buddah, and

Saint Francis. This almost prodigal hospitality, it must seem, came into being when Lindsay, as the result of his preachings, found the world drawing more and more sharply into divided parties—those who sympathized with him, or those with whom he sympathized, and, against them and him, the hostile ones. "For years," he recorded, "no one would have anything to do with me in Springfield but Willis Spaulding and the Swedenborgians; Frank Bode and the Liberal Democrats; George and Maydie Lee and their daughter Virginia and the Single Taxers; Mr. and Mrs. Duncan MacDonald and the Socialists; Rabbi Tedesche and the Jews; Rachel Hiller and Susan Wilcox and the English teachers; and the Honorable James M. Graham and the Knights of Columbus."[24] Such a list, with certain exceptions, indicated how close Lindsay's prophetic search had brought him to the native roots of the spirit of Liberation known to Masters, Sandburg, and Anderson.

The world of the Liberation in Chicago had become aware of Lindsay's existence as early as 1909 when he wrote to Floyd Dell, "If you can assure the dear public that I have a system, that I am not disorganized or irresponsible, that all I require is patience and a second hearing, I will be deeply grateful."[25] Three years later, still before the appearance of "General Booth," he was again writing Dell, and again concerned with his system, his evangelistic mission, and his faith. "I do not want to do anything prim or on the surface. And I do not think many men of my age—thirty-three years—are so free to serve their cause. I serve no woman but the Virgin Mary, reverence no knight but Galahad, pray to no God but the Christ-Apollo (despite much contrary advice in your publication)."[26] This correspondence suggests that Lindsay had stumbled upon the Chicago movement as a result of reading the *Friday Literary Review*, a publication whose spirit his prophetic soul could embrace even though its content seemed so foreign to his own schemes. At the same time, Harriet Monroe was reading some verses of Lindsay which had appeared in the *Outlook* and was intrigued by Dell's account of "the vagabondish Nicholas" printed in the *Friday Review*. She wrote to Lindsay in 1912 asking to see some of his work, and the sheaf of poems he sent her included "General Booth." This poem,

she felt, was the finest first appearance ever to be made in *Poetry*
and was to be counted among the magazine's permanent triumphs.
It was given a prize in 1914 by the *Poetry* judges, and two years later
Lindsay took another award, the Levinson Prize, for "The Chinese
Nightingale." By its highest Chicago authority, Lindsay had been
declared a triumphant leader of the new poetry.

For the reading public and for Lindsay himself, however, Harriet
Monroe's recognition typed him as the author of vaudeville and
obscured his earlier work beyond notice. Partly, no doubt, the
judgment reflected Harriet Monroe's tendency to date any poet's
career from the time of his first appearance in her magazine. More
important, however, was the immense disparity between the basis
of the Chicago Liberation and of Lindsay's early work. He had been
born, Harriet could note with profound misunderstanding, "into a
rather thin and bloodless strain of Puritan thought." From this, she
felt, he had been snatched in the nick of time so that "his instinct
for beauty" could expand "into richer regions," and such a trunca-
tion of Lindsay's career became the generally accepted version. James
Stephens hailed "The Chinese Nightingale" as one of the two
greatest poems of the period "on the one subject which poetry has
any true concern with, the soul of man and its meaning and destiny."
It was precisely the generalized romantic fervor and the diffuse
romantic excitement of these later poems which intrigued Stephens,
the Chicago literary world, and now Lindsay himself.

There followed, between 1912 and 1917, the bulk of Lindsay's popular work printed in *General William Booth Enters into Heaven and
Other Poems* (1913), *The Congo and Other Poems* (1914), and
The Chinese Nightingale and Other Poems (1917). The question
of their relative quality apart, there can be no doubt that these verses
marked an abrupt change in Lindsay's production. If the aegis of
Blake had been dominant in Lindsay's earlier work, that of Poe,
and of Poe the jingle man, now took ascendance. Some of the
imagery of Lindsay's earlier work was still present, but it had sunk
to an ancillary level, taking its place as little more than a stereotyped
excuse for the sound-effects which were the real substance of his
work. Though apostles come to redeem the Congo from its voo-doo
religion, it was not the evangelistic vision which gave Lindsay's poem

its excitement, rather it was the voo-doo itself and the drumming refrain,

Boomlay, boomlay, boomlay, BOOM.

While Lindsay lamented the seeming misunderstanding of these poems, he never knew that he had in effect created that misunderstanding by reversing the order of importance of the parts of his work —putting an often over-eager and irrelevant trickiness of form ahead of substance.

Of all Lindsay's later poems, only those on political themes avoided such perversion. A number of these, such as "Abraham Lincoln Walks at Midnight," and "The Statue of Old Andrew Jackson," were seemingly excited by the ultra-patriotism of the first world war. At the same time, this vein had been one of long standing with Lindsay and, if his fondness for writing poems about heroic figures be included, it dated back to the years of his residence in New York. Lindsay's politics, however, like his religion, had two aspects, that of deep personal commitment and that of excitement whipped up for his verses. In such poems as "Why I Voted the Socialist Ticket," or "The Eagle That Is Forgotten," he managed a moving and convincing expression of his idealism, though one perhaps too simply acquiescent to rank as very sturdy poetry. But, in general, as his poems moved from earlier to later, they gained only in pretentiousness and superficiality.

It is impossible to blame Harriet Monroe or the Chicago renaissance for this process since it was one which Lindsay himself, for a time, enthusiastically advanced. But in so far as Chicago was responsible for his momentary concept of himself as the author of a triumphantly popular verse, its effect was incongruously to bind and emasculate his work. The success of 1913 precipitated him into his later life of lecturing and performing, and of writing poems which would help him succeed in these purposes. In 1920 he went abroad, and in England especially was lionized by poets and poetasters. The result was to give an immense lift to his reputation in America, and from that year until his death eleven years later he was scarcely ever free from the public demands which had created his excessively public poetry. His audiences asked from him an almost constant repetition of the vaudeville poems in lecture. His later books, however, were received with diminishing interest and regard, and at least one of them, *The Golden Whales of California*, drew strong adverse criticism.

Chicago was the occasion of a burden for Lindsay rather than a liberation. His own freedom had come in a way quite foreign to Chicago when he had seen and briefly accepted the Christian vision of reality. Chicago, in a sense, burdened him with poetic success and he had acquiesced in it. An act of affirmation had been made in his freedom, but his hydropic mind then ran off after half a dozen new streams of interest and so lost hold of its original gift. The vaudeville poems became the more elaborate, and even more hollow poem-games of his late books. He wrote verses for dancing. He adopted new sets of images and subjects for his later work, one growing out of his marriage and his honeymoon in the natural magnificence of Glacier National Park, and the other centering around the opposition in American life of two strains, those of Babbitt and those of "the Mohawk," the latter a symbol of all that was wild, free, and promising of individual fulfillment. Little of this later work achieved distinction. Lindsay's planning and desiring became steadily more frantic while his images and his convictions grew ever wilder and looser. Much of his later verse was outright rant.

> So, Babbitt, your racket is passing away.
> Your sons will be changelings, and burn down
>   your world.
> Fire-eaters, troubadours, conquistadors,
> Your sons will be born refusing your load,
> Thin-skinned scholars, hard-riding men,
> Poets unharnessed, the moon their abode,
> With the statesman's code, the gentleman's
>   code,
> With Jefferson's code, Washington's code,
> With Powhatan's code!
> From your own loins, for your fearful defeat
> The Virginians are coming again.

Equally, Lindsay's personal life after 1920 was one of growing unhappiness. His mother's death in 1922 was literally a staggering blow to her perennial bright child, and, after her death, the family home, following upon a family quarrel, was granted to his sisters. His teaching at Gulf Park College came to an end with an unhappy love affair and a quarrel with the college authorities. In the spring of 1924 he moved to Spokane where, for some five years, he led a curiously disjointed and unsatisfying existence as a local literary and artistic celebrity. He piled up large debts during this period under the impression that he was a guest of the city, an understanding different from that of Spokane's own, and these led to a violent and bitter break with Spokane in 1929. His return to Springfield in that year brought him little peace of mind and led to his groveling suicide, by drinking a bottle of Lysol, in 1931. The only point of relief and comfort during much of this time was his wife, Elizabeth Connor, whom Lindsay had married in 1925. Increasingly, he felt that the world had turned aside from him even as he was bound remorselessly to it by his incessant lecturing, his only means of support. His wife, he felt, was the only human being in existence who had any sympathy for his convictions and aims. In his last days, he lost even this faith. His behavior during the final dark years was so extreme that his sanity was brought into question by those nearest him, though a physician who had been sent for wrote to Harriet Monroe that the most he could say was that Lindsay had a paranoid trend and had become wholly irresponsible concerning the pecuniary affairs of his family.

Lindsay, like Anderson, Sandburg, and Masters, had been born into a native and midwestern romanticism from which he sought a personal and poetic support. His had been defined by Campbell, Swedenborg, Blake, and Poe rather than Shelley and Whitman, and so he became a religious visionary rather than a secular one. Where religion for his three compatriots was the anathema it could scarcely help but be for those awakened by Shelleyan trumpet blasts, religion of an increasingly personal and diffuse sort was the only unifying tie of Lindsay's career. In spite of this difference, however, there was, in a more purely literary way, a great bond sealing together the four midwestern writers. The romanticism which had formed the atmosphere of each was a free-floating affair, coming to them from various directions and divorced largely from the circumstances which had created its original validity. Their task as writers was the control of this detached balloon; each had to spin and wield a net if his impulses were to be caught and held within imaginative limits. In this sense, Masters' penetration of the firm realities of a small-town midwestern life in *Spoon River*, Anderson's discovery of sympathy and craft in the *Winesburg* stories, Sandburg's guidance by the absorbing and tragic personality of Lincoln, and Lindsay's commitment to the mystical vision of his earlier poetry, all these served a common end. They gave substance out of which literature could be made by a romantically freed imagination.

Like Anderson and Sandburg, Lindsay began in quest, and like them he found a personal order of things which seemed to suit his need. He differed from them, however, not only in the nature of what he had found but also in his inability to grow within his vision. Lindsay shared with Masters a collapse of his personal world after a brief fulfillment within it. Anderson and Sandburg were more fortunate. Their acts of affirmation, though far from achieving perfection, stood better the weathering of time and changed circumstances than the abortive realism of *Spoon River* or the religious idealism of Lindsay. All four, however, voiced a common and regional concern, and despite their variety, a literary effort common to their place and time. In terms both of what they sought and of what they found, a romantic view of life and an imaginative medium for romantic literature, they differed only as individual natures and according to individual fortunes.

Impresarios, Authors, Critics, and Columnists

TWO other centers of the Liberation, the theater and the Chicago newspaper world, require treatment before its story can be ended. Neither of these, with such exceptions as have already been noted, produced major writing, but both filled important sectors in the life of liberation and so played a large part in the texture of the Chicago community. Like its predecessor, the later Chicago movement was one in which the fact of a common life took precedence over any other, whether of ideas, literary technique, or professional success, and such social institutions as the theater and the newspaper bore a corresponding weight. Harry Hansen, describing his contemporaries in *Midwest Portraits*, could proceed quite reasonably by an almost exclusive treatment of persons and groups, for these were the elements by which the Liberation most naturally recognized itself. By the same token, as the years drew on into the early twenties, they showed most plainly the signs of its diminishing social and creative force.

I

More than any other part of the Chicago renaissance, the theater was to move in direct continuity from the earlier generation to the later. Not only was the Fine Arts building a center of dramatic effort in both groups, but among the actual plays produced, Shaw, Maeterlinck, and Greek tragedy made up a common staple for the Chicago Little Theatre of 1912 to 1917 as well as for the Little Room productions of the turn of century. As Anna Morgan had created a personal center for the earlier productions, so did Maurice Browne and the Chicago Little Theatre for the later. The two were of different generations and undoubtedly would have found much to differ about. But they also shared much in common. Both found their labors made possible by the patronage of the Chicago gentry, and there was some carryover of personnel from the earlier group to the later. Both thought first in terms of the "art theater," rather than those of the "little theater" of the later twentieth century. For each, a chief aim of theatrical production was "beauty," a concept deeply involved in romantic antecedents and involving an explicit detachment from everyday life to the point where it was easy to run far astray in poeticized playwriting, theatrical whimsy, and shimmering fantasy. For each, Maeterlinck was more than a producable playwright; he was almost a definitive symbol. And the character of his plays marked the tone of both Miss Morgan's and Browne's productions as that of Eugene O'Neill did the work of the later and more fully developed little theater movement. For neither one did the concept of the amateur theater as an expressive community hold a chief place. Their efforts, rather, were like those of the writers of the genteel protest. They were uplifters, raising the taste of their audience to a preconceived level of perfection rather than spokesmen expressing something presumed to be common and indigenous to the intellectual life of their time and place.

At the same time, the Chicago Liberation had grown in part from theatrical roots of its own. In 1900 there had been founded at Jane Addams' Hull House a theater which was to provide a center of vitality for more than one member of the Chicago renaissance. It introduced both Floyd Dell and Francis Hackett to intellectual Chicago. It undertook production of plays by Chicago writers including Oren Taft, Jr., Mary Aldis, Kenneth Goodman, Ben Hecht, and Martyn Johnson, and, in an emphasis upon plays of a sociological cast and a liberated point of view, it spoke directly and forcefully for the chief concern of the early Liberation. Unlike the efforts of either Miss Morgan or Maurice Browne, productions at the Hull House theater had an intellectual rather than an art-theater tone. It favored Galsworthy, Ibsen, Masefield, and St. John Irvine among playwrights. And its work stood always as the dramatic aspect of the enlightened humanitarianism upon which Hull House itself was built. It was the voice of a social and intellectual attitude, as the

Friday Review was to be, rather than the center of a deep artistic commitment for its own sake.

In this way it differed also from a second theatrical enterprise indigenous to the Liberation, the Players' Workshop, located in one of the Fifty seventh street studios and presided over by Elizabeth Bingham. The Workshop, founded in 1916, shared with Hull House a lack of interest in the art-theater preoccupation with poetic drama and impressionistic scenery, but in turn it found a center of its own. That was, appropriately for the Liberation which it voiced, one of experimentation. Its program centered around plays produced by their own authors, who necessarily, were largely of the Chicago group. It confined itself to first performances only, and sought dramatists, stage directors, and players who would be given a chance to prove their ideas working with fellow artists and assistants, mutually interested in testing, under favorable conditions, one another's efforts to secure variety and beauty along new lines. The authors of its plays were almost all familiar to the Chicago group,—Maxwell Bodenheim, William Saphier, Ben Hecht, Kenneth Sawyer, Elisha Cook, and Alice Gerstenberg among others.

But in the full development of the Chicago Little Theatre, despite Browne's own predilection for the art theater, all three of the theatrical types prevalent in Chicago were to combine. During his Chicago years, from 1912 to 1917, Browne achieved the most successful and influential theatrical venture of the entire renaissance. The Little Theatre's membership, at its height, exceeded 400 persons. It occupied comfortable quarters on the fourth floor of the Fine Arts building which included not only its theater, limited to ninety-three spectators, but also meeting rooms, production rooms, and a tea shop which was open each afternoon for Little Theatre members. It produced plays by Euripides, Ibsen, Strindberg, Schnitzler, Wilde, Mrs. Havelock Ellis, Yeats, Shaw, W. W. Gibson, Maurice Baring, Lord Dunsany, and a number of the Chicago playwrights. Its example was influential in the formation of the Provincetown Players, through George Cram Cook's connection with it, and the Washington Square Players, upon their formation, sent representatives to study its methods and achievements. As Browne's later career might suggest, it was more professionalized in its methods and ideals than were the other Chicago ventures, and was conducted with a developed sense of theatrical responsibility, artistic, educational, and commercial. During its life it housed the institution of the theater in Chicago more fully than any other effort.

Browne had been born in Reading, England, in 1881, and after graduating from Cambridge was drawn into the new movement in literature which led him, with Harold Monro, to the founding of the Samurai Press. A little later, while traveling in Florence, he met Ellen Van Volkenburg of Chicago and became engaged to her. Proceeding to Chicago for his wedding, he remained there to found and direct the Little Theatre. Miss Van Volkenburg had a strong interest in the theater which made their combined efforts a happy inevitability. She served as assistant director in the Chicago Little Theatre (while her mother managed the front of house), originated its puppet theater for which she wrote many plays, and was one of its acting company. An early associate of the Brownes was Mary Aldis, who had operated a private theater on the grounds of her home in Lake Forest since 1911 and who provided for them a natural entry into Chicago's upper-class world. The Brownes proceeded to their efforts thus in terms of a substantial foundation and one at first having little in common with such more fully liberated institutions as the Hull House theater. Like both Francis Hackett and Harriet Monroe, they set out upon their task with the interest and backing of Chicago aristocracy in what was essentially a genteel effort. They were neither bohemians nor rebels. Rather, like The Little Room or the Contributors' Club before them, they proposed to make high culture prevail in Chicago.

The two objectives announced for the Little Theatre in its prospectus struck well its original character. The first was "to create and produce a poetic drama,"[1] which, in 1912, meant still a Maeterlinckian and romantic effort different from that of the socially conscious realists or the intellectualism of such as Shaw. The second aim was "to promote free discussion of life and the arts,"[2] which aim, if it veered nearer a great love of the Liberation, still lay well within its more conservative bounds. Plans for the theater included weekly lectures by Mr. Browne on the plays which were under production, or on "cognate subjects,"—a schoolmastering interest wholly consistent with the genteel ideal. Equally so was the proposed establishment of a Little Theatre salon which would be held throughout the season "at the homes of the social committee," and the proposal of a discussion circle, "open to members," which would meet weekly throughout the season at 10:30 A.M. The membership would be limited to 250 persons and would cost $10.00 a year. Those philanthropically inclined or able could become supporting members at $50.00 a year or life members at $100.00 a year. But especially did the original appeal of the theater to genteel-aesthetic circles become apparent in the list of plays first proposed for production. These included works by Euripides, Maeterlinck, Schnitzler, Swinburne, Wilfred Gibson, Browne himself, and a dramatization of a short story by a Chicago writer, Alice Brown. Like Harriet Monroe, Browne sought financial support from the Chicago gentry which was forthcoming in a few large contributions, $500 from Mrs. Chauncey Blair and $1500 from Mrs. Ogden Armour both of whom were numbered among Chicago's Society leaders, and in a sizeable list of contributing and life members among whom were Arthur Aldis, Mrs. Blair, Arthur Davison Ficke, Mrs. Albert Loeb, and Mrs. Julius Rosenwald.

But, again like Harriet Monroe's *Poetry*, the Chicago Little Theatre, once established, drifted almost inevitably toward the Liberation because in that force lay the real creative potency of Chicago. Arrangements were made with *Poetry* to produce the best poetic drama submitted to that magazine each year. This led, particularly, to the production of Cloyd Head's *Grotesques*, a liberated view of human character in free verse. In addition, the Little Theatre inaugurated a series of Sunday evening receptions for guests of honor which were ordinarily capped with a lecture and which brought to Chicago not only such theatrical luminaries as Sara Allgood of the Abbey Theater and John Barrymore, but also Jo Davidson, Theodore Dreiser, Emma Goldman, and John Cooper Powys whose ideas became perhaps the single most important prop of the *Little Review* and the extreme wing of the Liberation. Moreover, a number of the members of the Little Theatre's acting company, like Jane Heap or Lou Wall Moore, were notable for their pronounced individualism.

When, in 1917, Browne drew up a repertory from which he hoped to select that year's productions, the change of tenor in playwrights from those listed in his first prospectus was suggestive. Now it was Synge, Yeats, Shaw, and Paul Claudel, who dominated his list and whose plays the Little Theatre produced most successfully during its five active years.

At its height, the Little Theatre gave to the Liberation a lively and even glamorous center. Its intimate auditorium fenced out the unlovely world of Chicago, while on the stage, in a play one knew must be intellectually and imaginatively challenging, those brave spirits who made up the company chanted, danced, declaimed, and acted in bizarre costumes or even on one occasion in silhouette. Though Browne lacked the funds and the space required for all the very latest devices in staging, his stage manager, C. Raymond Johnson, tolerated no shabby makeshifts or mundane realism. Footlights were banned along with representational scenery, and impressionistic sets and costumes, gauzy, grotesque, or gay as the occasion required, were lit with a mixture of soft colors against the requisite art-theater sky dome. Each Tuesday, Wednesday, and Thursday night during the season, one might find at the Chicago Little Theatre the Chicago Liberation's most fully performed act of aesthetic independence from the claims of the city itself. What otherwise existed only in idea or print, here became fulfilled dramatic reality.

By the season of 1915-1916, the Little Theatre had achieved a considerable scope of operation as was indicated by its proposed budget for that year which totaled $23,440.00. Of this the largest part, $11,576.00 was for salaries, $3750.00 for advertising, and $3200 for rent of the Fine Arts building headquarters. Only $2000.00 was spent directly on production, and the remainder went for individual overhead charges. A separate budget was drawn up for touring expenses, which by this time had also reached a considerable sum. The Theatre had done well during its first years. After the first season, Browne was able to announce that members would no longer be charged for admission to Little Theatre productions, and in the budget of 1915-1916 he was indicating the inadequacy of certain of the allocations. But by the opening of the 1917-1918 season he deemed it advisable to change the financial basis of the theater's operations. Instead of relying on yearly memberships he sought the establishment of a three-year subscription endowment fund which would give a longer term to his financial expectancies and would spread to a broader base the burden of the theatre's cost. The campaign for the endowment fund went well enough so that it finally totaled more than five hundred persons pledged to three-year subscriptions. And, by 1917, the need for such support had become apparent.

Late 1916 and early 1917 were marked by a sharp controversy with Charles Curtis, manager of the Fine Arts building, which culminated in the eviction of the Little Theatre from the building for non-payment of rent, though this was not done without a stormy correspondence involving a number of friends of the theatre. Then, in April, 1917, the United States went to war, and in the consequent excitement, the Little Theatre dropped from the minds of many. Browne faced the situation as squarely as possible. His announcement for 1917 and 1918 declared that the Little Theatre, now to produce its plays only "periodically" at the Central Music Hall, would concentrate upon the repertory it had established over the past five years in order to scrutinize the place of art, of a search for beauty, in times of public crisis. It abandoned much of its elaborate program and submitted itself to the needs of the hour. Such a tactic, however, was not enough to save it. As the season opened, with Shaw's *Candida* and Euripides' *Medea*, some sixty per cent of the subscribers were in default on their pledges, and ninety-five per cent failed to attend the productions. Under such circumstances only one course remained, and on December 7, 1917, the Brownes announced the closing of the Little Theatre. Its books, they announced, had been audited and were open to scrutiny; there would be a pro-rata distribution of any remaining funds; and they begged, with sincere gratitude, to thank all who had supported the venture.

Browne's Little Theatre had been a bright and influential achievement of the Chicago renaissance. In later times its founder could write, "As I look back over seventy years, the 1910-1920 decade in Chicago was incomparably the most mentally exciting decade of my life (not excluding "Journey's End" and all the rest of it in New

York and London)."³ The place of his venture in American theatrical history was a secure one, and its value to the Chicago movement had been attested in many ways. Most obviously, it had provided a full-fledged theater for the Liberation which that movement otherwise would have lacked. Even more pointedly, in its creation of a community of interest, in the liberating and invigorating effect of its plays, and in the special contribution of its lecturers it had been in itself a source of vitality. As the reviews, the writers, and the publishers were contributors to the renaissance, builders of it rather than derivers of its strength, so the Chicago Little Theatre could take a place in their ranks. It too had served as a creative force.

II

Meanwhile, across town at the corner of Madison and Wells, the Chicago *Daily News*, with the advent of Henry Justin Smith as its news editor, was about to stir up a last current in the life of the Liberation. The reasons for a localization of confused but plentiful literary energy in a newspaper staff were several, but they focused most sharply, perhaps, in the person of Smith himself. The *Daily News*, after its original guiding spirit, Melville Stone, departed from Chicago journalism for other enterprises in 1888, had been in the conservative hands of Victor F. Lawson; and during Lawson's tenure, though it continued as a sound newspaper, little was done to hold or to shape the aspiring writers who in one way or another drifted to its staff. Only the editorial encouragement of Charles Dennis provided a partial exception. Smith himself had graduated from the University of Chicago and had become a *News* reporter in 1899. He rose successively to its city editorship in 1901 and to the assistant managing editorship in 1906. Seven years later when he was made news editor he had achieved a position where, as hirer of reporters and directors of news-writing policies, he could exercise his strong taste for a combination of the literary and the journalistic. This was to be manifested throughout his own novels and stories, particularly in *Deadlines*, published in Chicago by Covici-McGee in 1922. Here he did much to shape what was becoming a dominant image of newspaper work—that of a romantic, bohemian, and lumpen-intellectual profession attractive to vagrant and brilliant spirits as providing a place specifically for them in an otherwise stodgy world. One of his own protegés, Ben Hecht, was later to produce with Charles MacArthur the definitive statement of this view in *The Front Page*. For Smith, however, newspaper work was more than farce and melodrama. It was specifically a literary occupation. Its chief functionaries, in his view, were its writers, not the "journalists" of a later and more technological generation, and as such they had, ideally, to be men of letters, however much that concept might be tailored to the demands of daily publication.

As a result, Smith made a practice of hiring and encouraging reportorial aspirants who could make some convincing show of general literacy. The result was an almost unique combination of city room and salon. If the *News* men tended too often to believe that the whole Chicago renaissance had taken place in their office, they at least had the excuse of having contributed to it more variously and as colorfully as any other single group. The whole number of them who had a perceptible share in the Chicago movement ran to nearly twenty. In addition to Smith himself they included the literary editors of the *News* from 1916 to 1926, Henry Blackman Sell and Harry Hansen; an original and omnivorous reader and bookman in Vincent Starrett; the learned, gentle, and witty Keith Preston, classicist and conductor of a popular column, "The Periscope;" Carl Sandburg; Ben Hecht, a wit and ubiquitous man of letters; Tubman K. Hedrick, a former editor of Reedy's *Mirror* and a short story writer; Edgar Ansel and Paul Scott Mowrer, later to be known as news analysts; Wallace Smith, litterateur and illustrator; Lloyd Lewis, historian and essayist; John V. A. Weaver, the colloquial poet; and Richard Atwater and Victor Yarros, readers, writers, and critics. In addition, the *News* was to draw contributions from a large number of the Liberation's figures of both East and West including Mencken, Carl Van Vechten, Burton Rascoe, Sherwood Anderson, Maxwell Bodenheim, and Eunice Tietjens.

It was the *News* men chiefly who supported what was to become perhaps the best known institution of the later renaissance, the Round Table at Schlogl's restaurant, located a short distance down

Wells street from the *News* office itself. The table, a center of good food and of elaborately intellectualistic conversation, had been established by Harry Blackman Sell about the time he became editor of the *News'* first fully developed literary page in 1916. Schlogl's restaurant was expensive and not in the least a bohemian center. Rather it was well known in Chicago as a home of excellent professional cooking of a Germanic and heavily masculine sort. Hasenpfeffer with paprika, baby turkey and *sauce meuniere*, eel in aspic, roast venison, and even, Harry Hansen has recorded, "Owls to order," were staples of its *carte du jour*. As a regular dining place, Schlogl's was beyond the ordinary means of working newspapermen. But once a week, for Saturday lunch and thence for much of the afternoon, Schlogl's could be afforded as a special indulgence gratifying both to the gustatory appetite and that for ambitious and elaborate talk. Schlogl's certainly was something of a forum. Ben Hecht dazzled the company with what almost succeeded in being coruscating tirades against modern civilization and letters. Sherwood Anderson enlarged his reputation as a master story-teller. Carl Sandburg, with a square cap pulled over his eyes and his coat hung over his shoulders, maintained a dogged pursuit of populistic and proletarian values. And Maxwell Bodenheim spoke the same artificially elaborate language that characterized his verse. But Schlogl's was as much, perhaps more, a stage on which one wing of the Liberation could parade to its own considerable satisfaction its enfranchisement and dazzle its visitors who, as time passed, were trotted regularly to Schlogl's to see the Chicago writers in action. Harry Hansen's *Midwest Portraits*, an effort to translate the Schlogl's atmosphere to the printed page, was characterized throughout by a natural but too enormous gratification with the originality, the wit, and the perspicuity of the Schloglites. The Schlogl group as such created little in the life of the Chicago movement. As a show window it had its virtues, but it was hardly more than a striking arrangement of the wares already existing in the Liberation itself and pre-dating the Schlogl luncheons by some six or eight years. The round table was a blossom of the Liberation rather than a seed.

As the variety of interests at Schlogl's would suggest, the center of activity of the *Daily News* men can be defined only with some difficulty. Actually, perhaps, there was no center except that of the diffused force of the Liberation itself. In one direction, Keith Preston's column carried on the News tradition of classically tinged, personal composition inaugurated by Eugene Field. In another direction lay the predominantly historical interests of Lloyd Lewis and of Henry Justin Smith who collaborated, among their other literary activities, on what remains a standard and delightful treatment of their city, *Chicago, The History of Its Reputation*. In a third direction, Carl Sandburg's poetry, as well as his writing for the News itself, reached out toward a visionary, nativistic goal. Yet no one of these interests dominated, nor was there any clearly marked hierarchy of value. The Liberation, granting to each man his own talent and his own interest, could scarcely have had it another way.

In historical perspective, however, two lines of activity among the News men can be singled out as ones of special point for the conduct and development of the Liberation. The first of these was the editorial activity of Sell and Hansen as directors, in sequence, of the *Daily News* book page from 1916 to the point of Hansen's departure for New York in 1926. Writers and books had not been of great editorial interest to the News before 1916. In the years just preceding, there had been occasional columns on "Books of the Day" and some literary gossip of an insignificant sort. But, unlike the *Post*, or even the *Tribune*, in this regard, the News had no visibly established literary staff or practice. When Sell was made literary editor, however, a radically new policy ensued. Each Wednesday a full page was given over to literary matters. Much, of course, was book reviewing, but there were critical and repertorial columns as well, guest contributors, and some creative writing. The tenor of Sell's book page was wholly within the spirit of the Liberation. A large part of it was the work of the various members of the News staff, and only those acceptable to its taste were asked to contribute from outside. Conrad Aiken served for a time as reviewer of poetry. Edgar Lee Masters, Sherwood Anderson, and Eunice Tietjens wrote reviews. And Harriet Monroe, in 1917, inserted a plea for continued support of *Poetry*, which was promptly forthcoming.

The journalistic leadership which the *Friday Literary Review* had given the Liberation during its early years had now shifted largely to the *Daily News*. Under Llewellyn Jones, the *Friday Review* had taken on a conservative tone which occasioned it and its editor considerable disfavor from the livelier and somewhat younger *News* men, and these worked to reestablish the air of fervent iconoclasm and eloquent special pleading which had been the role of the *Review*. No contributor lagged behind Ben Hecht in this regard. He was omnipresent in Sell's page and the constant champion of revolt. "Huysmans," he shouted, "is the antithesis of American culture. . . . His work, from beginning to end a fulgurating panorama of phrases, forms the rarest and most precious pages in the thought of France. To him may all stylists be compared. Verlaine, de Gourmont, Barres, Nietzsche, Louys, Pater. For beside the flame of his strong genius the Salome of Wilde, jeweled phrased courtesan that she is, pales to a shadowy bawd."⁴ And, though Hecht's too newly won exuberance for the decadence was here displayed in full, he could reach out an equal hand to Carl Sandburg or to Sherwood Anderson despite their homespun garments. "Let the mandarins in London and New York unleash the pious yelp of derision. If Sandburg's a kangaroo, I'm a kangerbooster."⁵ Sandburg himself made an occasional appearance, one to plug Reedy's *Mirror*, "a weekly paper I have read every week for thirteen years . . . of St. Louis, Mizzoura;"⁶ to support the Wisconsin Players of Laura Sharry and Zona Gale, "Altogether, the Wisconsin Players sort of belong with middle-west things, along with Sell and his book pages, Reedy and his *Mirror*, Cliff Raymond and his poetic almanac, and H. Monroe and 543 Cass Street,"⁷ or, more often, to review books of social import. Sherwood Anderson, in an article on "Chicago Culture," made a valuable point for the midwestern group. "There is a good deal of danger in too much talk of a distinctive mid-American culture. If we are not careful we shall sink into the vulgarity of taking ourselves as seriously as Germany or Washington Square in New York. It is my own prayer that the day when Chicago has expressed itself may be for a long time put off. May the Lord leave us at least our cow town innocence and naivity."⁸ Carl Van Vechten explained that he had learned to write from John Reed by being told to express himself. "Reading over a letter I had written he said, 'Why are your letters so much better than your journalism? You put yourself into your letters, but you keep yourself out of your published writing;"⁹ And Conrad Aiken, in the kind of hoax so admired by his contemporaries, demolished in a review one of his own volumes of poetry.

Under Hansen, from 1920 to 1926, the *News* book page changed little in essential character. Though it became less parochial in its concerns, added a larged number of writers outside the *News* staff itself, and spread its interests to include a booming of John Maynard Keynes' *Economic Consequences of the Peace*, a New York letter, a spate of favorable writing on Fitzgerald's *This Side of Paradise*, and recognition by John V. A. Weaver of O'Neill's *Beyond The Horizon*, "as near perfect as anything the American drama has produced,"[10] these excursions outside the immediate Chicago orbit, betokened more a change of circumstances than a change of procedure. For the Liberation, which up to 1920 had possessed so fervent a center in Chicago, was now lessening in intensity there. The earliest phase of modern Literary culture was giving way to "the twenties," and "the twenties" were to find centers for its life which were to leave Chicago in the rear rather than the vanguard of change. Hansen's editorship of the *News* book page was important, but it marked the phase during which Chicago became culturally less conscious of its own nature as it grew more conscious of a national movement. Its own status was altering from that of whole to part, or from that of one of several isolated islands of liberation, to just another spot on the continent of the twenties.

In addition to its book page the *Daily News* group was to achieve one other significance in the liberation, that of the distinct change of interest, marked especially in Vincent Starrett and Ben Hecht with the addition of Maxwell Bodenheim, from a basically native effort at liberation to a reliance chiefly upon foreign allies, particularly writers of the European decadence. These had figured somewhat in earlier years, a little *Yellow Book*, a little Maeterlinck, but their influence was to become perhaps the chief distinguishing mark of the later effort. Hecht's admiration for Huysmans has already been noted, but one must add to his enthusiasms the American Stephen Crane, Arthur Machen, Arthur Symons, Theophile Gautier, and Remy de Gourmont. A character in his novel, *Humpty Dumpty*, who greatly resembles his author, thus rearranges his bookcase according to a supposedly matured taste. " 'This Nietzsche set,' " he tells a friend, " 'is rare. There are only a dozen in town. It makes a charming museum piece. Like an obsolete Spanish cannon. How it roared in its youth! Now we admire its ornamental iron work. . . . All the Stephen Crane in [shelf] number one. The first American to write English. . . . Now here we come to the shock troops of mediocrity. That box is full of last year's enchantments. Shaw. Wells. Bennett . . . I liked them all once. Stick Conrad with them. Grocery store classics. I'll sell you the eight Galsworthy volumes for two bits apiece.' "[11] This drastic change of taste away from the revered masters of the early *Friday Review* was not perhaps characteristic of the whole *News* group, but in a vocal and influential sub-group it became almost a ruling passion and marked as clearly as any other internal sign the beginning of the end of the Liberation as Chicago had known it.

The inaugurator of much of this new enthusiasm among the *News* men was the Canadian born Vincent Starrett whose importance in the group was that of pervasive influence. He was possessed of an independent and discerning taste which ranged at will over a field of reading wide enough to suit an omnivorous appetite. The Chicago writers had, perhaps, heard of the Europeans, but it was most often Starrett who put their volumes under the noses of such as Ben Hecht and so precipitated an excitement which was to be some years in running its course. He had been raised in Chicago where he began a newspaper career in 1905 on the *Inter-Ocean*. From 1906 to 1916 he served on the *Daily News* and after the latter date became a free-lance writer until 1942 when he joined the *Tribune* to write a weekly literary column, "Books Alive." Starrett's influence was well summed up by Burton Rascoe. "He was always reading . . . books by authors the reporters had never heard of—Stephen Crane, Ambrose Bierce, W. C. Morrow, Richard Middleton, Hubert Crackanthorpe, John Davidson, Arthur Cosslett Smith, Haldane Macfall, Arthur Machen. . . . It was in this manner that Ben Hecht and Wallace Smith and, I think, Sherwood Anderson first heard of Stephen Crane. . . . And so too they learned of writers like Edgar Saltus and Lafcadio Hearn, and Arthur Symons and Havelock Ellis."[12] Starrett was schoolmaster to a whole wing of the Chicago movement.

He reached a somewhat wider audience with published volumes on

Crane, Bierce, and Arthur Machen, and indeed, during the early twenties, kept the shelves of Covici-McGee filled with an assortment of volumes of essays, stories, and poetry. Starrett's literary energy, however, was as diverse as his tastes and flowed off into half a dozen channels ranging from the mystery yarn to bibliography so that his mark on the Liberation was most plainly seen in other writers. Particularly did his influence reach Ben Hecht whose early works, *Erik Dorn*, *Gargoyles*, and *Fantazius Mallare* would have been unthinkable without the kind of tutelage Starrett provided. There was more significance to Starrett's influence than that of a stray meteor however. The eager interest which his taste, genuine and wholly natural on his part, aroused in other Chicagoans bespoke a growingly apparent failure of power in the original forces of the Liberation. What had begun as a drive toward an aggressive and even too conscious sanity, and against a warping inhibition of the self, had by the time of Starrett, Hecht, Bodenheim, Wallace Smith, and the other late bohemians, turned off once again into the creation of a private and, finally, frenetic world. As in the case of the lyric poets, the Liberation, which had commenced in attack and in construction, was concluding in a retreat. This was not necessarily bad in itself. The positive forces of the Liberation had spread themselves very thin and had managed to catch only a small handful in their nets. The later interest could have been the withdrawal necessary to a new return except that it was to meet an overwhelming counter force, an abandonment of the ideal of liberation altogether, before it had much opportunity to collect itself.

In this last phase, the *Daily News* group played something of the same role as had The Little Room in its time, forming the center and common ground of a widely dispersed number of activities. It was the backbone of the Schlogl luncheon group. Ben Hecht's *Chicago Literary Times* grew, partly by way of secession, from its interests and activities. It formed the mainstay of the bookselling and publishing activities of Pascal Covici, conducted at first in partnership with Billy McGee and later by Covici himself. It gave support to Jack Jones' Dill Pickle Club, and made up the community from which Burton Rascoe, as literary editor of the *Tribune*, was to draw much of his strength. All these activities came into being during the latter part of the Liberation, between 1916 and the early twenties, and all were characterized, though in varying degrees, with the qualities of the later movement as exemplified in Starrett and Hecht. All of them, in melancholy fashion, were to be touched also with the fate of dissolution. They made, as a group, the last concerted try of the Chicago renaissance.

Indeed, the *terminus ad quem* of the whole course of the Chicago renaissance can most clearly be marked by the short lived *Chicago Literary Times*, published and edited by Ben Hecht between March 1, 1923 and May 15, 1924. This fantastic and rambunctious sheet had been started by Hecht as a house organ for Covici-McGee when the latter began as a publishing firm. Hecht had left the *News* in 1923 because of the storm aroused by the censorship for obscenity of his *Fantazius Mallare* and turned immediately to the *Times* for occupation and support. The former involved writing much of the paper's content as well as setting type and printing each issue, but the rewards from this activity were startlingly generous for a bohemian literary organ. Hecht lived from its income, cleared about $300 a week, and toward the end of the *Times'* life was circulating fifteen to seventeen thousand copies. He broke the paper off in 1924 because he felt something had ended in Chicago, and the sardonic joy had too largely gone out of his work.

Hecht had by no means depended entirely on the *Daily News* for his literary apprenticeship. He had begun newspaper work in Chicago in 1910 on the *Journal* and had proceeded to the *News* in 1914. His acquaintance among the city's newspapermen was large and of importance to him. Men whose names otherwise meant little developed his tastes, his ideas, and his talents. While on the *Journal* he had written plays which were accepted by the Players' Workshop leaders, Elizabeth Bingham, Lou Wall Moore and Maxwell Bodenheim. He had staged a number of literary quarrels with Burton Rascoe, one over James Branch Cabell and another over Joyce's *Ulysses*. And his reading had been widened by an older group of Chicago newspapermen, Sherman Duffey, George Wharton, and Ronald Miller, all of whom united in an admiration for H. L. Mencken. Hecht's intellectual position might best be described as nihilistic—possessed of a Menckenian conviction that the leader of every cause was a scoundrel and that principles were mostly pretense. His upbringing had been that of a wandering performer, his tastes were incorrigibly bohemian, and his great desire in life was complete independence.

During his earlier Chicago years he had been in frequent attendance at the 57th Street salon, perpetuated by Margery Currey after Dell's departure for New York, and there made his erratic friendship with Maxwell Bodenheim, with Stanislaus Szukalski, and with Lou Wall Moore.

This extreme bohemian background was immediately reflected in the *Literary Times*. Szukalski, Herman Brosse, Wallace Smith, and George Grosz contributed numerous fantastic illustrations. Hecht and Maxwell Bodenheim, who was the only other regular contributor to the paper, outvied each other in a wild and regularly pointless prose, while the occasional contribution of Vincent Starrett and Lloyd Lewis struck a grotesque note of sanity in an otherwise wholly abandoned enterprise. Each issue was printed on paper of a different color. Magenta, bright yellow, and vivid green were the favorites. The contents were for the most part unimportant. They had no center and practically no purpose except that of shock, in which they succeeded. Maxwell Bodenheim serialized his autobiography, advertised as "merciless and unedited," and stood as the almost unique recipient of the *Times*' praise. Christopher Morley was "a sliding Billy Watson in cap and gown," and Sherwood Anderson, who now bored Hecht, became "the genius of the average man . . . betraying the essential lowbrowness of his temperament."[13] Eliot's *Waste Land*, according to Bodenheim, spoke like "intellect engaging in a drunken commotion, and erudition prattling with the husky candor of a vagrant in the back room of a saloon."[14] Dada, however, promised more. "It is a large kick in the pants for the holy arts. It is the first revolt of artists not against the bourgeoisie nor the ideas of the bourgeoisie, but against art."[15] The dadaism of the *Times* itself burst forth in an indignant headline, поѣздка въ Россію съ Московскимъ „Art" Театромъ,[16] while the paper for issue after issue carried the installments of a lurid inanity called "Cutie, or The Warm Mamma."

The publishing firm which the *Times* had originally represented lagged far behind its house organ in cultivated insanity though it too possessed much color characteristic of the late Chicago renaissance. It was founded as a bookstore by Pascal Covici, an educated and bookish son of Roumanian immigrants, and Billy McGee who was a defrocked Roman Catholic priest, from their own private libraries. From 1921 to 1923 the book shop served as a center for the *News* group plus Burton Rascoe of the *Tribune* and Llewellyn Jones of the *Post*. Covici and McGee began publishing operations in 1923 with Hecht's 1001 *Afternoons in Chicago* and continued with volumes from Starrett, Bodenheim, Richard Aldington, and others. Covici initiated luxury book publishing with an elaborate volume of Stanislaus Szukalski's drawings, a venture upon which he lost $10,000, and proceeded as time drew on to a larger and much less localized list of authors. After 1925 McGee separated from the firm, but Covici maintained his activity until 1928 when, upon the formation of Covici-Friede, he moved to New York. Both his sales and his authors had been taking on an increasingly Eastern preponderance, and the move came as a wholly natural one.

On Tooker Alley, just off North State street, another institution opened about 1916 characteristic of the late renaissance. There had appeared in town a gentleman calling himself Jack Jones who maintained, among other claims, that he had been a safe-cracker. He rented the upper floor of a disused carriage house and there opened The Dill Pickle club which was to carry on operations for some ten years. The Dill Pickle suggested well enough the diminution of creative energy in Chicago. It was mainly bohemian in character and purpose, just intellectual enough to encourage the arty trade. Jones let his hair grow long, donned a flowing black tie, and opened his club to poets willing to read their verse, to the production of original plays, and to lectures upon presumably intellectual subjects. This bohemia, however, was a far cry from Floyd Dell's hopeful and active studio of 1912. It stimulated no significant work, played heavily to the tourists, and relied upon the formula which Jones once confided to Sherwood Anderson. "I give them the high-brow stuff until the crowd begins to grow thin and then I turn on the sex faucet."[17] The occasion of this disclosure was a lecture by an unnamed lady on "Men Who Have Made Love to Me." Hecht wrote some of the plays which were produced, and Bodenheim read his poetry there, but The Dill Pickle accomplished little beyond such temporary triumphs.

A last feature of the later renaissance, Burton Rascoe's book page in the *Tribune*, running from 1917 to 1920, was conducted with considerable liveliness and intelligence. This did not differ materially from Sell's and Hansen's literary department in the *News* except for Rascoe's particular pungent quality of mind. The new authors generally were praised and the issues of the Liberation itself hotly supported. Rascoe's assignment had emerged from the earlier literary editorship of Mrs. Elia Peattie and a column of Fanny Butcher. But where Mrs. Peattie was openly and incisively conservative, and Fanny Butcher somewhat coyly progressive, Rascoe opened full the gates of the *Tribune* to Chicago's renaissance. Under the general editorship of Joseph Medill Patterson the *Tribune* was then willing to recognize progressive causes so that Rascoe was able to bring his views to a paper in fundamental sympathy with them. He reprinted one of Mencken's tributes to Chicago, "Find me a writer who is indubitably an American and who has something new and interesting to say, and who says it with an air, and nine times out of ten I will show you that he has some sort of connection with the abattoir by the lake."[18] He upheld the essential soundness of midwestern writing against the "shrill, imitative, and anti-Semitic"[19] poetry of Pound. He opposed *Ulysses* as too specialized and inward, but greeted *This Side of Paradise* with great enthusiasm. He conducted in the *Tribune* the first full scale publicizing of Branch Cabell, "an artist to whom only one man is comparable . . . Anatole France,"[20] and defended the Chicago poets against the attack of Edgar Jepson which Margaret Anderson had reprinted from *The English Review*. More strictly perhaps than any of his contemporaries, Rascoe argued the cause and forwarded the accomplishments of the early Liberation. His energy and ability, however, were unavailing. Despite argument and exposition, that force seemed more and more clearly to be drawing to an end. Its downward course could not be stayed by any individual however great his zeal, nor altered by whatever amount of devoted enthusiasm.

The Dispersal

THERE can be no doubt that Chicago, by 1926, had been super-seded as an advanced creative center. It was not only dead but also old hat, and the latter charge, in 1926, damaged it perhaps more completely than the first. In that year Harry Hansen moved to New York and the *Herald-Tribune*. Sell had gone to *Harper's Bazaar* in 1920. Rascoe departed in the same year as Sell. The Little Theatre was finished in 1917, the *Little Review* had moved east in 1916, and the *Friday Review* had long been impotent as a liberating force. Only *Poetry* among the institutions of the later renaissance remained and *Poetry*, Samuel Putnam discovered in his article, had always been debilitated by a genteel taint. Herrick had left for the East in 1913 and Garland in 1915. Masters departed in 1919. Anderson in 1920, and Lindsay was little in the city after 1921. Ben Hecht left in 1924. Bodenheim had been much out of Chicago for some years. All the chief personnel of the Liberation, in effect, were gone, and, most significant, no younger figures appeared to take their places.

The reasons for collapse have been much discussed. But the con-clusion most often reached, despite a seeming weight, cannot be taken as sufficient. The Chicago writers did not, as a group, move to New York because of a superiority of publishing centers in that city. The newspapermen, no doubt, found New York jobs more attractive and better paying than their Chicago counterparts, but the Chicago renaissance had not been the exclusive creation of newspapermen. Many of the Chicagoans who moved eastward came to use New York only as a temporary or part-time base. Only three of Chicago's more important novelists or poets, Garland, Masters, and Dell, settled in or near New York. Fuller, Herrick, Sandburg, Anderson, and Lindsay stayed largely apart from New York all their days, having no taste for the city and little need to go there.

The renaissance was not stolen away from Chicago by New York but by two forces largely ideological. First, the intellectual heart of its being and growth, which had been formed by the militant ideas of personal liberation and personal fulfillment, seemed inadequate to younger writers and, in great part, proved finally unsatisfying to the older men. Such nostalgia for the Chicago days as was expressed in Sherwood Anderson's *Memoirs* or Edgar Lee Masters' correspondence did not obviate their authors' movement away from the simple idea of liberation which had been the chief force in their earliest work. As the idea of liberation grew less meaningful to the group, and finally even burdensome, its community grew less organic. The distance from Hackett's or Dell's idealism to Hecht's nihilistic dadaism was precisely the measure of its exhaustion. Second, the intellectual forces of the twenties, though much indebted to the Liberation for a ground-clearing operation, were developing new directions. In 1921, recorded the young Malcolm Cowley, the newer writers were "not gathered in a solid phalanx behind H. L. Mencken to assault our American puritanism. Certainly they are not puritans themselves, but they are willing to leave the battle to their elder cousins and occupy themselves elsewhere. In the same way the controversy about Queen Victoria does not excite them. She died when they were still in bloomers, and the majority of the Browning Clubs died with her. Time has allowed enough perspective for them to praise Tennyson a little and Browning a great deal." New idols, mainly learned of through European guides like Flaubert, the de Gourmont of "The Dissociation of Ideas," Eliot, or Joyce were making a claim upon the rising generation. "Before the War the belief was rapidly gaining ground that literature and the drama began together on that night when Nora first slammed the door of the doll's house." Now, "the youngest writers not only prefer to read Shakespeare: they may even prefer Jonson, Webster and Marlowe, Racine and Moliere. They are more interested in Swift and Defoe than in Samuel Butler. Their enthusiasm for the New Russians is temperate, even lukewarm. In other words, the past that they respect ended about forty years ago—not long after Nora slammed the door." And a new kind of writing was capturing their taste. "Form, simplification, strangeness, respect for literature as an art with traditions, abstractness . . . these are the catchwords repeated most often among the younger writers. They represent ideas that have characterized French literature hitherto, rather than English or American. They are the nearest approach to articulate doctrine of a generation without a school and without a manifesto."

If Cowley's exhilist views seemed extreme, and they were not so for a large number of the rising generation, one may turn to see what had become of the force of liberation itself. Ludwig Lewisohn, though he built upon essentially Freudian foundations in his *Liberation of American Literature*, could still dismiss the whole battle from final importance. "I am unwilling," he said, "to leave this record of the central critical debate in American literature a purely negative one. . . . Amid the clamorous pseudo-certainties of the extremists the voice of humanity and of reason has not been very clearly heard. And in a confused and brawling and spiritually mist-swept age few influences have fortified a serener criticism, and its practitioners have been less pertinacious and loud than those in the divided and embattled camps." If this was a repudiation of literary conservatism, it was equally one of the grounds upon which the Chicago movement had flourished.

Likewise the idealist but vague and hopeful Socialism of the early Liberation was to suffer the contempt for all middle-class phenomena of the more sternly Marxist V. F. Calverton. "If the vitality of [the new poetry] died within the next decade [the twenties], it was not because the native elements in it provided insufficient impetus for its inspiration. The native elements survived even after its individualistic spirit was abandoned. . . . It was not the native aspects of the movement that died, then, but the individualistic energy, derivative of the petty bourgeois revolt, which had endowed it with vigor. The twenties saw the end of that last spurt of individualistic energy which inspired the poetic revolt of the teens. The petty bourgeois at last was crushed on every front. The face of rugged individualism could hardly conceal any longer the ghostlike visage that trembled behind its verbal masque." Such new voices as these of Cowley's, Lewisohn's and Calverton's were possessed not only of novelty of doctrine but also of an authenticity of style, urbane or intellectual, which silenced once and for all the essentially homegrown optimism as such, and even the home grown despair, of the Chicago school. New ideas of literature had been formed to which the midwesterners could only aspire. They had, however willingly, to become followers rather than leaders.

An undue emphasis upon the decline of the Chicago movement however, in favor of all that followed, may well lead to a radical misestimation of the movement's character and worth. Even so recent and perspicacious a writer as Irving Howe would maintain that it was "a historical curiosity that in the Chicago bohemia of 1912-1915 the populist values of 19th-century mid-America received such thorough, but already obsolete, expression and criticism." And equally, "The sense of Europe which was to disturb American literary life in the 1920's did not yet exist in the Chicago of 1912-1916." If this was half true, it was at once to make "populism" the sole force of the Chicago Liberation and to minimize out of all proportion the impact upon the movement of European thought. Such a judgment neglects and distorts both the complexity and the reality of the Chicago years. For the renaissance was precisely the first characteristic modern instance in which American literary romanticism re-encountered Europe. Where Whitman, with too protestant an innocence, had turned his back upon the old world, Chicago attempted a bridge. The tentative aestheticism of *The Chap Book*, Henry Fuller's cosmopolite criticism of American life, Francis Hackett's application of Fabianism to American culture, Dell's and Sandburg's Socialism, Harriet Monroe's openness of taste, Maurice Browne's equal enthusiasm for continental and midwestern drama, Anderson's use of George Borrow and Gertrude Stein, Margaret Anderson's espousal of anarchism, and Vincent Starrett's undivided taste for European and American authors, each of these marked precisely an effort to wed a native rebelliousness and intransigeance to a more committed and more profoundly dissenting vocabulary and attitude. It is thus no exaggeration to say that the group reality of twentieth-century American literature began in Chicago because in Chicago a chief strain which has formed our modern writing was first recognized. The first stage of Chicago's renaissance joined hands with the second to define a literary culture deliberately hostile to and liberated from the dominant forces of a modern business America. This was the legacy of the Chicago renaissance to the following decades, and it combined native and foreign impulses. With increasing sophistication, its successors have proceeded beyond the Chicago generation in understanding and accomplishment. It will not do, however, for them to attempt disavowal or patronage of the Chicago group. At the very least, they are the heirs of its peculiar problem. Like the Chicagoans, they are self-dispossessed devotees of a separatist art and separatist lines of thought. What they will finally make of them must in part be determined by the original romantic act of dispossession from which they have grown.

But what is there in the Chicago renaissance, after modern criticism has done its work, that is of use to these later days? Great room is needed for individual perceptions. One might suggest, however, that the ironic and elegant realism of Henry Fuller, the radical estrangement of the *Spoon River Anthology*, the striving mythopoesis of Sandburg's *Lincoln*, or the padded but precise feet of Anderson's best prose offer possible and viable choices. If to these one add the slim achievement of Garland's realistic sketches, the intense dedication of Herrick's Chicago novels, the exaltation of Lindsay's mystical moments, and the freshness of impression in Dell's *Moon Calf* and *Briary Bush*, he has perhaps the largest part of Chicago's literary success before him. Whether he will treat it with propriety, or turn impatiently back to his own self-defined horizon, may, in the last analysis, be not so much a measure of Chicago as of his own special and immediate needs.

Comments on the
Principal Sources

CHAPTER 1: THE LARGER PATTERN

THE chief scholarly history of Chicago is that of Prof. Bessie Pierce of the University of Chicago entitled, *A History of Chicago*. Volume I appeared in 1937 and Volume II in 1940. Volume III, as of this writing, is still in preparation. Passages on Chicago's earlier history here and elsewhere in my study are especially indebted to the detailed summary and the statistical reporting which are Miss Pierce's great contributions. For more recent Chicago history, that to be covered by Miss Pierce's third volume, the reader must rely largely on Lewis and Smith's *Chicago: A History of Its Reputation* (1929), which is useful for the whole period also, and on magazine articles which can be located through the appropriate indices. The same impulse toward the popular history of Chicago which produced Lewis and Smith's work has also yielded Ernest Poole's *Giants Gone, Men Who Made Chicago* (1943), summaries of the careers of leading citizens, and Wayne Andrews' *Battle For Chicago* (1946), a brief history of the city in terms of the struggles for power within it. Bessie Pierce's *As Others See Chicago* (1933) is a valuable collection of traveler's accounts while Harvey Zorbaugh's *The Gold Coast and the Slum* is an early but readable and discerning sociological study of that city within a city, Chicago's near north side. Of the older treatments, A. T. Andreas' *History of Chicago* (1886), Moses and Kirkland's *History of Chicago* (1895), and *Chicago Yesterdays*, a collection of memoirs edited by Caroline Kirkland in 1919, have all proved useful for particulars. Hobart Chatfield-Taylor's *Chicago* of 1917 and Edgar Lee Masters' *The Tale of Chicago* (1933) are impressionistic volumes revealing more about their authors than they do about the city, but they are useful within their limits.

CHAPTER 2: THE FIRST ESTATE

THE development of Chicago newspaper writing remains as yet a largely unstudied matter. The only attempt at a comprehensive account is Henry Justin Smith's brief *Gallery of Chicago Editors* (1933). In addition to using Smith, I have relied chiefly on personal narrative, especially Melville E. Stone's *Fifty Years a Journalist* (1921), Slason Thompson's *Way Back When* (1931), and Franc B. Wilkie's *Personal Reminiscences of Thirty-Five Years of Chicago Journalism* (1891). An account of the *Tribune* will be found in Philip Kinsley's *The Chicago Tribune: Its First Hundred Years* (Vol. I, 1943; Vol. II, 1945). The extensive collection of Victor Lawson's papers in the Newberry Library contains much detailed material pertaining to the *Daily News* and its associated papers.

For Eugene Field I have chiefly relied on Slason Thompson's *Eugene Field: A Study in Heredity and Contradictions* (1901). Thompson's later volume, *The Life of Eugene Field, The Poet of Childhood* (1927), and Charles Dennis' *Eugene Field's Creative Years* (1924) do not displace Thompson's earlier and more comprehensive study though they add to it in part.

Only one volume apiece on the life and work of Finley Dunne and George Ade exists. For the former there is Elmer Ellis' *Mr. Dooley's America: A Life of Finley Peter Dunne.* The comparable volume on Ade is Fred C. Kelly's *George Ade: Warmhearted Satirist* (1947). There is supplementary material on Ade, however, in the preface he wrote for Franklin J. Meine's selection of *Stories of the Streets and of the Town* (1941).

CHAPTER 3: HENRY FULLER

HENRY FULLER'S life and literary career have been summarized by Constance Griffin in *Henry Blake Fuller* (1939). A later study, more fully informed and governed by a critical interest, will be found

in an unpublished dissertation by Bernard Bowron, *Henry B. Fuller,
A Critical Study* (Harvard University, 1948). Hamlin Garland's
Daughter of the Middle Border and his *Roadside Meetings* (1930)
contain anecdotal material on Fuller. There are a number of critical
and scholarly articles. In addition to these I have made use of the
Henry Fuller collection at the Newberry Library which, though
spotty, is a chief primary source, and I was aided by a conversation
with Mr. Ralph Fletcher Seymour. Occasional Fuller letters are to
be found in other collections of the Newberry, in the Robert Herrick
collection at the University of Chicago, and in the University of
Pennsylvania's Dreiser Collection.

CHAPTER 4: THE GENTEEL PROTEST

THERE has been no study made of Chicago genteelism. A brief
contemporary survey of it will be found in Henry Fuller's article,
"The Upward Movement in Chicago," *Atlantic Monthly*, LXXX
(1897), 534-547. William Morton Payne's "Chicago's Higher Evolution" in the *Dial* for October 1st, 1892, is an even briefer survey while
his "Literary Chicago" in the *New England Magazine* of July, 1893,
touches upon the strictly literary aspect. Other sources for my essay
have been Henry Fuller's stories collected in *Under The Skylights*
(1901) which are largely concerned with the life of Chicago's "artistic gang;" Hobart Chatfield-Taylor's *Chicago* (1917); Anna Morgan's
My Chicago (1918), a particularly full report; Mrs. Carter H. Harrison's *Strange To Say* (1939); Hamlin Garland's *A Daughter of the
Middle Border* (1921); the earlier chapters of *A Poet's Life* (1938) by
Harriet Monroe; and Ralph Fletcher Seymour's *Some Went This
Way* (1945). Mr. Seymour obliged me greatly by giving me further
memories in conversation with him.

For my study of The Little Room I have used many of the references quoted above plus the Newberry Library's collection of
miscellaneous records of The Little Room. My chief resource for
America was Slason Thompson's memoirs, *Way Back When* (1931),
plus the files of *America* itself. The *Dial* has been ably studied by
Frederick Mosher in an unpublished dissertation, *Chicago's "Saving*

Remnant;" Francis Fisher Browne, William Morton Payne, and the Dial (University of Illinois, 1950). This work, plus files of the magazine and the Newberry's Francis Fisher Browne collection, were my chief sources. The activities of Stone and Kimball have been definitively described by Sidney Kramer in A History of Stone and Kimball (1940).

CHAPTER 5: HAMLIN GARLAND

THE chief sources of information for Hamlin Garland exist in his autobiographical writing, A Son of The Middle Border (1917), A Daughter of The Middle Border (1921), Back Trailers From The Middle Border (1928), Roadside Meetings (1930), Companions on The Trail (1931), My Friendly Contemporaries (1932), and Afternoon Neighbors (1934). These, though very full, are contradictory and unreliable in detail. In addition, I have used the numerous Garland letters contained in the Century collection of the New York Public Library and occasional Garland letters appearing in other collections cited for this study.

CHAPTER 6: THE REAL WORLD

THE nearest approach to a survey of American realistic fiction is to be found by indirection in Walter F. Taylor, The Economic Novel in America (1942), and in Alfred Kazin, On Native Grounds (1942). I have had to dissent in part from both these authors.

A thorough-going body of information about Joseph Kirkland has been amassed by Clyde Henson in an unpublished doctoral dissertation, The Life and Works of Joseph Kirkland, With an Edition of Zury (Western Reserve University, 1950). I have used also the Newberry Library's collection of Kirkland papers. No studies of Will Payne exists apart from the comments of Walter Taylor as cited above, but a few of his letters, from which I have quoted, are contained in the Harper Library of the University of Chicago's Robert Herrick collection. The fullest treatment of William Vaughn Moody is in David

D. Henry's *William Vaughn Moody: A Study* (1934) while Daniel Gregory Mason's *Some Letters of William Vaughn Moody* (1913) has been a helpful primary source. The best information about Robert Morss Lovett is contained in his autobiography, *All Our Years* (1948). This book has also been useful for other purposes in my study through its comment on Moody and Herrick. A considerable body of Lovett's letters is contained in the Herrick collection of the University of Chicago. I. K. Friedman has not been studied.

CHAPTER 7: ROBERT HERRICK

HERRICK'S writing has been treated from a critical angle by Blake Nevius in an unpublished dissertation, *The Novels of Robert Herrick* (University of Chicago, 1947), and there are brief though helpful comments by Robert Lovett in *All Our Years* (1948). But the chief source of information is the very full collection of Herrick papers at the Harper Library of the University of Chicago which contains manuscripts, letters, notebooks, press cuttings, and unpublished autobiographical essays.

CHAPTER 8: WORLD AND SELF

THE essay on the Liberation utilizes a number of the sources to be described in succeeding comments. Of particular value, however, were the Floyd Dell collection of the Newberry Library, Dell's autobiography, *Homecoming* (1933), Sherwood Anderson's *Memoirs* (1941), and Margaret Anderson's *My Thirty Years War* (1930) for the general texture of the Liberation movement.

CHAPTER 9: Edgar Lee Masters, The Advent of Liberation

THE chief published source of information for Masters' life is his autobiography, *Across Spoon River* (1936). I have supplemented and at points corrected the incomplete record there contained with information culled from Masters' revealing letters in the Dreiser collection of the University of Pennsylvania Library and the Eunice

Tietjens collection at the Newberry. Some material on Masters is obtainable from the memoirs of his acquaintance. Eunice Tietjens' *The World at My Shoulder* (1938) and Harriet Monroe's *A Poet's Life* (1938) contain useful accounts though both are censored and selected in deference to Masters' stormy life.

The best account of the Chicago Press Club I could find was in Opie Read's *I Remember* (1930). Reedy's *Mirror* remains unstudied and I have relied on files of the magazine for my account of it.

CHAPTER 10: THREE VOICES OF THE LIBERATION

LITTLE of consequence has been written on the *Friday Literary Review* except the comments contained in Floyd Dell's *Homecoming*. I have used these plus the files of the *Review* itself and the Floyd Dell collection at the Newberry as my chief sources. A conversation with Mr. Francis Hackett was most illuminating as to his part in the *Review* and its early years. Likewise, Harriet Monroe's *A Poet's Life* (1938) represents the chief published account of *Poetry's* early years. The files of that magazine and the extensive material contained in the Harriet Monroe collection at the University of Chicago yielded most of my information. Summary accounts of the *Little Review* have appeared in print, especially in Hoffman, Allen, and Ulrich, *The Little Magazine* (1946), which also includes material on *Poetry*, but I am chiefly in debt to Margaret Anderson's *My Thirty Years War* (1930) and to files of *The Little Review*. Conversation with persons active in the Liberation and occasional letters and notes contained in the collections elsewhere cited for this study have helped to complete my record.

The Harriet Monroe collection contains letters and manuscripts from most of the midwestern lyricists. The Floyd Dell collection at the Newberry includes a large bulk of letters from Ficke, though he is also represented at the Newberry by a collection of his own. The Eunice Tietjens collection at the Newberry is useful for her own work and for that of a number of other midwesterners, Sara Teasdale especially.

CHAPTER 11: THE STRUGGLE FOR AFFIRMATION

THE primary material available for a study of Sherwood Anderson is considerable. It is dominated by the very full Sherwood Anderson collection at the Newberry, a portion of which is now available in Howard Mumford Jones and Walter Rideout, *The Letters of Sherwood Anderson*, and includes Anderson's own semi-autobiographical writings, *A Story Teller's Story* (1924), *Tar* (1926), and *Sherwood Anderson's Memoirs* (1942). The collections of midwestern authors cited elsewhere have also yielded scattered information on Anderson. Of the secondary material, two unpublished doctoral dissertations are of major importance, William Sutton's *Sherwood Anderson's Formative Years* (The Ohio State University, 1943), and William Phillips' *Sherwood Anderson's Winesburg, Ohio* (University of Chicago, 1949). I have used both of these extensively in my own work. Two book-length studies of Anderson have appeared since my investigation began: Irving Howe's *Anderson* (1951), and James Scheville's *Sherwood Anderson, His Life and Work* (1951).

For material on Carl Sandburg's life I am greatly in debt to Karl Detzer's *Carl Sandburg: A Study in Personality and Background* (1941); Sandburg's autobiographical volume, *Always the Young Strangers* (1953); and his preface to his *Complete Poems* (1951). Only a very few of Sandburg's letters are to be found in the collections of midwestern authors, and they are largely without importance.

Much information on Vachel Lindsay remains out of scholars' hands, but one large and revealing group of letters is to be found in the University of Chicago's Harriet Monroe collection. Otherwise, the chief source is Edgar Lee Masters' *Vachel Lindsay* (1953). Masters is especially helpful because of voluminous quotations from Lindsay's notebooks and other records. Lindsay's own comment in the two prefaces to his *Collected Poems* (1925), along with *Adventures While Preaching the Gospel of Beauty* (1928) are also essential.

Although there are several studies of Alexander Campbell and the Disciples of Christ, I have found Campbell's own *The Christian System* (1839) most suggestive for the impact of his thought on Lindsay's.

CHAPTER 12: IMPRESARIOS, AUTHORS, CRITICS, AND COLUMNISTS

THE best information now available on the Chicago Little Theater is that contained in the Maurice Browne-Ellen Van Volkenburg collection of the University of Michigan library. I have used this and am indebted to Mr. Browne for a friendly and detailed correspondence. My information on the Hull House Theater and the Players' Workshop is drawn chiefly from Constance Darcy MacKay's *The Little Theater in the United States* (1917).

My comments on the *Daily News* group are drawn from a variety of sources, but chiefly from conversation with Mr. Hecht, Mr. Starrett, Mr. Covici, and the late Lloyd Lewis. Talks by Harry Hansen and Llewellyn Jones before the Friends of Literature in Chicago were helpful, while Mr. Hansen's *Midwest Portraits* (1923) is the chief record in print of this group. Burton Rascoe's *Before I Forget* (1937), *We Were Interrupted* (1947), and *A Bookman's Daybook* contain much information on himself and penetrating sidelights on others. The only approach to a sustained account of the Dill Pickle Club I have found is in *Sherwood Anderson's Memoirs* (1942). Files of the *Daily News*, *The Chicago Literary Times*, and the *Chicago Tribune* completed my sources.

CHAPTER 13: THE DISPERSAL

MENCKEN'S chief salutes to Chicago were two in number. The first appeared in the Chicago *Tribune* for October 28, 1917, where it was reprinted from the New York *Evening Mail*. The second, entitled "The Literary Capital of the United States" was printed in the London *Nation*, April 17, 1920. The quotations used in this concluding essay from Malcolm Cowley, Ludwig Lewisohn, V. F. Calverton, and Irving Howe are, respectively, from *Exile's Return* (1934), *Expression in America* (1932), *The Liberation of American Literature* (1932), and *Sherwood Anderson* (1951).

Sources of Quotations

CHAPTER 2: THE FIRST ESTATE

[1] Franc B. Wilkie, *Personal Reminiscences of Thirty-Five Years of Journalism* (Chicago, 1891), 194.
[2] Melville E. Stone, *Fifty Years a Journalist* (New York, 1921), 52.
[3] Stone, 115.
[4] Slason Thompson, *Eugene Field, A Study in Heredity and Contradictions*, 2 v., (New York, 1901), I, 188.
[5] Hamlin Garland, *Roadside Meetings* (New York, 1930), 244.
[6] *The Complete Tribune Primer* (Boston, 1901), 67.
[7] *Primer*, 74.
[8] *Primer*, 25.
[9] Thompson, I, 344.
[10] George Ade, *Stories of the Streets and of the Town*, ed. Franklin J. Meine (Chicago, 1941), xxiii.
[11] Fred C. Kelly, *George Ade, Warmhearted Satirist* (Indianapolis, 1947), 122.
[12] Kelly, 124.
[13] *Artie* (Chicago, 1898), 170.
[14] Elmer Ellis, *Mr. Dooley's America: A Life of Finley Peter Dunne* (New York, 1941), 69.
[15] Elmer Ellis (ed.), *Finley Peter Dunne: Mr. Dooley At His Best* (New York, 1938), 150.
[16] Ellis, *Dooley At His Best*, 1.

CHAPTER 3: HENRY FULLER

[1] October 1, 1892, 206.
[2] Wayne Andrews, *Battle For Chicago* (New York, 1946), 95.

[3] "The Upward Movement in Chicago," *Atlantic Monthly*, LXXX (1897), 534.

[4] Andrews, 30.

[5] Andrews, 95.

[6] Bessie Louise Pierce, *As Others See Chicago: Impressions of Visitors, 1673-1933* (Chicago, 1933), 399.

[7] Andrews, 30.

[8] Miscellaneous Journal, Henry Fuller Collection, Newberry Library.

[9] European Journal, II, January 25, 1880, Fuller Collection.

[10] European Journal, I, November 6, 1879, Fuller Collection.

[11] *Modern Self-Consciousness* (Notes for a lecture), Fuller Collection.

[12] Constance M. Griffin, *Henry Blake Fuller* (Philadelphia, 1939), 29.

[13] *The Chevalier of Pensieri-Vani* (Boston, 1890), 168.

[14] Chevalier, 89.

[15] *The Cliff Dwellers* (New York, 1893), 44.

[16] *Cliff Dwellers*, 50-51.

[17] *Cliff Dwellers*, 242-243.

[18] *Cliff Dwellers*, 54.

[19] *With the Procession* (New York, 1895), 248.

[20] *The Last Refuge* (New York, 1900), 26.

[21] *Last Refuge*, 152-153.

CHAPTER 4: THE GENTEEL PROTEST

[1] Slason Thompson, *Way Back When* (Chicago, 1931), 288-289.

[2] II (1889), 58, 167.

[3] II (1889), 62, 299.

[4] II (1890), 72, 631.

[5] IV (1891), 129, 689.

[6] *The Wind In the Corn* (New York, 1917), 50.

[7] *Valeria and Other Poems* (Chicago, 1892), 213.

⁸ Valeria, 219.

⁹ *Loc. cit.*
¹⁰ Valeria, 290.
¹¹ Garland to Browne, 1893, Francis Fisher Browne Collection, Newberry Library.
¹² Browne to Garland, 1893, Browne Collection.

CHAPTER 5: HAMLIN GARLAND

¹ *Son of the Middle Border* (New York, 1928), 346.
² *Roadside Meetings* (New York, 1930), 119.
³ Garland to Gilder, n.p., n.d., Richard Watson Gilder Collection, New York Public Library.
⁴ Garland to Gilder, Boston, n.d., Gilder Collection.
⁵ Garland to Gilder, Boston, n.d., Gilder Collection.
⁶ *Crumbling Idols* (Chicago 1894), 69.
⁷ *Daughter of the Middle Border* (New York, 1921), 28.
⁸ *Daughter*, 87.
⁹ *Daughter*, 94.
¹⁰ *Daughter*, 155.

CHAPTER 6: THE REAL WORLD

¹ *Zury, The Meanest Man In Spring County* (Boston and New York, 1887), 24.
² Winifred Wilson, *Joseph Kirkland*, unpublished M. A. thesis, Northwestern University, 1939.
³ Kirkland to his family, July 4, 1887, Joseph Kirkland Collection, Newberry Library.
⁴ *Rose of Dutcher's Cooly* (New York and London, Border Edition, n.d.), 156.
⁵ *The Gospel of Freedom* (New York, 1898), 131.
⁶ *Jerry the Dreamer* (New York, 1896), 173.

[7] *Jerry*, 188.

[8] Payne to Herrick, n.p., [1916] Robert Herrick Collection, Harper Library, University of Chicago.

[9] *The Money Captain* (Chicago, 1898), 159.

[10] *Money Captain*, 273.

[11] Daniel Gregory Mason, *Some Letters of William Vaughn Moody* (Boston, 1913), 36-37.

[12] Mason, 56.

[13] *Poems* (Boston and New York, 1901), 49-54.

[14] Mason, 32-33.

[15] Payne to Herrick, n.p., May 16, 1900, Herrick Collection.

[16] Payne to Herrick, n.p., November 25, 1901. Herrick Collection.

[17] Preface *To Fiction* (Chicago, 1931), 11.

CHAPTER 7: ROBERT HERRICK

[1] *The Gospel of Freedom* (New York and London, 1898), 149.

[2] *Gospel*, 153.

[3] *Gospel*, 267.

[4] *The Common Lot* (New York and London, 1904), 338.

[5] *Common Lot*, 338.

[6] Blake Nevius, *Robert Herrick, A Critical Study*, unpublished dissertation, University of Chicago, 1947, 23.

[7] *Myself*, Robert Herrick Collection, Harper Library, University of Chicago.

[8] *Myself*.

[9] *Myself*.

CHAPTER 8: WORLD AND SELF

[1] Dell to Ficke, Chicago, May 26, 1913, Floyd Dell Collection, Newberry Library.

[2] Van Wyck Brooks, *Three Essays On America* (New York, 1934), 98.

[3] John Macy, *The Spirit of American Literature* (New York, n.d.), 17.

CHAPTER 9: EDGAR LEE MASTERS

[1] *Across Spoon River* (New York, 1936), 337.

[2] *I Remember* (New York, 1930), 93.

[3] *Loc. cit.*

[4] Masters to Harriet Monroe, New York, June 9, 1925, Harriet Monroe Collection, Harper Library, University of Chicago.

[5] Masters to Eunice Tietjens, New York, May 12, 1937, Eunice Tietjens Collection, Newberry Library.

[6] *Across Spoon River*, 84.

[7] *Across Spoon River*, 209-210.

[8] V (1914-15), 6, 280.

[9] Masters to Dreiser, Chicago, November 27, 1912, Theodore Dreiser Collection, University of Pennsylvania Library.

[10] Masters to Dreiser, Chicago, March 10, 1919, Dreiser Collection.

[11] *Across Spoon River*, 338.

[12] *Across Spoon River*, 352.

[13] *Selected Poems* (New York, 1925), 169.

CHAPTER 10: THREE VOICES OF THE LIBERATION

[1] *Friday Literary Review*, June 6, 1913.

[2] August 2, 1912.

[3] *Loc. cit.*

[4] March 8, 1912.

[5] January 26, 1912.

[6] February 2, 1912.

[7] February 9, 1912.

[8] *Loc cit.*

[9] February 23, 1912.

[10] April 25, 1913.

[11] May 16, 1913.

[12] July 31, 1914.

[13] *The Briary Bush* (New York, 1921), 55.

[14] *Briary Bush*, 34.

[15] Dell to Rabbi Fineshriber, [Fall, 1913], Floyd Dell Collection, Newberry Library.

[16] *A Poet's Life* (New York, 1938), 252.

[17] D. D. Paige (ed.), *The Letters of Ezra Pound, 1907-1941* (New York, 1950), 9.

[18] Paige, 15.

[19] Masters to Harriet Monroe, February 2, 1915, Harriet Monroe Collection.

[20] *The Collected Poems of Sara Teasdale* (New York, 1937).

[21] *Little Review*, I, 2, 16.

[22] I, 1, 13.

[23] I, 7, 5.

[24] I, 9, 14.

[25] I, 11, 16.

[26] II, 1, 12.

[27] II, 3, 3.

[28] II, 4, 20.

[29] II, 5, 14.

CHAPTER 11: THE STRUGGLE FOR AFFIRMATION

[1] Anderson to Dell, July 27, 1915. Floyd Dell Collection, Newberry Library.

[2] Anderson to Dreiser, January 1, 1935. Sherwood Anderson Collection, Newberry Library.

[3] Howard Mumford Jones, in association with Walter B. Rideout, *Letters of Sherwood Anderson* (Boston, 1953), 42.

[4] Jones and Rideout, 20.

[5] *Sherwood Anderson's Memoirs* (New York, 1942), 235.

[6] "The New Note," *Little Review*, I (1914), 1, 23.

[7] Jones and Rideout, 274-275.

[8] *The Modern Writer* (San Francisco, 1925), 29.

[9] *Modern Writer*, 44.

[10] "A Writer's Concept of Realism," quoted from Paul Rosenfeld (ed.), *A Sherwood Anderson Reader* (Boston, 1947), 344.

[11] Jones and Rideout, 78.

[12] *Mid-American Chants* (New York, 1918), 81.

[13] Jones and Rideout, 79.

[14] *A Story Teller's Story* (New York, 1924), 300-301.

[15] Quoted from Harry Hansen, *Midwest Portraits* (New York, 1923), 41.

[16] Karl Detzer, *Carl Sandburg, A Study In Personality and Background* (New York, 1941), 49.

[17] Masters to Dreiser, April 13, 1914, Theodore Dreiser Collection, University of Pennsylvania Library.

[17a] From *Chicago Poems* by Carl Sandburg. Copyright, 1916, by Henry Holt and Company, Inc. Copyright, 1944, by Carl Sandburg. By permission of the publishers.

[18] Quoted from Harriet Monroe, *A Poet's Life* (New York, 1938) 312.

[19] Lindsay to Harriet Monroe, February 3, 1917, Harriet Monroe Collection, Harper Library, University of Chicago.

[20] Alexander Campbell, *The Christian System* (Cincinnati, 1839), 159.

[21] Campbell, 60.

[22] Quoted from Edgar Lee Masters, *Vachel Lindsay* (New York, 1935), 67.

[23] *Adventures While Preaching the Gospel of Beauty* (New York, 1928), 16-17.

[24] "Adventures While Preaching Hieroglyphic Sermons," *Collected Poems* (New York, 1925), xxxvi.

[25] Lindsay to Dell, September 6, 1909, Dell Collection.

[26] Lindsay to Dell, December 1, 1912, Dell Collection.

CHAPTER 12: IMPRESARIOS, AUTHORS, CRITICS, AND COLUMNISTS

[1] Original prospectus for the Chicago Little Theatre, Maurice Browne and Ellen Van Volkenburg Collection, University of Michigan Library.

[2] Loc cit.
[3] Maurice Browne to the author, November 22, 1950.
[4] Chicago Daily News, July 25, 1917.
[5] October 25, 1918.
[6] January 9, 1918.
[7] June 5, 1918.
[8] February 2, 1918.
[9] March 13, 1918.
[10] May 26, 1920.
[11] Humpty Dumpty (New York, 1924), 223-224 passim.
[12] A Bookman's Daybook (New York, 1929), 158.
[13] The Chicago Literary Times, March 15, 1923.
[14] May 1, 1923.
[15] March 1, 1924.
[16] April 15, 1923.
[17] Sherwood Anderson's Memoirs, 270.
[18] Chicago Tribune, October 28, 1917.
[19] February 23, 1918.
[20] April 6, 1918.

Index